the freelance
photographer's
market handbook
2011

the freelance photographer's market handbook 2011

Edited by
John Tracy
& Stewart Gibson

 BFP BOOKS London

A catalogue record for this book is available from the British Library

ISBN3: 978-0-907297-62-8

27th Edition

Published for the Bureau of Freelance Photographers by BFP Books, Focus House,
497 Green Lanes, London N13 4BP. Typesetting and page layout by BFP Books.
Text set in New Century Schoolbook. Printed in Great Britain by the MPG Books Group.

CONTENTS

PREFACE

The past 12 months has seen economic conditions continuing to restrain growth in the publishing sector and recent sales figures provide unhappy reading for many publishers.

The effects of the recession and competition from the Internet, in a market already saturated with competing titles, continues to hurt many publications.

Over the past decade, overall UK magazine sales have declined by some 25 per cent, though real decline only really set in around five years ago. Inevitably this coincided with the rise of the Internet as a primary source for news and other information.

However, while newspapers and many general magazines have lost sales over recent years, many upmarket or specialist magazines have actually been increasing them.

A major reason would appear to be that these titles have only a limited presence online. Readers have to buy them to read them, and many remain happy to do so.

Print still provides a more rewarding experience for many readers, especially when it comes to high-quality picture display and information for the dedicated enthusiast.

As we write, figures released by the Audit Bureau of Circulations (ABC) gave an indication of an improving outlook for the UK consumer magazine sector.

Total circulation for audited titles in the first half of 2010 increased by 0.3 per cent compared with the same period in 2009. A small increase to be sure, but an increase nonetheless.

Given the economic climate and those continuing pressures from the Internet, this is rather reassuring for print publishers.

The results appear to underline a continued high level of consumer demand for magazines in the face of both economic pressures and the availability of an increasing array of media choices.

Unsurprisingly though, launch activity has remained at a standstill. Publishers are still unprepared to take the risk of chancing a brand-new title in a marketplace that seems to be content with what it already has.

But compared to previous years, significant closures have been remarkably few. Those titles that have managed to survive so far, seem destined to go on doing so.

The picture agency scene also remains subdued. There have been fewer launches, fewer closures and fewer acquisitions than for some time.

One of the more encouraging events of 2010 was the collapse of the attempt by the giant Getty Images – which has been swallowing up rivals large and small for many years – to acquire the old-established Rex Features, one of the UK's most venerable picture agencies. This followed a referral of the proposed deal to the Competition Commission by the Office of Fair Trading.

If this event signals an end to the reduction of competition and the consequent forcing down of fees paid by picture buyers, then it can only be beneficial as far as both the independent agency and the freelance contributor are concerned.

Overall it remains true that despite the many ups and downs of the past several years, the market for freelance photography continues to expand, both online and off.

ABOUT THE BFP

Founded in 1965, the Bureau of Freelance Photographers is today the major body for the freelance photographer. It has a worldwide membership, comprising not only full-time freelances, but also serious amateur and semi-professional photographers. Being primarily a service organisation, membership of the Bureau is open to anyone with an interest in freelance photography.

The most important service offered to members is the *Market Newsletter,* a confidential monthly report on the state of the freelance market. A well-researched and highly authoritative publication, the *Newsletter* keeps freelances in touch with the market for freelance work, mainly by giving information on the type of photography currently being sought by a wide range of publications and other outlets. It gives full details of new magazines and their editorial requirements, and generally reports on what is happening in the publishing world and how this is likely to affect the freelance photographer.

The *Newsletter* also includes in-depth interviews with editors, profiles of successful freelances, examples of successful pictures, and other general features to help freelances in understanding and approaching the marketplace.

The *Newsletter* is considered essential reading for the freelance and aspiring freelance photographer, and because it pinpoints launches and changes in the marketplace as they occur, it also acts as a useful supplement to the *Handbook*. The *Handbook* itself is an integral part of BFP membership services; members paying the full annual fee automatically receive a copy every year as it is published.

Other services provided to members for the modest annual subscription include:

● Advisory Service. Individual advice on all aspects of freelancing is available to members.

● Mediation Service. The Bureau tries to protect its members' interests in every way it can. In particular, it is often able to assist individual members in recovering unpaid fees and in settling copyright or other disputes.

● Exclusive items and special offers. The Bureau regularly offers books and other useful items to members, usually at discount prices.

● In the Services section of this *Handbook* can be found a number of companies providing special discounts to BFP members on production of a current membership card. Amongst various services members can obtain comprehensive photographic insurance cover at competitive rates.

For further details and an application form, write to Bureau of Freelance Photographers, Focus House, 497 Green Lanes, London N13 4BP, telephone 020 8882 3315, e-mail mail@thebfp.com, or visit the BFP website at www.thebfp.info. Or if you wish to join right away, you'll find an application form at the back of this book, after the main index.

HOW TO USE THIS BOOK

Anyone with the ability to use a camera correctly has the potential to make money from their pictures. Taking saleable photographs isn't difficult; the difficulty lies in finding the market. It isn't enough for you, the photographer in search of a sale, to find what you think *might* be a suitable market; rather you must find *exactly* the right magazine, publisher, agency or whatever for your particular type of work. Many a sale is lost when work which is, in itself, technically perfect fails to fulfil the total requirements of the buyer.

The Freelance Photographer's Market Handbook has been designed to help resolve these difficulties. It puts you in touch with major markets for your work, telling you exactly what each is looking for, together with hints and tips on how to sell to them and, wherever possible, an idea of the rates they pay.

The *Handbook* covers five big markets for your pictures: magazines (by far the largest), newspapers, book publishers, picture agencies, and companies producing cards, calendars, posters and other print products. There are three ways of using the book, depending on the way you need or wish to work:

1. If you are out to sell to magazines and you can offer coverage on a theme particularly applicable to a certain type of publication (eg gardening, angling, sport) turn to the magazine section and look for the subject. The magazines are listed under 36 categories, each of which has a broad heading covering specific magazines. The categories are in alphabetical order, as are the magazines within those categories. You need only read through them to discover which is best for your type of work.

2. If you have a set of pictures that fall into a specific photographic category (landscapes, children, celebrities etc), turn to the subject index on page 21.

Look up your chosen subject and there you will find a list of all the magazines with a strong interest in that particular type of picture. You then have only to look up each one mentioned in the appropriate section for precise details of their requirements. (If in doubt as to where to find a particular magazine consult the general index at the back of the book.) There are separate subject indexes for book publishers and agencies on pages 152 and 175 respectively.

3. If you are looking for the requirements of a specific magazine, book publisher, agency, card or calendar publisher, whose name is already known to you, simply refer to the general index at the back of the book.

Some points to remember

With this wealth of information open to you, and with those three options for finding the right market, there is no reason why you shouldn't immediately start earning good cash from your camera. But before you rush off to submit your images, here are some points worth bearing in mind and which will help you to more successful sales:

1. The golden rule of freelancing: don't send people pictures they don't want. Read the requirements listed in the various parts of this directory and obey them. When, for instance, a Scottish magazine says they want pictures of all things Scottish with the exception of kilts and haggis, you can be sure they are over-stocked with these subjects. They are not going to make an exception just for you, however good you think your pictures might be.

2. Digital images supplied on disc are the norm nowadays, but always check preferred image file format and size with your chosen market in advance. Small selections of low-resolution files may be sent as initial samples via e-mail, but e-mail is rarely an acceptable method of submission for larger files or batches of material intended for publication. If still working with colour film, and unless the listing states otherwise, always supply transparencies rather than prints.

3. When submitting pictures, make sure they are accompanied by detailed captions. And don't forget to put your own name and address on each photograph/CD.

4. If you have an idea for a picture or feature for a particular publication, don't

be afraid to telephone or e-mail first to discuss what you have in mind. Nearly every editor or picture buyer approached when the *Handbook* was being compiled said they would much prefer to hear from potential freelances in advance, rather than have inappropriate pictures or words landing on their desks.

5. If seeking commissions, always begin by making an appointment with the appropriate person in order to show your portfolio and/or cuttings. Do not turn up at a busy editor's office unannounced and expect to be met with open arms.

6. Enclose a stamped addressed envelope if you want a posted submission returned if unsuccessful.

APPROACHING THE MARKET

You've chosen your market, taken the pictures and written the captions. Full of hope and expectation, you put your work in the post. A week later, it comes back with a formal rejection slip. Why? Where did you go wrong?

You have only to look through the pages of this book to see that there are a lot of markets open to the freelance photographer, yet the sad fact remains that a great many of those who try their hand at editorial freelancing fail the first few times, and many never succeed at all. That isn't meant to be as discouraging as it might sound. On the contrary, because so many freelances fail, *you*, with the inside knowledge gleaned from these pages, stand a better chance of success than most. What's more you can gain from the experience of others.

So let's take a look at some of the areas where the inexperienced freelance goes wrong. Knowing the common mistakes, you can avoid them and consequently stand the best chance of success with your own work.

The first big mistake made by the novice is in the actual form of the pictures they supply.

Images taken with digital cameras are acceptable to all markets, but really need to be produced on a well-specified digital SLR in order to provide the quality parameters necessary for high-quality reproduction. For submission to picture markets they must also be of a suitable high resolution (usually 300dpi) and large file size. Picture buyers will expect the images to be submitted on CD or DVD, not via e-mail.

In the case of film, high-quality prints or slides may still be acceptable to some markets. But if you are shooting on film, bear in mind that most buyers in the publishing world will prefer to receive digital files scanned from your slides or negatives, not original film material.

Most publications are all-colour, but a number of smaller magazines still use some black and white, while many up-market titles like to use a proportion of high-quality monochrome imagery. In this case, high-quality black and white digital files or prints will usually be required.

A few markets – such as calendars and greetings cards, or certain specialist magazines and picture libraries – do continue to favour film, often in the form of larger format transparencies for ultimate reproduction quality.

The quality of your work must be first class. Images should be pin-sharp and perfectly exposed to give strong, saturated colours. Slight under-exposure of around one-third to half a stop may be acceptable, but over-exposure never. *Never* send over-exposed, washed-out pictures.

While all markets now accept images in digital form, each will have specific technical requirements or preferences that should be ascertained before submission. File format and image size preferences do vary, so always check with your chosen market for their precise requirements in each case.

Unless otherwise stated in an individual entry, it can be assumed that all the markets listed here accept both digital and film submissions.

So much for picture format, but what of the actual subject of your pictures? Here again, a lot of fundamental mistakes are made. The oldest rule in the freelancing book is this: don't take pictures, then look for markets; find a market first and then shoot your pictures specifically with that market in mind.

Every would-be freelance knows that rule; yet the many who ignore it is frankly staggering. Remember that rule and act accordingly. First find your market, analyse it to see the sort of pictures it uses, then go all out to take *exactly* the right type of picture.

Editors see a lot of pictures every day, and the vast majority are totally unsuited to their market. Of those that are suited, many are still rejected because, despite being the right *type* of pictures, the subjects are still uninspiring. They are subjects the editor has seen over and over again; and the type that the magazine will already have on file. So once again, the work gets rejected.

Remember this and learn from it. Most of the pictures that fall on an editor's desk are pretty ordinary. If you want to make yours sell, you have to show them something different. It might be a fairly straightforward view of an unusual subject, or it might be a more common subject, seen and photographed from a new angle. Either way, it will be different.

So when you set out to take your pictures, really look at your subject and, even before you press the shutter, ask yourself, why am I taking this picture? Why will an editor want to buy it? What's so different or unusual about it? How can I make a few changes here and now to give it a better chance of success?

Good, traditional picture composition also plays a part in a picture's chances. Many would-be freelances submit pictures of people in which the principal subject is far too small and surrounded by a wealth of unwanted, distracting detail. So make a point, whenever you shoot, of moving in close and really filling the viewfinder with your subject.

Many potentially saleable landscapes are ruined by a flat perspective. So watch out for, and try to include, foreground interest in such pictures.

People at work on a craft or a hobby can be good sellers, but a good many pictures depicting such subjects are shot candidly without the necessary thought needed to really show the subject to its best. Always pose pictures like these before you take them.

Finally, a word about presentation. It's true that a good picture can often find a sale, no matter how badly it is presented; but it is equally true that bad presentation can have a negative influence on an editor or picture buyer and so ruin your chances of success. So why make things difficult for yourself?

When you send prints or CDs, make sure they are stiffly packed between thick card or in cardboard envelopes. Present any slides in plastic filing wallets and make them easy to view with the minimum of fuss.

With digital submissions, an editor will always appreciate a print-out of thumbnail images for quick reference.

If you are sending words – either captions to pictures or a full-blown article – always submit a "hard copy" print-out as well as including your text and/or caption files on the CD.

Send your submission with a brief covering letter, not with pages of explanations about the work. The sale will stand or fall by your pictures and/or words, never by the excuses you offer as to why certain pictures might not be too good. If they're not good enough, they won't sell.

Give your editors what they want. Give them originality and sparkle, and present the whole package in the best way you can. Learn the rules and you'll be on your way to a good many picture sales.

But don't think that anyone is going to break those rules just for you. If your pictures don't measure up to what is required, there will always be another submission right behind full of pictures that do. And there are no prizes for guessing which submission is going to make the sale.

MAGAZINES

The British magazine market is vast. Anyone who doubts that has only to look at the racks of periodicals in any major newsagent. And this is only the tip of the iceberg, the largest section of the consumer press. Beneath the surface there is the trade press, controlled circulation magazines and many smaller publications that are never seen on general sale. At the last count more than 8,000 magazines were being published on a regular basis in Britain.

In this section you will find detailed listings of magazines which are looking for freelances. Some pay a lot, others are less generous, but all have one thing in common – they are here because they need freelance contributions on a regular basis and they are willing to pay for them.

When you come to start looking at these listings in detail, you might be surprised by the number of magazines of which you have never heard. Don't let that put you off. What the newcomer to freelancing often fails to realise is that there are as many, if not more, trade magazines or small specialist titles as there are major consumer publications, and very few of these are ever seen on general sale.

Trade magazines, as the term implies, are aimed at people whose business is making money from the particular subject concerned. As such, their requirements are usually totally different to their consumer counterparts.

As an example, consider boating. A consumer magazine on that subject will be aimed at the boat owner or enthusiast and could contain features on boats and the way they are handled. A trade magazine on the same subject is likely to be more interested in articles about the profits being made by the boating industry and pictures of shop displays of boating accessories.

Trade magazines do not necessarily have a separate section to themselves. If the subject is a common one, such as the example above in which there are both trade and consumer publications, they have been listed for your convenience under a common heading. Despite that, however, there *is* a section specifically for trade. This contains trade magazines that have no consumer counterparts, as well as magazines whose subject is actually trade itself and trading in general.

As you go through these listings, therefore, it is important for you to realise that there is a very real difference between the two sides of the subject, but it is a difference which is explained under each publication's requirements. So don't ignore trade magazines of whose existence you were not previously aware. Very often such a magazine will have just as big a market for your pictures and the fees will be just as good, if not better, than those offered by the consumer press.

It is often a good idea for the freelance to aim at some of the more obscure publications listed here, be they trade magazines or the smaller hobbyist magazines. Simply because they are a little obscure they may not have been noticed by other freelances and, as such, your sales potential may well be higher even if fees paid by some of these publications are relatively low.

When you are looking through the entries, don't stop at the section on illustrations. Read what the magazine needs in the way of text too. A publication that might appear to have a very small market for individual pictures often has a larger potential for illustrated articles, and all you need to do to make a sale is add a few words.

You will also find that many publications talk about needing mainly commissioned work. Don't be misled by this. The commissions are given to freelances and, although this means they won't consider your work on spec, they could well be interested in giving you a commission if you can prove you are worth it. That's where previous experience comes in. When trying for commissions, you should always have examples of previously published work to show an editor.

Many of the larger magazines employ a specific editor to deal with picture submissions and with photographers. They may go under various titles – picture editor, art editor, art director – but this is the person directly responsible for picture selection and for commissioning photographers for specific jobs. This, therefore, is the person you should approach when sending pictures or seeking photographic assignments. When sending written material though – illustrated or not – your approach is best made direct to the editor.

The magazine market is one of the largest available to the freelance. You might not receive as large a fee per picture as you would from, say, the calendar market, or for certain sales that might be made on your behalf by an agency, but what this field does offer is a *steady* income, especially once you have made a breakthrough with one or more titles.

There are so many magazines, covering so many different subjects, that freelances who have their wits about them would be hard put *not* to find one to which their own style and interests can be adapted. Make yourself known to a few chosen magazine editors, let them see that you can turn out good quality work on the right subject, at the right time, and there is no reason why this market shouldn't make you a good, regular income, either part time or full time.

New Listings, Changes & Deletions

The following is designed to alert readers to possible new markets as well as to important changes that have taken place since the last edition of the *Handbook*.

'New Listings' includes magazines that have been launched since the last edition appeared as well as established titles that appear in the *Handbook* for the first time. 'Title Changes' lists publications that have changed their names (previous titles in brackets). 'Deletions' lists publications that appeared in the previous edition but are omitted from this one. Publications under this heading have not necessarily ceased publication – they may have been deleted because they no longer offer a worthwhile market for the contributor.

To find the page number for any particular magazine, refer to the main index at the back of the book.

New Listings

How It Works
Practical Sportsbikes
Rotorhub

Title Changes

Visordown (Two Wheels Only)
Master Photography
   (Master Photo>Digital)
Waitrose Kitchen
   (Waitrose Food Illustrated)
Prima Baby & Pregnancy (Prima Baby)

Deletions

Building Services Journal
Chemistry & Industry
Flypast
Go Flying!
Hardware & Garden Review
Horse & Pony
House & Garden
International Rugby News
Italy
Scotland Outdoors
Scouting Magazine
Snowboard UK
Traditional Boats & Tall Ships

Subject Index

Only magazines are included in this index, but it should be noted that many of these subjects are also required by agencies, book publishers and card and calendar publishers.

Separate subject indexes for book publishers and picture agencies appear in the appropriate sections, on pages 153 and 177 respectively.

To find the page number for any magazine, refer to the main index at the back of the book.

Agriculture

BBC Countryfile
The Countryman
Crops
Dairy Farmer
Eurofruit Magazine
Farmers Guardian
Farmers Weekly
Home Farmer
Poultry World
Waitrose Kitchen

Aircraft

Aeroplane
Air International
Airforces Monthly
Airliner World
Aviation News
Defence Helicopter
Flight International
Flyer
How It Works
Jane's Defence Weekly
Pilot
Rotorhub
Today's Pilot

Arts/Crafts

Best of British
Classic Stitches
Furniture & Cabinetmaking
Good Woodworking
Knitting
The Lady
This England
Woodcarving
Woodturning
The Woodworker

Birds

BBC Wildlife
Bird Watching
Birdwatch
The Falconers & Raptor Conservation
    Magazine
Parrots
Pet Product Marketing
Racing Pigeon Pictorial

Boats/Nautical

Boat International
Canal Boat
Canals & Rivers
Classic Boat
Coast
International Boat Industry
Jet Skier & PW
Marine Engineers Review
Motor Boat and Yachting
Motor Boats Monthly
RYA Magazine
Rowing & Regatta
Sailing Today
Sportsboat & RIB Magazine
Towpath Talk
Water Craft
Waterways World
Yachting Monthly
Yachting World
Yachts and Yachting

Buildings

Architecture Today
BD
Build It
Country Homes and Interiors
The English Home
FX

House Beautiful
Housebuilder
Icon
Municipal Journal
Period Living
Planning
RIBA Journal
SelfBuild & Design
Stadium & Arena Management
World of Interiors

Business

Accountancy Age
CA Magazine
CNBC European Business
Computer Weekly
Director
EN
The Economist
Financial Management
Marketing
People Management

Celebrities

Bella
Best
Closer
Glamour
Grazia
Heat
Hello!
Look
Mizz
More
Now
OK!
Radio Times
Red
Reveal
Saga
The Stage
Sugar
TV Times
Woman

Children

Mother & Baby
Nursery World
Prima Baby & Pregnancy
Right Start
Scholastic Magazines

Domestic/Farm Animals

Dairy Farmer
Dogs Today
Farmers Guardian
Farmers Weekly
Home Farmer
Horse
Horse & Rider
K9 Magazine
Kennel and Cattery Management
The Lady
Pet Product Marketing
Your Cat
Your Dog

Fashion

Bella
Best
Company
Condé Nast Customer Publishing
Drapers
Elle
Esquire
Essentials
FHM
Front
GQ
Glamour
Good Housekeeping
Grazia
Harper's Bazaar
The Lady
Loaded
Look
Marie Claire
Mizz
More
Prima
Red
Refresh
She
Woman
Woman's Own
Woman's Weekly

Flowers/Plants

BBC Gardeners' World
Country Homes & Interiors
The English Garden
The Garden

Garden Answers
Garden News
Garden Trade News
Gardens Illustrated
Gardens Monthly
Good Homes
Good Housekeeping
Homes & Gardens
Horticulture Week
House Beautiful
The Lady
Woman&Home

Food/Drink

Bella
Best
British Baker
Caterer & Hotelkeeper
Country Homes & Interiors
Decanter
Essentials
Eurofruit Magazine
Food & Travel
France
French Magazine
Good Housekeeping
Home Farmer
Homes & Gardens
House Beautiful
Italia!
Lifescape
Olive
Prima
Publican
Red
Restaurant
Scottish Licensed Trade News
Waitrose Kitchen
Woman&Home

Glamour/Erotic

Club International
Escort
FHM
Front
Loaded
Mayfair
Men Only
Nuts
Zoo

Homes/Interiors

Best
Build It
Coast
Country Homes & Interiors
Elle Decoration
The English Home
Essentials
Glamour
Good Homes
Good Housekeeping
Homes & Gardens
House Beautiful
Ideal Home
Period Living
Prima
Real Homes
Red
SelfBuild & Design
25 Beautiful Homes
Woman&Home
World of Interiors
Your Home

Industry

Chemist & Druggist
Director
Education in Chemistry
The Engineer
Engineering
Financial Management
Industrial Diamond Review
People Management
Planning
Post Magazine
Professional Engineering
Urethanes Technology International
Utility Week
Works Management

Landscapes

Amateur Photographer
Best of British
Bird Watching
Camping
Cheshire Life
Coast
Cotswold Life
Country Life
Country Walking
The Countryman

Cumbria
Dalesman
Dorset
Dorset Life
The Great Outdoors
Hertfordshire Countryside
The Lady
Lancashire Life
Lincolnshire Life
Outdoor Photography
Photography Monthly
PhotoPlus
Practical Photography
The Scots Magazine
Somerset Life
Sussex Life
TGO – The Great Outdoors
This England/Evergreen
Trail
Walk
Waterways World
Yorkshire Life

Military

Air International
Airforces Monthly
Defence Helicopter
Jane's Defence Weekly

Motor Vehicles

American Car World
Auto Express
Autocar
The Automobile
Automotive Management
Boys Toys
Classic American
Classic Cars
Classic & Sports Car
Classic Plant & Machinery
Classics Monthly
Coach and Bus Week
Commercial Motor
Driving Magazine
Evo
4x4
Fleet News
Jaguar
Land Rover Monthly
Land Rover Owner International

Maxpower
Motor Trader
Motoring & Leisure
Motor Sport
911 & Porsche World
Octane
Performance Ford
Redline
Roadway
Top Gear Magazine
Total911
Tractor
Tractor & Machinery
Triumph World
Truck and Driver

Motorcycles

Back Street Heroes
Bike
Classic Bike
The Classic Motor Cycle
Dirt Bike Rider
Moto Magazine
Motor Cycle News
Practical Sportsbikes
Redline
Ride
Scootering
Superbike
Visordown

Pop/Rock

Blues and Soul
Heat
Kerrang!
Keyboard Player
Loaded
Metal Hammer
MixMag
Mojo
New Musical Express
Q
Rhythm
Total Guitar

Railways

Engineering in Miniature
Heritage Railway

International Railway Journal
Rail
Rail Express
Railnews
The Railway Magazine
Steam Railway
Today's Railways UK
Traction

Sport

All Out Cricket
Athletics Weekly
Badminton
Boat International
Boxing Monthly
Cycle Sport
Cycling Plus
Cycling Weekly
Darts World
Dirt Bike Rider
Esquire
F1 Racing
Fieldsports
Fighting Fit
FourFourTwo
GQ
Golf Monthly
Golf World
Horse & Hound
Loaded
Martial Arts Illustrated
Match
Men's Health
Motor Boats Monthly
Motor Cycle News
Motor Sport
Mountain Biking UK
Nuts
Redline
Rowing & Regatta
Rugby World
Running Fitness
Shooting Gazette
Shooting Times & Country Magazine
Ski & Board
The Skier & Snowboarder Magazine
Snooker Scene
Spin
Sports Boat & RIB Magazine
Sports Shooter
Stadium & Arena Management
Swimming Times

Today's Golfer
Visordown
Windsurf Magazine
The Wisden Cricketer
Yachts and Yachting
Zoo

Travel

A Place in the Sun
Australia & New Zealand
Business Life
Business Traveller
Coach and Bus Week
Condé Nast Customer Publishing
Condé Nast Traveller
Food & Travel
France
French Magazine
Geographical
Good Housekeeping
Italia!
The Lady
Living France
Motorhome Monthly
Motoring & Leisure
Olive
Real Travel
Saga Magazine
Spain
Sunday Times Travel Magazine
Travel & Leisure Magazine
The Traveller
Wanderlust
Woman&Home
Yours

Wildlife

Amateur Photographer
BBC Countryfile
BBC Wildlife
Bird Watching
Birdwatch
Coast
Country Life
Country Walking
The Countryman
Cumbria
Dalesman
Dorset
The Falconers & Raptor Conservation
    Magazine

The Field
Geographical
The Lady
Natural World
Outdoor Photography
Photography Monthly

PhotoPlus
Practical Photography
The Scottish Sporting Gazette
The Shooting Gazette
Shooting Times and Country Magazine
Sporting Shooter

Angling

ANGLER'S MAIL
IPC Media Ltd, Blue Fin Building, 110 Southwark Street, London SE1 0SU.
Tel: 020 3148 4159. E-mail: tim_knight@ipcmedia.com
Editor: Tim Knight.
Weekly publication with news and features for followers of coarse and sea fishing in the UK.
Illustrations: Topical news pictures of successful anglers with their catches. Captions should give full details concerning weight and circumstances of capture. Covers: pictures of anglers with exceptional specimen fish or catches.
Text: Features on coarse and sea fishing topics only. Up to 800 words.
Overall freelance potential: Minimal for non-angling freelances.
Editor's tips: Contributors really need knowledge and experience of the subject; pictures and text seen from non-anglers are rarely acceptable.
Fees: By agreement.

ANGLING TIMES
Bauer Media, Bushfield House, Orton Centre, Peterborough PE2 5UW.
Tel: 01733 395106. E-mail: rich.lee@bauermedia.co.uk
Editor: Richard Lee.
Weekly newspaper format publication covering mainly coarse angling. Includes news, features and general instruction.
Illustrations: General angling images, especially newsworthy catches, action and scenics. Covers: "stunning" action shots featuring anglers in the environment.
Text: Illustrated features on all aspects of the hobby. Up to 800 words.
Overall freelance potential: A good percentage used each week.
Fees: By agreement.

COARSE FISHERMAN
Metrocrest Ltd, 2 Harcourt Way, Meridian Business Park, Leicester LE19 1WP.
Tel: 0116 289 4567. E-mail: info@conceptdesignltd.co.uk
Editor: Stuart Dexter.
Monthly magazine covering all aspects of coarse fishing.
Illustrations: Pictures of anglers in action or riverside/lakeside scenes where coarse angling takes place. Covers: colour pictures showing anglers displaying particularly fine catches.
Text: Articles of 1,000–2,000 words, most usually first person accounts of angling experiences.
Overall freelance potential: Excellent scope for angling specialists.
Fees: Pictures from £10 upwards. £25 per 1,000 words for text.

FLY FISHING & FLY TYING
Rolling River Publications Ltd, The Locus Centre, The Square, Aberfeldy, Perthshire PH15 2DD.
Tel: 01887 829868. Fax: 01887 829856. E-mail: markb.ffft@btinternet.com
Editor: Mark Bowler.
Monthly for the fly fisherman and fly-tyer.
Illustrations: Shots of fly fishermen in action, scenics of locations, flies and fly-tying, and appropriate insect pictures.
Text: Illustrated articles on all aspects of fly fishing.
Overall freelance potential: Fairly good.

Are you working from the latest edition of The Freelance Photographer's Market Handbook? It's published on 1 October each year. Markets are constantly changing, so it pays to have the latest edition

Editor's tips: Make an effort to avoid bland backgrounds, especially at watersides.
Fees: Colour from £24–£58; covers £50. Text £50 per 1,000 words.

IMPROVE YOUR COARSE FISHING
Bauer Media, Media House, Lynchwood, Peterborough PE2 6EW.
Tel: 01733 468000. Fax: 01733 468300. E-mail: kevin.green@bauermedia.co.uk
Editor: Kevin Green.
Monthly, inspirational, "hints and tips" style magazine for coarse fishing enthusiasts.
Illustrations: Photographs depicting all aspects of coarse fishing.
Text: Ideas for illustrated features from experienced angling writers always considered. 2,500 words; submit a synopsis first.
Overall freelance potential: Limited; much of the editorial content is produced in-house.
Editor's tips: Always query the editor before submitting.
Fees: £50 per picture unless supplied with article; articles £100 – £200 inclusive of pictures.

SEA ANGLER
Bauer Media, Media House, Lynchwood, Peterborough PE2 6EA.
Tel: 01733 468000. E-mail: mel.russ@bauermedia.co.uk
Editor: Mel Russ.
Monthly magazine dealing with the sport of sea angling from both boat and beach.
Illustrations: Good sea fishing and shore fishing pictures, scenic coastline pictures from around the country, and proud anglers with good catches. Covers: Head shots of individual sea fish and anglers displaying an exceptional catch (must be a fresh catch).
Text: Instructional features, fishing expeditions, match articles, etc. 1,000 words.
Overall freelance potential: 50 per cent of published material comes from freelance sources.
Fees: By negotiation; good rates for the right kind of material.

TROUT & SALMON
Bauer Media, Media House, Lynchwood, Peterborough PE2 6EA.
Tel: 01733 465783. E-mail: andrew.flitcroft@bauermedia.co.uk
Editor: Andrew Flitcroft.
Monthly magazine for game fishermen.
Illustrations: Digital files preferred. Photographs of trout or salmon waters, preferably with an angler included in the picture. Close-up and action shots to illustrate particular techniques. Captioned news pictures showing anglers with outstanding catches. Covers: attractive pictures of game fishing waters, always with an angler present.
Text: Instructional illustrated articles on all aspects of game fishing.
Overall freelance potential: Excellent for those who can produce the right sort of material.
Fees: Pictures inside according to use. Cover shots, £80. Text according to length.

TROUT FISHERMAN
Bauer Media, Bushfield House, Orton Centre, Peterborough PE2 5UW.
Tel: 01733 395131. E-mail: russell.hill@bauermedia.co.uk
Editor: Russell Hill.
Monthly magazine for the trout fishing enthusiast.
Illustrations: Colour. Photographs depicting any aspect of angling for trout – outstanding catches, angling locations, techniques, flies and equipment.
Text: Illustrated articles on all aspects of trout fishing, around 1,500 words.
Overall freelance potential: Excellent scope for top quality material.
Editor's tips: Too much angling photography is dull and uninteresting; an original and lively approach would be welcome.
Fees: On a rising scale according to size of reproduction or length of text.

Animals & Wildlife

BBC WILDLIFE

Bristol Magazines Ltd, 14th Floor, Tower House, Fairfax Street, Bristol BS1 3BN.
Tel: 0117 927 9009. Fax: 0117 934 9008. E-mail: sophiestafford@bbcmagazinesbristol.com;
wandasowry@bbcmagazinesbristol.com
Editor: Sophie Stafford. **Picture Researcher:** Wanda Sowry.
Heavily-illustrated magazine for readers with a serious interest in wildlife and environmental
matters. 13 issues per year.
Illustrations: Digital files preferred. Top-quality wildlife and environmental photography of all
kinds, mostly to illustrate specific features. Lists of available stock imagery should be sent to picture
researcher; suggestions for special portfolios or illustrated features to editor. See
www.bbcwildlifemagazine.com for submission guidelines.
Text: Feature suggestions considered from contributors who have a genuine knowledge of their
subject.
Overall freelance potential: Only for the very best quality work.
Fees: Pictures from £50 (under quarter-page) to £150 (dps); covers £300.

BIRD WATCHING

Bauer Active Ltd, Media House, Lynchwood, Peterborough PE2 6EA.
Tel: 01733 468419. E-mail: sheena.harvey@bauermedia.co.uk
Editor: Sheena Harvey.
Monthly magazine devoted to bird watching and ornithology.
Illustrations: Top quality photographs of birds in the wild, both in the UK and overseas. Prefer to
use pictures that illustrate specific aspects of bird behaviour. Also, landscape shots of British bird-
watching sites and of people watching birds. Always query editor before submitting.
Text: Illustrated features on all aspects of birds and bird watching.
Overall freelance potential: Excellent scope for wildlife specialists but much is obtained from
regular contributors.
Fees: By negotiation.

BIRDWATCH

Solo Publishing Ltd, B403A The Chocolate Factory, 5 Clarendon Road, London N22 6XJ.
Tel: 020 8881 0550. E-mail: editorial@birdwatch.co.uk
Editor: Dominic Mitchell. **Picture Editor:** Steve Young.
Monthly for all birdwatchers. Includes a strong emphasis on the photographic side of the hobby.
Illustrations: Digital files only. Good photographs of British and European birds in their natural
habitat. Those with collections of such material should send lists of subjects available.
Text: Well-illustrated features on birdwatching topics, including practical articles on bird
photography. 1,000–1,200 words, but send a synopsis first.
Overall freelance potential: Average.
Fees: According to use.

DOGS TODAY

Pet Subjects Ltd, The Dog House, 4 Bonseys Lane, Chobham, Surrey GU24 8JJ.
Tel: 01276 858880. Fax: 01276 858860. E-mail: enquiries@dogstodaymagazine.co.uk
Editor: Beverley Cuddy.
Monthly magazine for the pet dog lover.
Illustrations: News pictures or shots showing dogs in action, in specific situations, and interacting
with people (especially children). Will also consider exciting or amusing photo sequences and
pictures of celebrities with their dogs. No simple dog portraits unless displaying a strong element of

humour or sentiment. Shots of crossbreeds always needed.
Text: General illustrated features about dogs. Should be positive and have a "human interest" feel.
Overall freelance potential: Excellent for the right material.
Fees: According to use.

THE FALCONERS & RAPTOR CONSERVATION MAGAZINE

PW Publishing Ltd, Arrowsmith Court, Station Approach, Broadstone, Dorset BH18 8PW.
Tel: 0845 803 1979. Fax: 01202 659950. E-mail: steve@pwpublishing.ltd.uk
Editor: Peter Eldrett. **Art Editor:** Stephen Hunt.
Quarterly magazine devoted to falconry and birds of prey.
Illustrations: Images usually only required to illustrate specific articles as below. Covers: Striking images of birds of prey.
Text: Articles on falconry and related topics. 1,000–5,000 words.
Overall freelance potential: Little scope for individual photographs, but complete illustrated articles always welcome.
Editor's tips: Free author's guide available on request.
Fees: By negotiation.

K9 MAGAZINE

K9 Media Solutions, 21 High Street, Warsop, Mansfield, Notts NG20 0AA.
Tel: 08700 114 115. E-mail: mail@k9magazine.com
Editor: Ryan O'Meara.
Quarterly magazine plus extensive website (www.k9magazine.com), described as the only lifestyle magazine for British dog lovers.
Illustrations: Colour. Digital files preferred. High quality dog images – breeds, puppies, dogs with people, dogs in action, etc. Submit low-res samples via e-mail in the first instance. Some commissions available to experienced animal photographers.
Text: Illustrated features on aspects of dog behaviour and dog ownership.
Overall freelance potential: Only top quality material considered.
Fees: By negotiation.

KENNEL AND CATTERY MANAGEMENT

Albatross Publications, PO Box 523, Horsham, West Sussex RH12 4WL.
Tel: 01293 871201. Fax: 01293 871301. E-mail: newsdesk123@aol.com
Editor: Carol Andrews.
Bi-monthly magazine for boarding kennel/cattery proprietors, dog/cat breeders, rescue homes, etc.
Illustrations: Pictures depicting relevant subjects, but only required as part of a complete illustrated feature.
Text: Illustrated articles on any topic relating to the above, including cat/dog care.
Overall freelance potential: Limited.
Fees: By negotiation.

NATURAL WORLD

The Wildlife Trusts, The Kiln, Waterside, Mather Road, Newark, Nottinghamshire NG24 1WT.
Tel: 01636 670000. Fax: 0870 0360101.
Editor: Rupert Paul.
The magazine of The Wildlife Trusts, concerned with all aspects of wildlife and countryside conservation in the UK. Published three times per year.
Illustrations: Interesting shots of British mammals, amphibians, insects, flowers and trees.

As a member of the Bureau of Freelance Photographers, you'll be kept up-to-date with markets through the BFP Market Newsletter, published monthly. For details of membership, turn to page 9

Subjects must be wild; no pets or zoo animals.
Text: Short photo-features on wildlife or conservation topics particularly connected with local Wildlife Trusts. Around 300 words.
Overall freelance potential: Limited.
Fees: £35 minimum.

YOUR CAT
BPG (Stamford) Ltd, Roebuck House, 33 Broad Street, Stamford, Lincs PE9 1RB.
Tel: 01780 766199. Fax: 01780 766416. E-mail: s.parslow@bournepublishinggroup.co.uk
Editor: Sue Parslow.
Monthly magazine for all cat lovers. Covers every type of cat including the household moggie and pedigree cats.
Illustrations: Mostly by commission to accompany features as below. Limited scope for interesting, unusual or humorous single pictures.
Text: Illustrated news items and features on the widest variety of topics relating to cats: famous cats, cats in the news, readers' cats, rare cats, cats that earn a living, etc. Also authoritative articles on practical matters: behaviour, grooming, training, etc.
Overall freelance potential: Limited.
Fees: By negotiation.

YOUR DOG
BPG (Stamford) Ltd, Roebuck House, 33 Broad Street, Stamford, Lincs PE9 1RB.
Tel: 01780 766199. Fax: 01780 766416. E-mail: s.wright@bournepublishinggroup.co.uk
Editor: Sarah Wright.
Monthly magazine for "the everyday dog owner", with the emphasis on care and training.
Illustrations: Top quality pictures showing dogs and their owners in a practical context, i.e. walking, training, grooming; dogs in the news; amusing pictures. For covers pictures must be of the highest technical quality.
Text: Illustrated news stories, practical features, and articles on any interesting canine subject, i.e. working dogs, dog charities, celebrities and their dogs, etc. Always contact editor before submitting.
Overall freelance potential: Fair.
Editor's tips: Make sure that pictures are recent and not just something dug up from the back of the filing cabinet.
Fees: According to size of reproduction and by negotiation.

Architecture & Building

ARCHITECTURE TODAY
Architecture Today plc, 161 Rosebery Avenue, London EC1R 4QX.
Tel: 020 7837 0143. Fax: 020 7837 0155. E-mail: chris.f@architecturetoday.co.uk
Editor: Chris Foges.
Independent monthly for the architectural profession. Covers the most important projects in the UK and Europe, from art galleries to social housing and from interiors to urban design.
Illustrations: Most photography is commissioned, but interesting pictures of current architectural projects are always of interest on spec.
Text: Illustrated articles of genuine interest to a professional readership; submit ideas only first. 800–2,000 words.
Overall freelance potential: Some scope for specialists.
Editor's tips: Potential contributors must contact the editors before submitting anything.
Fees: £100 per 1,000 words; photography by arrangement.

BD (BUILDING DESIGN)

CMP Information, Ludgate House, 245 Blackfriars Road, London SE1 9UY.
Tel: 020 7921 5000. Fax: 020 7921 8244. E-mail: abaillieu@cmpi.biz
Editor: Amanda Baillieu. News **Editor:** Will Hurst.
Weekly newspaper for architects and architectural technicians.
Illustrations: News pictures may be considered on spec but most photography commissioned to illustrate major stories and features. Photographers should have a proven record in architectural photography and a demonstrable understanding of what it should capture. Submit samples of work along with details of experience.
Text: News pieces and features on all aspects of building design, by those with real understanding of the subject matter. Always make contact before submitting.
Overall freelance potential: Good for those with the requisite expertise.
Fees: Pictures variable according to use etc. Text around £160 per 1,000 words.

BUILD IT

Ocean Media Group Ltd, 19th Floor, 1 Canada Square, Canary Wharf, London E14 5AP.
Tel: 020 7772 8300. Fax: 020 7772 8584. E-mail: duncan.hayes@oceanmedia.co.uk
Editor: Duncan Hayes.
Monthly devoted to the self-build and home improvement market – ranging from those building a one-off home or converting old buildings to major extension and renovation projects.
Illustrations: Commissions available to experienced photographers to cover architecture, building work and interiors. Some interest in relevant stock photographs of housing and interior decoration subjects.
Text: Authoritative features on building, landscaping and interior design, plus specialised articles on finance, legal issues, weatherproofing, etc.
Overall freelance potential: Excellent for the experienced contributor in the architecture and interiors field.
Fees: Good rates for photographers; text negotiable.

BUILDERS' MERCHANTS JOURNAL

Faversham House Group, Faversham House, 232A Addington Road, South Croydon CR2 8LE.
Tel: 020 8651 7100. Fax: 020 8651 7117. E-mail: colinpetty@fav-house.com
Editor: Mark Rowland.
Monthly business to business magazine for the builders merchants industry – wholesale distributors of building products, including heating, bathroom and kitchen fixtures.
Illustrations: Always interested in unusual photography of merchants' yards, computers, showrooms and vehicles. Ongoing requirement for shots of house building/refurbishment work. Possible scope for creative still life shots of items such as bricks, blocks, timber, etc. Commissions also available, depending on geographic location – write in with details of experience and rates.
Text: Limited scope for freelance articles on suitable subjects – send business card and samples of published work in the first instance.
Overall freelance potential: Limited.
Editor's tips: Most commissions here tend to be rather mundane, usually involving quite general shots of a merchant's yard. Need photographers who can provide a more creative approach. Write in the first instance – do not telephone.
Fees: Photographs by negotiation. Text around £125 per 1,000 words.

Are you working from the latest edition of The Freelance Photographer's Market Handbook? It's published on 1 October each year. Markets are constantly changing, so it pays to have the latest edition

FX

Wilmington Business Information Ltd, 91 Charterhouse Street, London EC1M 6HR.
Tel: 020 7336 5213. Fax: 020 7336 5201. E-mail: tdowling@fxmagazine.co.uk
Editor: Theresa Dowling. **Art Editor:** Wesley Mitchell.
Monthly interior design business magazine for the retail, hotel and commercial sectors. Aimed at architects, designers and their clients.
Illustrations: By commission only; experienced architectural and interiors photographers with fresh ideas always welcome.
Text: Articles on commercial design matters and related business issues, only from those with real expertise in these areas.
Overall freelance potential: Good for the experienced worker.
Editor's tips: The magazine is very receptive to original ideas. Articles should be hard-hitting and possibly contentious.
Fees: Photography around £200–£250 per day. £160 per 1,000 words.

H&V NEWS

EMAP Trenton, Greater London House, Hampstead Road, London NW1 7EJ.
Tel: 020 7728 4652. Fax: 020 7391 3435. E-mail: claudia.hathway@emap.com
Editor: Dennis Flower.
Weekly for those who purchase or specify heating, ventilating and air conditioning equipment.
Illustrations: Pictures of installations and equipment in active use, preferably with a human interest element.
Text: News stories, installation stories regarding heating, ventilating and air conditioning equipment, stories on companies and people. 200–300 words. Longer features by negotiation.
Overall freelance potential: Good scope for newsworthy material.
Editor's tips: The more current the information supplied the better its chance of success.
Fees: £12 per 100 words; pictures by negotiation.

HOUSEBUILDER

Housebuilder Publications Ltd, Byron House, 7-9 St James's Street, London SW1A 1DW.
Tel: 020 7960 1630. Fax: 020 7960 1631. E-mail: ben.roskrow@house-builder.co.uk
Editor: Ben Roskrow.
Monthly journal of the House Builders Federation. Aimed at key decision makers, managers, technical staff, marketing executives, architects and local authorities.
Illustrations: Some scope for housebuilding coverage, but only by prior consultation with the editor.
Text: Features on marketing, land and planning, government liaison, finance, materials, supplies, etc. Always to be discussed before submission. 1,000 words.
Overall freelance potential: Around 50 per cent comes from freelances.
Editor's tips: Authoritative articles and news stories only. No PR "puffs".
Fees: £150 per 1,000 words; pictures by agreement.

ICON

Media Ten Ltd, National House, High Street, Epping, Essex CM16 4BD.
Tel: 01992 570030. Fax: 01992 570031. E-mail: justin@icon-magazine.co.uk
Editor: Chris Turner. **Art Editor:** Shazai Chaudry.
Monthly magazine covering architecture and design, aimed at both professionals and interested consumers.
Illustrations: Top quality architectural and design photography, mostly by commission. Submit ideas and samples in the first instance. Also runs a regular monthly showcase, "Icon Hang", for individual photographer's portfolios.
Text: Suggestions considered, but contributors must really know their subject.
Overall freelance potential: Fair.
Editor's tips: Potential contributors should really study the magazine first in order to "tune in" to

what it is trying to do.

LANDSCAPE
Wardour Publishing & Design, Walmar House, 296 Regent Street, London W1B 3AW.
Tel: 020 7016 2555. E-mail: jeff@wardour.co.uk
Editor: George Bull. **Art Director:** Steven Gregor.
Official magazine of The Landscape Institute. Aimed at professionals either producing or commissioning landscape architecture and designed to showcase the best work in the field.
Illustrations: Mostly by commission only; always happy to hear from photographers who can offer high-level skills in architectural work.
Text: Ideas for features will be considered.
Overall freelance potential: Good scope for experienced workers.
Editor's tips: Requirements are very specific, so in the first instance submit only a couple of samples as an indication of style.
Fees: By negotiation.

RIBA JOURNAL
Atom Publishing Ltd, 45/47 Clerkenwell Green, London EC1R 0EB.
Tel: 020 7490 5595. Fax: 020 7490 4957. E-mail: hugh@atompublishing.co.uk
Editor: Hugh Pearman. **Art Editor:** Mark Bergin.
Monthly magazine of the Royal Institute of British Architects. Covers general aspects of architectural practice as well as criticisms of particular buildings, profiles and interviews.
Illustrations: Pictures of buildings, old, new and refurbished. Covers: colour pictures connected with main feature inside. Best to send list of subjects initially.
Text: Illustrated features on architectural subjects and criticisms of particular buildings.
Overall freelance potential: Fair.
Fees: By arrangement.

SELFBUILD & DESIGN
WW Magazines Ltd, 151 Station Street, Burton-on-Trent DE14 1BG.
Tel/fax: 01584 841417. E-mail: ross.stokes@sbdonline.co.uk
Editor: Ross Stokes.
Monthly practical consumer magazine covering self-build housing, including conversions and major extensions.
Illustrations: Striking photographs of recently completed self-builds (interiors and exteriors), particularly those of an innovative design or in unusual or visually appealing locations. Coverage of new builds by celebrities also welcomed.
Text: Authoritative and well illustrated articles covering all aspects of building and renovation, including brief items of a quirky, amusing or informative nature. Telephone to discuss ideas before submission.
Overall freelance potential: Good.
Fees: By negotiation.

STADIUM & ARENA MANAGEMENT
Alad Ltd. Editorial: 4 North Street, Rothersthorpe, Northants NN7 3JB.
Tel: 01604 832149. E-mail: mark.webb@tesco.net
Editor: Mark Webb.
Bi-monthly, international news magazine covering all aspects of stadium and arena design, construction and management.
Illustrations: Photographs of new stadia or arenas internationally, but especially in Europe, preferably at the construction stage. Also newsworthy images involving stadia.
Text: News items always considered.
Overall freelance potential: Fair.
Fees: By negotiation.

Arts & Entertainment

HEAT
Bauer Media, Endeavour House, 189 Shaftesbury Avenue, London WC2H 8JG.
Tel: 020 7295 5000. Fax: 020 7817 8847. E-mail: john.robinson@heatmag.com
Editor: Sam Delaney. Picture Director: John Robinson.
Popular entertainment weekly with news, reviews and heavy celebrity content.
Illustrations: Interested in hearing from photographers covering live events throughout the UK.
Assignments available to shoot performances and behind-the-scenes coverage. Some scope for
paparazzi-type material.
Text: No scope.
Overall freelance potential: Good.
Fees: By negotiation.

RADIO TIMES
BBC Worldwide Publishing, Woodlands, 80 Wood Lane, London W12 0TT.
Tel: 020 8433 2000. Fax: 020 8433 3160. E-mail: roger.dickson@bbc.co.uk
Editor: Ben Preston. **Picture Editor:** Roger Dickson.
Weekly TV and radio listings magazine, containing news and features on mainly BBC productions
and personalities.
Illustrations: Coverage of broadcasting events, BBC productions, and TV personalities, usually by
commission.
Text: Commissioned features on TV personalities or programmes of current interest.
Overall freelance potential: Fair for commissioned work.
Fees: Various.

THE STAGE
The Stage Newspaper Ltd, 47 Bermondsey Street, London SE1 3XT.
Tel: 020 7403 1818. Fax: 020 7357 9287. E-mail: editor@thestage.co.uk
Editor: Brian Attwood.
Weekly newspaper for professionals working in the performing arts and the entertainment industry.
Illustrations: News pictures concerning people and events in the theatre and television worlds.
Text: Features on the theatre and light entertainment. 800 words.
Overall freelance potential: Limited.
Fees: Pictures by agreement, text £100 per 1,000 words.

TV TIMES
IPC Media Ltd, Blue Fin Building, 110 Southwark Street, London SE1 0SU.
Tel: 020 3148 5570. Fax: 020 3148 8115. E-mail: elaine_mccluskey@ipcmedia.com
Editor: Ian Abbott. **Art Director:** Steve Fawcett. **Picture Editor:** Elaine McCluskey.
Weekly television programme listings magazine, plus features on major programmes.
Illustrations: Usually commissioned or requested from specialist sources. Mainly quality colour
portraits or groups specific to current programme content.
Text: Articles on personalities and programmes.
Overall freelance potential: Between 50 and 75 per cent each week is freelance, but mostly from
recognised contributors.
Fees: Negotiable.

---

*As a member of the Bureau of Freelance Photographers, you'll be
kept up-to-date with markets through the BFP Market Newsletter,
published monthly. For details of membership, turn to page 9*

Aviation

AEROPLANE

IPC Media Ltd, Blue Fin Building, 110 Southwark Street, London SE1 0SU.
Tel: 020 3148 4100. E-mail: editoraero@ipcmedia.com
Editor: Michael Oakey.
Monthly aviation history magazine, specialising in the period 1909–1960. Occasional features on modern aviation.
Illustrations: Colour; B&W archive material. Photographs for use in their own right or for stock. Main interests – veteran or vintage aircraft, including those in museums; preserved airworthy aircraft; unusual pictures of modern aircraft. Action shots preferred in the case of colour material – air-to-air, ground-to-air, or air-to-ground. Covers: high quality air-to-air shots of vintage or veteran aircraft.
Text: Short news stories concerning preserved aircraft, new additions to museums and collections, etc. Not more than 300 words.
Overall freelance potential: Most contributions are from freelance sources, but specialised knowledge and skills are often necessary.
Editor's tips: The magazine is always in the market for sharp, good quality colour images of preserved aircraft in the air.
Fees: Colour photographs: full page £80; centre spread £100; covers £180. B&W from £10 upwards.

AIR INTERNATIONAL

Key Publishing Ltd, PO Box 100, Stamford, Lincolnshire PE9 1XQ.
Tel: 01780 755131. Fax: 01780 757261. E-mail: mark.ayton@keypublishing.com
Editor: Mark Ayton.
Monthly general aviation magazine covering both modern military aircraft and the civil aviation industry. Includes some historical topics. Aimed at both enthusiasts and industry professionals.
Illustrations: Topical single pictures or picture stories on aviation subjects worldwide, e.g. aircraft in active war zones, airliners in new livery, new aircraft at Heathrow, etc. Overseas material welcomed. Air show coverage rarely required.
Text: Illustrated features on topics as above, from writers with in-depth knowledge of the subject. Length variable.
Overall freelance potential: Very good for suitable material.
Editor's tips: Remember the magazine is read by professionals and is not just for enthusiasts.
Fees: B&W from £10; colour based on page rate of £75. Covers, up to £120 for full-bleed sole reproduction. Text £50 per 1,000 words.

AIRFORCES MONTHLY

Key Publishing Ltd, PO Box 100, Stamford, Lincolnshire PE9 1XQ.
Tel: 01780 755131. Fax: 01780 751323. E-mail: edafm@keypublishing.com
Editor: Alan Warnes.
Monthly magazine concerned with modern military aircraft.
Illustrations: Mostly colour. Interesting, up-to-date pictures of military aircraft from any country. Must be current; archive material rarely used.
Text: Knowledgeable articles concerning current military aviation. No historical matter.
Overall freelance potential: Good for contributors with the necessary knowledge and access.
Fees: £25 minimum for colour; £10 minimum for B&W; covers £120. Text by negotiation.

AIRLINER WORLD

Key Publishing Ltd, PO Box 100, Stamford, Lincs PE9 1XQ.
Tel: 01780 755131. Fax: 01780 757261. E-mail: tony.dixon@keypublishing.com
Editor: Tony Dixon.

Heavily-illustrated monthly for civil aviation enthusiasts.
Illustrations: Colour, some B&W. Always interested in topical photos covering the commercial airline scene, including business jets – new aircraft being rolled out, new liveries, new airlines, airport developments, etc. International coverage. Some archive material used; send stock lists.
Text: Will consider ideas for articles on any civil aviation theme, around 2,000 words. Contributors must have in-depth knowledge of their subject.
Overall freelance potential: Excellent.
Fees: Pictures from £20; text £50 per 1,000 words.

AIRPORT WORLD
Insight Media Ltd, Sovereign House, 26-30 London Road, Twickenham TW1 3RW.
Tel: 020 8831 7507. Fax: 020 8891 0123. E-mail: joe@airport-world.com
Editor: Joe Bates.
Bi-monthly trade journal published for the Airports Council International, circulated to airport operators worldwide.
Illustrations: Recent photographs taken in airports and airport terminals in any part of the world – must be high quality pictures with a creative approach. Before submitting photographers should first send details of airports they have on file.
Text: No scope.
Overall freelance potential: Fair.
Fees: By negotiation.

AIRPORTS INTERNATIONAL
Key Publishing Ltd, PO Box 100, Stamford, Lincs PE9 1XQ.
Tel: 01780 755131. Fax: 01780 757261. E-mail: tom.allett@keypublishing.com
Editor: Tom Allett.
Published nine times a year, dealing with all aspects of airport construction, management, operations, services and equipment worldwide.
Illustrations: Photographs related to airport operational affairs. Particularly interested in high quality images for cover use, and coverage of "exotic" overseas locations. Always contact the editor before submitting.
Text: Possible scope for overseas material, depending on region; Middle East, Asia-Pacific, South America and Africa of particular interest.
Overall freelance potential: Fair.
Fees: By negotiation.

AVIATION NEWS
Key Publishing, PO Box 100, Stamford, PE9 1XQ.
Tel: 01780 755131. E-mail:editor@aviation-news.co.uk
Editor: David Baker.
Monthly magazine covering aviation in general, both past and present. Aimed at both the industry and the enthusiast.
Illustrations: Colour; B&W archive material. Photographs of all types of aircraft, civil and military, old or new. Captioned news pictures of particular interest, but no space exploration or aircraft engineering.
Text: News items about current aviation matters. Historical contributions concerning older aircraft.
Overall freelance potential: About 45 per cent is contributed by freelances.
Fees: On a rising scale according to size of reproduction or length of text.

DEFENCE HELICOPTER/ROTORHUB
The Shephard Press Ltd, 268 Bath Road, Slough, Berkshire SL1 4DX.
Tel: 01753 727020 Fax: 01753 727002. E-mail: ts@shephard.co.uk
Editor: Tony Skinner.
Defence Helicopter is concerned with military and parapublic helicopter use. Rotorhub magazine

covers the civil, public service and corporate rotorcraft market.

Illustrations: Pictures of military, public service (police, coastguard, etc), civil and corporate helicopters anywhere in the world. Must be accurately captioned. Covers: high quality pictures of appropriate helicopters. Should preferably be exclusive and in upright format. No "sterile" pictures; must be action shots.

Text: News stories and features on helicopters in service use and helicopter technology. Up to 1,500 words.

Overall freelance potential: Moderate.

Fees: By negotiation.

FLIGHT INTERNATIONAL

Reed Business Information Ltd, Quadrant House, The Quadrant, Sutton, Surrey SM2 5AS.

Tel: 020 8652 3842. Fax: 020 8652 3840. E-mail: gareth.burgess@flightglobal.com

Editor: Murdo Morrison. Group **Art Editor:** Gareth Burgess.

Weekly aviation magazine with worldwide circulation, aimed at aerospace professionals in all sectors of the industry.

Illustrations: Weekly requirement for news pictures of aviation-related events. Feature illustrations on all aspects of aerospace, from airliners to satellites. Covers: clean, uncluttered pictures of aircraft – civil and military, light and business.

Text: News items always welcomed. Features by prior arrangement only; submit ideas in the first instance.

Overall freelance potential: Limited for those without contacts in the industry.

Editor's tips: News material should be submitted on spec. Pictures should always be as new as possible or have a news relevance.

Fees: B&W, £19.61; colour, £56.38 up to 30 sq.in., £65.93 to £106.93 30–60 sq. in.; £223.30 for cover. News reports, minimum £7.07 per 100 words; commissioned features by negotiation.

FLYER

Seager Publishing Ltd, 9 Riverside Court, Lower Bristol Road, Bath BA2 3DZ.

Tel: 01225 481440. Fax: 01225 481262. E-mail: ianw@flyermag.co.uk

Editor: Ian Waller.

Monthly magazine for private pilots.

Illustrations: Attractive and striking photographs of light aircraft of the type commonly used by the private pilot, mainly required for DPS feature "Opening Shot". Details of material available should be sent first, rather than speculative submissions.

Text: News items and illustrated articles from those with good knowledge of the subject, with the aim of entertaining and amusing as much as conveying facts. Anecdotal personal experiences always of interest. 1,500–3,000 words for major features.

Overall freelance potential: Limited – mainly provided by established contributors.

Editor's tips: All contributors should have a genuine understanding of the flying scene.

Fees: By negotiation.

PILOT

Archant Specialist, 3 The Courtyard, Denmark Street, Wokingham, Berkshire RG40 2AZ.

Tel: 0118 989 7246. Fax: 01799 544201. E-mail: nick.bloom@pilotweb.co.uk

Editor: Nick Bloom.

Monthly publication for the general aviation (i.e. business and private flying) pilot.

Illustrations: Pictures on topics associated with this field of flying.

Text: Features, preferably illustrated, on general aviation. 2,000–4,000 words.

Overall freelance potential: Excellent. Virtually all of the editorial matter in the magazine is contributed by freelances.

Editor's tips: Read a copy of the magazine before submitting and study style, content, subject and coverage.
Fees: £150–£800 for features. Pictures inside £30; covers £250.

TODAY'S PILOT
Key Publishing Ltd, PO Box 100, Stamford, Lincs PE9 1XQ.
Tel: 01780 755131. Fax: 01780 757261. E-mail: dave.unwin@keypublishing.com
Editor: David Unwin.
Monthly aimed at both private and commercial pilots, those learning to fly, and general aviation enthusiasts.
Illustrations: Will consider any news-based or unusual photographs likely to be of interest to the readership.
Text: Always interested in well-illustrated, authoritative articles on any aspect of private or commercial flying, ranging from travelogues to technical pieces. Submit suggestions only in the first instance
Overall freelance potential: Good scope for illustrated articles.
Fees: By negotiation.

Boating & Watersport

BOARDS
Yachting Press Ltd, 1 West Smithfield, London, EC1A 9JU
Tel: 020 7332 9700.. E-mail: editorial@boards.co.uk
Editor: Dave White.
Monthly magazine devoted to boardsailing and windsurfing.
Illustrations: Good clear action shots of boardsailing or windsurfing; pictures of attractive girls in a boardsailing context; any other visually striking material relating to the sport. Covers: good colour action shots always needed.
Text: Articles and features on all aspects of the sport.
Overall freelance potential: Very good for high quality material.
Editor's tips: Action shots must be clean, clear and crisp.
Fees: By negotiation.

BOAT INTERNATIONAL
Boat International Media, First Floor, 41-47 Hartfield Road, Wimbledon, London SW19 3RQ,
Tel: 020 8545 9330. Fax: 020 8545 9333. E-mail: amandam@boatinternationalmedia.com
Editor: Amanda McCracken.
Monthly glossy magazine focusing on the top, luxury level of sailing and power vessels.
Illustrations: Will consider images of world class yacht racing and luxury cruising.
Text: Mostly staff produced or commissioned from top writers in the field.
Overall freelance potential: Excellent for the best in boating photography and marine subjects.
Editor's tips: Only the very best quality is of interest.
Fees: By negotiation.

BOATING BUSINESS
Mercator Media Ltd, The Old Mill, Lower Quay, Fareham, Hants PO16 0RA.
Tel: 01329 825335. Fax: 01329 825220. E-mail: pnash@boatingbusiness.com
Editor: Peter Nash.
Monthly magazine for the leisure marine trade.
Illustrations: News pictures relating to the marine trade, especially company and overseas news.

Some scope for commissioned work.
Text: Features on marine trade topics; always consult the editor first.
Overall freelance potential: Limited.
Fees: Photographs from £20; text £100 per 1,000 words.

CANAL BOAT

Archant Specialist, 3 The Courtyard, Denmark Street, Wokingham, Berkshire RG40 2AZ.
Tel: 0118 989 7215. E-mail: nick.wall@archant.co.uk
Editor: Nick Wall.
Monthly specialist title covering inland boating especially on canals, looking at boats, boat ownership and cruising.
Illustrations: Photographs depicting colourful boats, attractive waterways, scenery and seasonal elements, but mainly published as part of an illustrated article.
Text: Good opportunities for illustrated features on canal boats and boating personalities.
Overall freelance potential: Good opportunities for good freelance photojournalists.
Editor's tips: Good ideas will be enthusiatically received, but study the magazine before making contact.
Fees: According to use of material.

CANALS & RIVERS

A E Morgan Publications Ltd. Editorial: PO Box 618, Norwich NR7 0QT.
Tel: 01603 708930. E-mail: chris@themag.fsnet.co.uk
Editor: Chris Cattrall.
Monthly publication aimed at inland waterway enthusiasts and canal holidaymakers.
Illustrations: Photographs of all inland waterway subjects. Covers: colour pictures of attractive waterways subjects, preferably with an original approach.
Text: Illustrated articles on canals, rivers, boats and allied subjects.
Overall freelance potential: Good, especially for material with an original approach.
Fees: By negotiation.

CLASSIC BOAT

IPC Country & Leisure Group, Leon House, 233 High Street, Croydon CR9 1HZ.
Tel: 020 8726 8000. Fax: 020 8774 0943. E-mail: cb@ipcmedia.com
Editor: Dan Houston. **Art Editor:** Peter Smith.
Monthly magazine for the enthusiast interested in traditional or traditional-style boats from any part of the world. Emphasis on sailing boats, but also covers traditional power boats, steam vessels and modern reproductions of classic styles.
Illustrations: Digital files and transparencies accepted. Pictures to accompany features and articles. Single general interest pictures with 100 word captions giving full subject details. Particular interest in individual boat photo essays. Covers: spectacular sailing images, but exceptional boat building shots may be used. Upright format with space for logo and coverlines.
Text: Well-illustrated articles covering particular types of boat and individual craft, combining well-researched historical background with hard practical advice about restoration and maintenance. Some scope for humorous pieces and cruising articles involving classic boats. Always send a detailed synopsis in the first instance.
Overall freelance potential: Good for those with specialist knowledge or access.
Editor's tips: Well-documented and photographed practical articles do best.
Fees: £90-£100 per page pro rata; covers £200.

Are you working from the latest edition of The Freelance Photographer's Market Handbook? It's published on 1 October each year. Markets are constantly changing, so it pays to have the latest edition

---

INTERNATIONAL BOAT INDUSTRY

IPC Country & Leisure Media Ltd, Leon House, 233 High Street, Croydon CR9 1HZ.
Tel: 020 8726 8134. Fax: 020 8726 8196. E-mail: ed_slack@ipcmedia.com
Editor: Ed Slack.
Business publication dealing with the marine leisure industry worldwide. Eight issues a year.
Illustrations: Pictures of boat building and moulding, chandlery shops, showrooms, new boats and equipment. Also marinas.
Text: News items about the boat industry are always of interest.
Overall freelance potential: Good for those in touch with the boat trade.
Editor's tips: This is strictly a trade magazine – general pictures of cruising or racing are not required.
Fees: Linear scale – £100 per page down.

JET SKIER & PW

CSL Publishing Ltd, Alliance House, 49 Sydney Street, Cambridge CB2 3HX.
Tel: 01223 460490. Fax: 01223 315960. E-mail: spicer@jetskier.co.uk
Editor: Sue Baggaley.
Monthly magazine devoted to small, powered water craft and related sports activity. Features jet skis, wetbikes and other personal watercraft.
Illustrations: Spectacular action shots and pictures of unusual individual craft and uses. Events coverage usually by commission.
Text: Some scope for illustrated articles from those with good knowledge of the subject. Submit ideas only in the first instance.
Overall freelance potential: Good.
Fees: By negotiation.

MOTOR BOAT & YACHTING

IPC Media Ltd, Blue Fin Building, 110 Southwark Street, London SE1 0SU.
Tel: 020 3148 4651. Fax: 020 3148 8128. E-mail: mby@ipcmedia.com
Editor: Hugo Andreae. **Deputy Editor:** Stewart Campbell. **Art Editor:** Caroline Creighton-Metcalf.
Monthly magazine for owners and users of motor cruisers.
Illustrations: Mostly required as part of feature packages as below. May consider pictures of motor cruisers at sea, harbour scenes, workboats, people enjoying life on motor boats, but check with editor before submitting.
Text: Features on interesting, unusual or historic motor boats; first-person motor boat cruising accounts; technical motor boating topics. 1,500–2,500 words.
Overall freelance potential: Around 40 per cent of features and 20 per cent of pictures are freelance contributed.
Fees: Good; on a rising scale according to size of reproduction or length of article.

MOTOR BOATS MONTHLY

IPC Inspire, Blue Fin Building, 110 Southwark Street, London SE1 0SU.
Tel: 020 3148 4664. Fax: 020 3148 8128. E-mail: mbm@ipc.co.uk
Editor: Carl Richardson. **News Editor:** Sally Coffey.
Monthly magazine for all motorboating enthusiasts, but mainly aimed at owners of boats of up to 60 feet. Covers all aspects, from top level powerboat racing to inland waterway cruising.
Illustrations: Digital files preferred. News pictures, motor boat action, and shots of cruising locations, both in UK and overseas.
Text: Illustrated articles on any motorboat-related topic, UK and worldwide.
Overall freelance potential: Fairly good.
Fees: On a rising scale according to size of reproduction or length of text.

PRACTICAL BOAT OWNER
IPC Magazines Ltd, Westover House, West Quay Road, Poole, Dorset BH15 1JG.
Tel: 01202 440820. Fax: 01202 440860. E-mail: pbo@ipcmedia.com
Editor: Sarah Norbury. **Art Editor:** Kevin Slater.
Monthly magazine for yachtsmen, sail and power.
Illustrations: Up to date pictures of boats, harbours and anchorages. Covers: Action shots of cruising boats up to about 40ft (preferably sail). Must have strong colours.
Text: Features and associated illustrations of real use to the people who own boats. Subjects can cover any aspect of boating, from buying a boat through to navigation, seamanship, care and maintenance.
Overall freelance potential: About 25 per cent bought from contributors.
Fees: On a rising scale according to size of reproduction or length of feature.

RYA MAGAZINE
Royal Yachting Association, RYA House, Ensign Way, Hamble, Southampton SO31 4YA.
Tel: 023 8060 4100. E-mail: deborah.cornick@rya.org.uk
Editor: Deborah Cornick.
Quarterly publication for personal members of the RYA, affiliated clubs and class associations.
Illustrations: Digital files preferred. Pictures of boats, yachting events and personalities, used either in their own right or as illustrations for reports and articles. Covers: seasonal/topical shots of yachting subjects.
Text: Reports and articles on yachting.
Overall freelance potential: Moderate.
Fees: By arrangement.

ROWING & REGATTA
British Rowing Ltd, 6 Lower Mall, London W6 9DJ.
Tel: 020 8237 6700. Fax: 020 8237 6749. E-mail: wendy.kewley@britishrowing-rowing.org
Covers rowing and sculling – competitive, recreational and technical. Nine editions annually.
Illustrations: Any coverage of the subject considered, especially action pictures of rowing and rowing in scenic settings.
Text: Short, illustrated articles and longer features on all aspects of rowing. Technical topics such as coaching, training and boat-building.
Overall freelance potential: Good.
Fees: By arrangement with editor.

SAILING TODAY
Edisea, Swanwick Marina, Lower Swanwick, Southampton SO31 1ZL.
Tel: 01489 585209. Fax: 01489 565054. E-mail: stewart.wheeler@sailingtoday.co.uk
Editor: Duncan Kent. **Art Editor:** Stewart Wheeler.
Practical monthly for active sail cruising enthusiasts.
Illustrations: Dynamic action shots of cruising yachts from 30-55ft, from home waters to blue waters. Sunny Mediterranean shots, sailing or at anchor, always required for library. Contact sheets/thumbnails accepted for library.
Text: Well-illustrated features on boat improvements and cruising.
Overall freelance potential: Good.
Fees: By negotiation.

SPORTSBOAT & RIB MAGAZINE
CSL Publishing Ltd, Alliance House, 49 Sydney Street, Cambridge CB2 3HX.
Tel: 01223 460490. Fax: 01223 315960. E-mail: editor@sportsboat.co.uk
Editor: Alex Smith.
Monthly publication covering sports boats from 14–50 feet.
Illustrations: Top quality action shots of small sports boats. Also stylish pictures that show boats

as glamorous and exciting. Commissions may be available to illustrate major features. Covers: colour action shots with plenty of impact.
Text: Illustrated articles on all aspects of sports boats and waterskiing will always be considered. 500–3,000 words.
Overall freelance potential: Excellent.
Fees: By negotiation.

WATER CRAFT
Pete Greenfield Publishing, Bridge Shop, Gweek, Helston, Cornwall TR12 6UD.
Tel: 01326 221424. Fax: 01326 221728. E-mail: ed@watercraft-magazine.com
Editor: Pete Greenfield.
Bi-monthly magazine devoted to traditional small boats and boat building.
Illustrations: Photographs mainly required as part of complete feature packages, but interesting or unusual singles and sequences considered if accompanied by detailed caption information.
Text: Well-illustrated features on suitable subjects
Overall freelance potential: Limited at present; much is produced by regular contributors.
Fees: Around £60 per published page inclusive of pictures.

WATERWAYS WORLD
Waterways World Ltd, 151 Station Street, Burton-on-Trent DE14 1BG.
Tel: 01283 742950. Fax: 01283 742957. E-mail: editorial@waterwaysworld.com
Editor: Richard Fairhurst.
Monthly magazine that covers all aspects of canal and river navigations (not lakes) in Britain and abroad. Aimed at inland waterway enthusiasts and holiday boaters.
Illustrations: No scope for stand-alone pictures except for cover use. Covers: colourful canal or river scenes with boating activity prominently in the foreground.
Text: Well-illustrated features on inland waterways, 500–2,000 words. Send for or see website for contributors' guide.
Overall freelance potential: Around 20 per cent freelance contributed.
Fees: Covers £75.

WINDSURF MAGAZINE
Arcwind Ltd, The Blue Barns, Tew Lane, Wootton, Woodstock, Oxon OX20 1HA.
Tel: 01993 811181. Fax: 01993 811481. E-mail: mark@windsurf.co.uk
Publishing Editor: Mark Kasprowicz.
Published ten times a year. Aimed at the enthusiast and covering all aspects of windsurfing.
Illustrations: Sequences and singles of windsurfing action. Top quality shots always considered.
Text: Illustrated articles on any aspect of windsurfing.
Overall freelance potential: Excellent.
Fees: £5–£15 for B&W; up to £35 for full-page colour; £60 for centre-spread; £60 for covers.

YACHTING MONTHLY
IPC Media Ltd, Blue Fin Building, 110 Southwark Street, London SE1 0SU.
Tel: 020 3148 4872. Fax: 020 3148 8128. E-mail: yachting_monthly@ipcmedia.com
Editor: Paul Gelder. **News Editor:** Dick Durham. **Art Editor:** Simon Fevyer.
Monthly magazine for cruising yachtsmen.
Illustrations: News pictures considered for immediate use; location pictures for stock; pictures illustrating seamanship, navigation and technical subjects to illustrate features. Top quality images also considered for regular "Opening Shot" double-page spread and for covers (sailing boats, 25–45ft, under sail, at anchor or in harbour). No motorboats or dinghies.
Text: Articles relevant to cruising yachtsmen, and short accounts of cruising experiences. 1,000–2,250 words. Submit synopsis to the editor in the first instance.
Overall freelance potential: Around 40 per cent comes from outside contributors, but most are

experienced specialists.

Fees: Dependent upon size of reproduction or length of feature. Normally around £50–£110 for colour; £200 for covers. Text from £75 per 1,000 words.

YACHTING WORLD

IPC Media Ltd, Blue Fin Building, 110 Southwark Street, London SE1 0SU.
Tel: 020 3148 4835. Fax: 020 3148 8128. E-mail: david_glenn@ipcmedia.com
Editor: David Glenn. **Picture Editor:** Vanda Woolsey.
Monthly magazine for informed yachtsmen.
Illustrations: Digital files only. Pictures of general yachting techniques or types of boat; pictures of events and occasions; location shots and mood pictures. Major feature photography commissioned from known specialists. Covers: top quality pictures of yachts in 35ft+ range – action pictures on board, at sea.
Text: Informative or narrative yachting articles; technical yachting features; short humorous articles; and news. 1,000–1,500 words and 2,000–2,500 words. Send for writers' guidelines.
Overall freelance potential: Around 30 per cent comes from freelances.
Editor's tips: Contributors must know the subject and know the market. The most successful photographers we use are the ones who work the hardest.
Fees: Inside pictures according to size, from £16. Text up to £160 per 1,000 words.

YACHTS & YACHTING

PO Box 445, Southampton SO31 0BD.
Tel: 07855 849273. E-mail: gael@yachtsandyachting.com
Editor: Gael Pawson.
Fortnightly publication covering all aspects of racing, including dinghies and offshore racers.
Illustrations: Pictures of racing dinghies, yachts and general sailing scenes. Covers: Action shots of relevant subjects.
Text: Features on all aspects of the race sailing scene. 1,000–2,000 words.
Overall freelance potential: Quite good.
Fees: Negotiable.

Business

ACCOUNTANCY AGE

Incisive Media, 32–34 Broadwick Street, London W1A 2HG.
Tel: 020 7316 9000. Fax: 020 7316 9250. E-mail: accountancy_age@vnu.co.uk
Editor: Gavin Hinks.
Weekly publication for qualified accountants.
Illustrations: All commissioned, but new photographers are always welcome.
Text: News and features coverage for accountants. Synopsis preferred in first instance. 1,200 words.
Overall freelance potential: Fairly good for commissioned photography. About 25 per cent of the features come from freelances.
Editor's tips: To gain acceptance, articles must contribute something which cannot be provided by the in-house staff.
Fees: By agreement.

CA MAGAZINE

Connect Communications Ltd, Studio 2001, Mile End, Paisley PA1 1JS.
Tel: 0141 560 3145. Fax: 0141 561 0400. E-mail: rob@connectcommunications.co.uk
Editor: Rob Outram. **Art Editor:** Renny Hutchison .
Scottish financial and management magazine incorporating monthly journal of The Institute of Chartered Accountants of Scotland.

Illustrations: Will consider creative and innovative images which can be related to the subject and which attract readers' attention.

Text: Articles on accounting and auditing, company law, finance, taxation, management topics, company/personal profiles, the financial and management scene in the UK and overseas, investment, computer science, etc. Length: 1,200–3,000 words.

Overall freelance potential: Fair for business specialists.

Fees: By arrangement.

CNBC EUROPEAN BUSINESS

Future Inc Ltd, 141-143 Shoreditch High Street, London E1 6JE.
Tel: 020 7613 8777. Fax: 020 7613 8776. E-mail: lisa.jacobs@ink-publishing.com
Editor: Boyd Farrow. **Picture Editor:** Lisa Jacobs
London-based business monthly offering an entirely European perspective on business in Europe. Allied with CNBC Europe, the only pan-European television network devoted to financial and business news.

Illustrations: European-based business images, but mainly people-oriented, focusing on the individuals behind businesses rather than the companies themselves. Some stock material used but prefer not to use standard "grey suit" business imagery. Photographers available for shoots overseas should contact picture editor in the first instance.

Text: Will consider relevant articles from those who know about business and can write in a lively style. Articles are kept fairly short and have to be written so that they are easy to comprehend for non-native English speakers. Contact the editor with details of experience in the first instance.

Overall freelance potential: Good, especially for freelances based on or regularly visiting the Continent.

Editor's tips: Try to get away from "grey suits" and show business people in a more original and stimulating way.

Fees: By negotiation.

DIRECTOR

Director Publications Ltd, 116 Pall Mall, London SW1Y 5ED.
Tel: 020 7766 8950. Fax: 020 7766 8840. E-mail: director-ed@iod.co.uk
Group **Editor:** Richard Cree. **Art Director:** John Poile.
Monthly journal for members of the Institute of Directors.

Illustrations: B&W and colour. Top quality portraits of company chairmen or major business personalities. Covers: portraits as above or top quality business/industry subjects. More creative, avant-garde illustrations also used.

Text: Interviews; management advice; company profiles; business controversies; EC affairs.

Overall freelance potential: Good.

Fees: By negotiation.

EN

Entrepreneur Business Publishing, Portland Buildings, 127-129 Portland Street, Manchester M1 4PZ.
Tel: 0161 236 2782. Fax: 0161 236 2783. E-mail: martin.regan@excelpublishing.co.uk
Editor: Martin Regan.
Glossy business monthly for entrepreneurs, with separate editions for the North West and Yorkshire regions, aimed at owner-managed companies with turnover between £0.5m–£40m.

Illustrations: Captioned news pictures about developments in private businesses as above. General business/industrial photography by commission, mainly portraiture but some general

As a member of the Bureau of Freelance Photographers, you'll be kept up-to-date with markets through the BFP Market Newsletter, published monthly. For details of membership, turn to page 9

business/industrial work.
Text: Topical articles of interest to business people in the region – hard-edged, readable, jargon-free. Newsy items only.
Overall freelance potential: Quite good for the freelance with a professional and creative approach.
Editor's tips: Prefer a creative, even off-the-wall, style. Happy to consider newcomers as long as they are thoroughly professional and reliable.
Fees: By negotiation.

FINANCIAL MANAGEMENT

Caspian Publishing Ltd, 198 King's Road, London SW3 5XX.
Tel: 020 7368 7177. Fax: 020 7368 7201. E-mail: rp1@caspianpublishing.co.uk
Editor: Ruth Prickett.
Monthly publication for financial managers. Published for the Chartered Institute of Management Accountants.
Illustrations: B&W and colour. Regular profile photography to accompany business-related articles.
Text: Occasional freelance market for articles on management/accountancy subjects.
Overall freelance potential: Good.
Fees: By agreement.

MEED (MIDDLE EAST BUSINESS INTELLIGENCE)

EMAP, Greater London House, Hampstead Road, London NW1 7EJ.
Tel: +971 4390 0045. E-mail: colin.foreman@meed-dubai.com
Editorial Director: Richard Thompson. **News Editor:** Colin Foreman.
Weekly business journal covering the affairs of Middle Eastern countries. Now edited from Dubai.
Illustrations: Pictures of current major construction projects in the Middle East and stock shots of important personalities (politicians, leading businessmen) in the region. Recent general views of particular locations occasionally used. Covers: colour pictures of contemporary Middle East subjects, preferably with an obvious business flavour. Also, high-quality colour abstracts.
Text: Specialist articles on relevant business matters.
Overall freelance potential: Limited.
Fees: On a rising scale according to size of reproduction or length of text.

MARKETING

Haymarket Business Publications Ltd, 174 Hammersmith Road, London W6 7JP.
Tel: 020 8267 4048. Fax: 020 8267 4504. E-mail: lucy.barrett@haymarket.com
Editor: Gareth Jones. **News Editor:** Alex Brownfell.
Weekly publication for marketing management, both client and agency.
Illustrations: Requires only experienced business photographers for commissioned coverage of subjects relating to marketing.
Text: News and features with a marketing angle and objective case histories.
Overall freelance potential: Limited; for business specialists only.
Editor's tips: Photographers must be able to work accurately to a brief.
Fees: Negotiable.

NORTH EAST TIMES

North East Times Ltd, 5-11 Causey Street, Gosforth, Newcastle-upon-Tyne NE3 4DJ.
Tel: 0191 284 9994. Fax: 0191 284 9915. E-mail: info@accentmagazines.co.uk

---

Are you working from the latest edition of The Freelance Photographer's Market Handbook? It's published on 1 October each year. Markets are constantly changing, so it pays to have the latest edition

---

Editor: Richard Holmes.
Monthly up-market business magazine.
Illustrations: Digital files preferred. Any general interest pictures connected with the North East of England.
Text: Features on business, fashion, property, motoring, wining and dining, sport, etc, all with North East connections. Around 750 words with two pictures.
Overall freelance potential: Fully committed to freelances.
Fees: By agreement.

PEOPLE MANAGEMENT
Personnel Publications Ltd, 17 Britton Street, London EC1M 5TP.
Tel: 020 7880 6200. Fax: 020 7336 7635. E-mail: sam.kesteven@redactive.co.uk
Editor: Rob Maclachlan. **Picture Editor:** Sam Kesteven.
Fortnightly magazine of the Chartered Institute of Personnel and Development. Covers all aspects of staff management and training.
Illustrations: Photographs of people at work in business and industry, particularly any depicting staff education and training. Detailed lists of subjects available welcomed. Some commissions may be available to experienced workers.
Text: Ideas for articles always welcome; submit a short written proposal first.
Overall freelance potential: Quite good – a lot of stock pictures are used. Contributions here might also be used in Supply Management, a similar title produced by the same team for the Chartered Institute of Purchasing and Supply.
Fees: By negotiation.

POST MAGAZINE
Incisive Media, 32–34 Broadwick Street, London W1A 2HG.
Tel: 020 7316 9321. Fax: 020 7484 9992. E-mail: jonathan.swift@incisivemedia.com
Editor: Jonathan Swift. **Group Art Editor:** Nicky Brown.
Weekly publication covering insurance at home and abroad.
Illustrations: Digital files preferred. Pictures of traffic, houses, offices, building sites, damage (including fire and motoring accidents), shipwrecks or aviation losses, etc. Also political and industry personalities.
Text: News and features on insurance, including general insurance, reinsurance, financial services, investment, marketing, technology, offices and personnel areas.
Overall freelance potential: Most news and features are contributed by freelances.
Fees: By negotiation.

Camping & Caravanning

CAMPING
Warners Group Publications plc, The Maltings, West Street, Bourne, Lincs PE10 9PH.
Tel: 01778 392442. Fax: 01778 392422. E-mail: cliveg@warnersgroup.co.uk
Editor: Clive Garrett.
Monthly magazine covering all aspects of tent camping. Emphasises the range of activities that camping makes available.
Illustrations: Single pictures considered for cover use, strong images of campers obviously enjoying themselves on a family or lightweight camping holiday. Other pictures only used as an integral part of features as below.
Text: Picture-led features that show camping as "a means to an end" and illustrate the range of people and lifestyles that camping embraces. Always check with the editor before submitting.
Overall freelance potential: Excellent for covers.
Fees: £70 per published page, £100 for covers.

CAMPING & CARAVANNING

The Camping and Caravanning Club, Greenfields House, Westwood Way, Coventry CV4 8JH.
Tel: 02476 475274. Fax: 02476 475413. E-mail: magazine@thefriendlyclub.co.uk
Editor: Simon McGrath.
Monthly magazine concerning all aspects of tent camping, caravanning and motorhoming, exclusive to C&CC members.
Illustrations: Limited scope for good shots of camping and caravanning scenes, but usually only required in conjunction with feature articles.
Text: Illustrated features on camping and caravanning in Britain, around 1,200 words. Contact the editor with ideas only in the first instance.
Overall freelance potential: Fair.
Fees: By agreement.

CARAVAN

IPC Focus Network, Leon House, 233 High Street, Croydon CR9 1HZ.
Tel: 020 8726 8000. Fax: 020 8726 8299. E-mail: caravan@ipcmedia.com
Editor: Victoria Bentley.
Monthly magazine for all caravanners.
Illustrations: Occasional need for general illustrations of touring and caravan-related subjects to illustrate features. Send list of subjects and low-res samples in the first instance. Some opportunities for commissioned work, though in-house photographers handle much of this.
Text: Well-illustrated accounts of touring in specific areas, or more general caravanning-related items with a human interest angle. Call or write with ideas first.
Overall freelance potential: Fair, but most content is supplied by regulars.
Fees: By negotiation.

CARAVAN INDUSTRY

A.E.Morgan Publications Ltd, 8a High Street, Epsom, Surrey KT19 8AD.
Tel: 01372 741411. Fax: 01372 744493. E-mail: teamwork@ukonline.co.uk
Editor: David Ritchie.
Monthly publication for manufacturers, traders, suppliers and park operators in the caravan industry.
Illustrations: News pictures of interest to the industry – new caravan park developments, new models, new dealer depots, etc.
Text: Company profiles on park owners and their businesses, traders and manufacturers. 900–1,200 words.
Overall freelance potential: Up to 30 per cent of the content comes from freelance contributors.
Fees: By agreement.

MOTORHOME MONTHLY

Stone Leisure Ltd, Andrew House, 2a Granville Road, Sidcup, Kent DA14 4BN.
Tel: 020 8302 6150/6069 and 020 8300 2316. Fax: 020 8300 2315. E-mail: mhm@stoneleisure.com
Editor: Bob Griffiths.
Monthly magazine about motorhomes and their use. Covers travel, lifestyle, etc.
Illustrations: Good photographs related to above subjects will always be considered.
Text: Illustrated features on travel and motorhoming. 500–1,000 words. Also reports on shows or other relevant events.
Overall freelance potential: Good.
Editor's tips: Preference for copy that requires a minimum of subbing or rewriting.
Fees: Around £50 for illustrated articles.

PARK HOME & HOLIDAY CARAVAN

IPC Media, Leon House, 233 High Street, Croydon CR9 1HZ.
Tel: 020 8726 8252. Fax: 020 8726 8299. E-mail: alex_melvin@ipcmedia.com

Editor: Alex Melvin.
Monthly covering residential park homes and caravan holiday homes.
Illustrations: Always interested in good photographs of park homes, static holiday caravans (not touring caravans), residential and holiday parks.
Text: Illustrated features on the above.
Overall freelance potential: Fair.
Fees: According to use.

PRACTICAL CARAVAN
Haymarket Consumer Media, Teddington Studios, Broom Road, Teddington, Middlesex TW11 9BE.
Tel: 020 8267 5629. Fax: 020 8267 5725. E-mail: practical.caravan@haymarket.com
Editor: Nigel Donnelly. **Art Editor:** Simon Mortimer.
Monthly for caravanning holidaymakers.
Illustrations: Mostly commissioned to accompany specific features, but interesting or unusual caravanning images may be considered on spec.
Text: Feature ideas and first-person stories always considered.
Overall freelance potential: Only for those with experience.
Fees: Commissions start at £250 rising according to suitability and quality.

PRACTICAL MOTORHOME
Haymarket Publishing Ltd, Teddington Studios, Broom Road, Teddington, Middlesex TW11 9BE.
Tel: 020 8267 5629. Fax: 020 8267 5725. E-mail: practical.motorhome@haymarket.com
Editor: Rob Ganley. **Art Editor:** Elizabeth Paterson.
Monthly for all motorhome holidaymakers and enthusiasts.
Illustrations: Mostly commissioned to accompany specific features, but interesting motorhome images may be considered on spec.
Text: Feature ideas and first-person stories always considered.
Overall freelance potential: Only for those with experience.
Fees: Commissions £250–£350 per day; other material negotiable.

Children & Teenage

MIZZ
Panini UK Ltd, Brockbourne House, 77 Mount Ephraim, Tunbridge Wells TN4 8BS.
Tel: 01892 500100. Fax: 01892 545666. E-mail: mizz@panini.co.uk
Editor: Karen O'Brien. **Picture Researcher:** Kirsty Grant.
Fortnightly magazine aimed at girls in the 10–14 age group.
Illustrations: Youth celebrity pictures always of interest (young TV stars, boy/girl bands, etc). Most other photography by commission for specific features, but some scope for stock images that could illustrate "real life" situations encountered by teenage girls. Some scope for single captioned pictures of a humorous nature.
Text: Lively illustrated features on almost any topic that could be of interest to the the target age group. Text should be informative as well as entertaining. A detailed synopsis should always be submitted in the first instance.
Overall freelance potential: Good for the experienced contributor.
Fees: By negotiation.

SUGAR
Hachette Filipacchi (UK) Ltd, 64 North Row, London W1K 7LL.
Tel: 020 7150 7000. Fax: 020 7150 7001. E-mail: deborah.hughes@hf-uk.com
Editor: Annabel Brog. **Art Director:** Deborah Hughes.
Monthly for teenage girls.
Illustrations: Fashion, beauty, still-life and portraiture, all commissioned for specific features.

Some scope for celebrity stock.
Text: No scope.
Overall freelance potential: Only for experienced specialists.
Fees: Basic rate £350 per day.

County & Country

BBC COUNTRYFILE
BBC Magazines Bristol, 9th Floor, Tower House, Fairfax Street, Bristol BS1 3BN.
Tel: 0117 314 8849 (editor); 0117 314 8372 (pictures). E-mail: picturedesk@bbcmagazines.com; editor@bbccountryfile.com
Monthly magazine celebrating the British countryside. Linked to the popular BBC TV programme.
Editor: Fergus Collins. **Picture Editor:** Tor McIntosh.
Illustrations: Photographers based in rural areas often required for specific assignments. Also occasional need for photographers specialising in outdoor activities. Submit a few sample images in the first instance. No scope to submit general countryside or landscape pictures on spec.
Text: Mostly produced by regular specialists, but ideas always considered.
Overall freelance potential: Good possibilities for those with suitable skills.
Fees: By negotiation.

CHESHIRE LIFE
Archant Life, 3 Tustin Court, Port Way, Preston PR2 2YQ
Tel: 01772 722022. Fax: 01772 760905. E-mail: louise.taylor@cheshirelife.co.uk
Editor: Louise Taylor.
Monthly up-market county magazine specialising in regional features.
Illustrations: Prints and digital files accepted. Pictures of the Cheshire region, mainly to accompany features on topics such as property, antiques, wildlife, society, arts and crafts, sport. Picture postcard scenes of Cheshire also of interest – landscapes, towns, villages, heritage, etc.
Text: Articles and features on regional topics. Always consult the editor in the first instance.
Overall freelance potential: Good.
Fees: By negotiation.

COTSWOLD LIFE
Archant Life, Archant House, 3 Oriel Road, Cheltenham GL50 1BB.
Tel: 01242 216050. Fax: 01242 255116. E-mail: mike.lowe@archant.co.uk
Editor: Mike Lowe.
Monthly showcasing "the best of the Cotswolds".
Illustrations: Pictures of local scenes and events, preferably with some life in them. Covers: Medium format colour of lively local scenes, with clear space at top for title logo.
Text: Illustrated articles of varying lengths, on local people, places, events, etc.
Overall freelance potential: Most material comes from regular freelance contributors but new contributors always considered.
Fees: Cover shots £50. Articles and other illustrations negotiable.

COUNTRY LIFE
IPC Media Ltd, Blue Fin Building, 110 Southwark Street, London SE1 0SU.
Tel: 020 3148 4421. Fax: 020 3148 8129. E-mail: dominic_walters@ipcmedia.com
Editor: Mark Hedges. **Picture Editor:** Dominic Walters.
Weekly magazine for a general readership.

Illustrations: Pictures of British countryside, wildlife, interiors, country pursuits. Covers: Top quality pictures of landscapes, rural and urban.
Text: No scope.
Overall freelance potential: Limited; around 80 per cent of the magazine comes from regular suppliers.
Fees: Good; on a rising scale according to size of reproduction. Covers, £300–350.

COUNTRY WALKING
Bauer Active Ltd, Media House, Lynchwood, Peterborough PE2 6EA.
Tel: 01733 468208. E-mail: jonathan.manning@bauermedia.co.uk
Editor: Jonathan Manning.
Monthly magazine for all walkers who enjoy great days out in the countryside.
Illustrations: Pictures depicting walkers in attractive locations, who must be wearing proper outdoor gear. Also top quality landscapes of suitable parts of the country, historic locations, landscapes with elements of walking interest (eg. stile, path), nature and wildlife. Covers: seasonal pictures of very attractive landscape settings.
Text: Well-illustrated articles and features on any walking or countryside topics. Strong emphasis on inspiration and entertainment and capturing the essence of why people walk.
Overall freelance potential: Limited, as much is produced by regulars or obtained from picture libraries.
Editor's tips: The emphasis is always on getting enjoyment from walking and the countryside.
Fees: By negotiation.

THE COUNTRYMAN
Country Publications Ltd, The Water Mill, Broughton Hall, Skipton, North Yorkshire BD23 3AG.
Tel: 01756 701381. Fax: 01756 701326. E-mail: editorial@thecountryman.co.uk
Editor: Paul Jackson.
Monthly covering all matters of countryside interest other than blood sports.
Illustrations: Sequences of pictures about particular places, crafts, customs, farming practices, kinds of wildlife, etc. Must be accompanied by ample caption material. Only limited scope for single stock pictures, but always seeking high-quality wildlife/countryside images for covers.
Text: Well-illustrated articles of 800–1,200 words, on such subjects as mentioned above. Must be accurate, and usually based on the writer's own experience.
Overall freelance potential: Excellent; almost all photographs, and most articles, are from freelance contributors.
Fees: £30 upwards for photographs inside; £150 for cover. Text according to length and merit.

CUMBRIA
Country Publications Ltd, The Water Mill, Broughton Hall, Skipton, North Yorkshire BD23 3AG.
Tel: 01756 701381. Fax: 01756 701326. E-mail: editorial@dalesman.co.uk
Editor: Kevin Hopkinson.
Monthly countryside magazine for Cumbria and the surrounding area.
Illustrations: Attractive shots of local landscapes, rural characters, wildlife, country pursuits and heritage.
Text: Illustrated articles on any aspect of Lakeland country life. 800–1,200 words.
Overall freelance potential: Excellent.
Fees: Half-page £20; full-page £30; covers £100.

Are you working from the latest edition of The Freelance Photographer's Market Handbook? It's published on 1 October each year. Markets are constantly changing, so it pays to have the latest edition

DALESMAN
Country Publications Ltd, The Water Mill, Broughton Hall, Skipton, North Yorkshire BD23 3AG.
Tel: 01756 701381. Fax: 01756 701326. E-mail: editorial@dalesman.co.uk
Editor: Paul Jackson. **Picture Editor:** Eleanor Morton.
Monthly countryside magazine for Yorkshire.
Illustrations: Attractive shots of local landscapes, local characters, wildlife and heritage.
Text: Illustrated articles on any aspect of Yorkshire life. 800–1,200 words.
Overall freelance potential: Excellent.
Fees: Half-page £20; full-page £30; covers £100.

DORSET
Archant Life, Archant House, Babbage Road, Totnes, Devon TQ9 5JA.
Tel: 01803 860920. E-mail: helen.stiles@archant.co.uk
Editor: Helen Stiles.
Monthly for people who like to explore the Dorset region.
Illustrations: Good stock photographs of the region: people, places, landscapes, natural history, culture and heritage.
Text: Local news and illustrated articles on Dorset subjects as above, around 1,000 words.
Overall freelance potential: Good.
Fees: Pictures from £25–£45; text £75 per 1,000 words.

DORSET LIFE
Dorset County Magazines Ltd, 7 The Leanne, Sandford Lane, Wareham, Dorset BH20 4DY.
Tel: 01929 551264. Fax: 01929 552099. E-mail:office@dorsetlife.co.uk
Editor: John Newth.
Monthly magazine for the Dorset area.
Illustrations: Interesting and original photographs of the region, but usually required as part of an article, not in isolation. Covers: Attractive local scenes, suitable for upright reproduction. Must be original.
Text: Well-illustrated articles on any topic relating to Dorset, around 1,000 words.
Overall freelance potential: Most contributions come from regular freelance contributors but new contributors always considered.
Fees: According to size of reproduction and length of text.

THE FIELD
IPC Media Ltd, Blue Fin Building, 110 Southwark Street, London SE1 0SU.
Tel: 020 3148 4777. Fax: 020 3148 8179. E-mail: rebecca_hawtrey@ipcmedia.com
Editor: Jonathan Young. **Art Editor:** Rebecca Hawtrey.
Monthly publication concerned with all rural and country sports interests.
Illustrations: Digital files required. Good pictures illustrating relevant topics as below. Most used for article illustration but good single pictures always considered for cover use. Commissions available to specialists.
Text: Illustrated features on country and country sporting subjects, especially shooting, fly-fishing, working dogs (gundogs, terriers). Length according to article, in the range 1,000–2,000 words.
Overall freelance potential: Around 80 per cent comes from outside contributors, many of whom are specialists, but opportunities are good for the right material.
Fees: According to merit.

As a member of the Bureau of Freelance Photographers, you'll be kept up-to-date with markets through the BFP Market Newsletter, published monthly. For details of membership, turn to page 9

HERTFORDSHIRE COUNTRYSIDE
Beaumonde Publications, PO Box 5, Hitchin, Herts SG5 1GJ.
Tel: 01462 422014. Fax: 01462 422015. E-mail: martin_small@btconnect.com
Editor: Sandra Small.
Monthly county magazine for the named area.
Illustrations: B&W and colour. People, places, and events in the county. Covers: colourful local countryside views.
Text: Topical articles, of a cultural nature, on any aspect of the county.
Overall freelance potential: Limited because much is supplied by regular freelance contributors.
Fees: By negotiation.

LANCASHIRE LIFE
Archant Life, 3 Tustin Court, Port Way, Preston PR2 2YQ.
Tel: 01772 722022. Fax: 01772 736496. E-mail: roger.borrell@lancashirelife.co.uk
Editor: Roger Borrell.
Monthly up-market county magazine specialising in regional features, covering Lancashire and the Lake District.
Illustrations: Pictures of the Lancashire and the South Lakes region, mainly to accompany features. Pictures of nationally known personalities with a Lancashire connection. Covers: top quality regional scenes.
Text: Articles and features on regional topics. Always consult the editor in the first instance.
Overall freelance potential: Around 20 per cent is from freelance sources.
Editor's tips: Unlikely to be interested unless there is a definite Lancashire or Lake District angle.
Fees: By negotiation.

LINCOLNSHIRE LIFE
County Life Ltd, County House, 9 Checkpoint Court, Sadler Road, Lincoln LN6 3PW.
Tel: 01522 527127. Fax: 01522 842000. E-mail: editorial@lincolnshirelife.co.uk
Editor: Josie Thurston.
Monthly magazine, dealing with county life past and present from the Humber to the Wash.
Illustrations: Pictures of people and places within the county of Lincolnshire Covers: portrait format colour pictures of local landscapes, architecture, people, street scenes, etc. Submissions for annual calendar also accepted.
Text: Features on people and places within the appropriate area. No more than 1,600 words. Contact editor first to discuss.
Overall freelance potential: Fifty per cent of the magazine comes from freelance sources.
Fees: £50 for covers, other material by agreement.

THE SCOTS MAGAZINE
D. C. Thomson and Co. Ltd, 80 Kingsway East, Dundee DD4 8SL.
Tel: 01382 575178. E-mail: mail@scotsmagazine.com
Editor: Lorraine Wilson.
Monthly magazine for Scots at home and abroad, concerned with Scottish subjects.
Illustrations: Scottish scenes, but avoid the obvious. Non-Highland subjects particularly welcome. Scenics with one or more figures preferred to "empty pictures". Ongoing requirement for good vertical scenes for possible front cover use.
Text: Features on all aspects of Scottish life past and present. 500–1,500 words. E-mail outlining idea in the first instance.
Overall freelance potential: Around 80 per cent of the magazine comes from freelances.
Fees: Variable.

SCOTTISH FIELD
Craigcrook Castle, Craigcrook Road, Edinburgh EH4 3PE.
Tel: 0131 312 4550. Fax: 0131 312 4551. E-mail: editor@scottishfield.co.uk
Editor: Richard Bath.
Monthly magazine reflecting the quality of life in Scotland today for Scots at home and abroad.
Illustrations: Varied subjects of Scottish interest; must be accompanied by appropriate text.
Text: Illustrated features with a Scottish dimension. 850–1,200 words. Submit only ideas initially, rather than completed articles.
Overall freelance potential: There are only limited openings for new contributors.
Editor's tips: Market study is essential.
Fees: Negotiable.

SOMERSET LIFE
Archant Life, Archant House, Babbage Road, Totnes, Devon TQ9 5JA.
Tel: 01803 860914. Fax: 01803 860926. E-mail:
rachel.lovell@archant.co.uk/natalie.vizard@archant.co.uk
Editors: Rachel Lovell/Natalie Vizard.
Monthly magazine for Somerset and Bristol area.
Illustrations: Interesting and original photographs of the area, usually only required as part of a words and pictures package. Covers: always on the lookout for portrait-format shots that will carry the title and coverlines, preferably seasonal pictures of recognisable Somerset scenes.
Text: Well-illustrated articles on any topic relating to Somerset, around 1,000 words.
Overall freelance potential: Keen to find new contributors with photographic skills who can also write well.
Fees: By arrangement.

SUSSEX LIFE
Sussex Life Ltd, Baskerville Place, 28 Teville Road, Worthing, West Sussex BN11 1UG.
Tel: 01903 604208. Fax: 01903 820193. E-mail: jonathan.keeble@sussexlife.co.uk
Editor: Simon Irwin.
Monthly county magazine.
Illustrations: Stock photographs always welcomed, but complete illustrated articles are preferred. Covers: medium format transparencies of Sussex scenes, usually depicting landscapes, but houses, activities, interiors and personalities from Sussex also welcome.
Text: Well illustrated features on any topic relevant to the county. 1,000–2,000 words.
Overall freelance potential: Quite good.
Fees: 1,000-word article plus pics, £150.

TGO – THE GREAT OUTDOORS
Newsquest Magazines, 200 Renfield Street, Glasgow G2 3QB.
Tel: 0141 302 7700. Fax: 0141 302 7799. E-mail: emily.rodway@tgomagazine.co.uk
Editor: Emily Rodway.
Monthly magazine for walkers in the UK. Covers hill and mountain walking, and related topics.
Illustrations: Digital files preferred. Material required for stock – mostly landscapes featuring walkers; no towns or churches. Plus pictures to illustrate features. Covers: colour pictures in upright format considered independently of internal content. Photographs of walkers, backpackers and fell walkers in landscape settings. Must be contemporary, well-equipped people in photos; action shots preferred.
Text: Features on the subjects mentioned above. 2,000 words.
Overall freelance potential: Most of the magazine comes from freelance sources.
Editor's tips: Too many freelances send material which is outside the scope of the magazine – not interested in low level rambling. Send e-mail for guidelines.
Fees: Articles, £150–£450 depending on length and number of illustrations; covers, around £200.

THIS ENGLAND/EVERGREEN
This England Publishing Ltd, PO Box 52, Cheltenham, Gloucestershire GL50 1YQ.
Tel: 01242 537900. Fax: 01242 537901. E-mail: editor@thisengland.co.uk
Editor: Stephen Garnett. **Deputy Editor:** Angeline Wilcox.
Quarterly magazines about England and the United Kingdom respectively, mainly its people, places, customs and traditions and with strong emphasis on nostalgia.
Illustrations: Town, country and village scenes, curiosities, craftsmen at work, nostalgia, patriotism. Prefer people in the picture, but dislike modernity etc. Pictures for stock or use in their own right.
Text: Illustrated articles on all things traditionally British. 1,000–1,500 words.
Overall freelance potential: Around 50 per cent comes from freelance sources.
Editor's tips: Send SAE or e-mail for contributor guidelines.
Fees: By negotiation.

TRAIL
Bauer Active Ltd, Media House, Lynchwood, Peterborough PE2 6EA.
Tel: 01733 468363. E-mail: trail@bauermedia.co.uk
Editor: Matt Swaine.
Monthly magazine aimed at the more adventurous walker, plus rock climbers and mountain bikers.
Illustrations: Well-composed pictures of walkers, backpackers, climbers and mountain bikers in attractive and dramatic landscapes, UK or overseas, high viewpoints preferred. Walkers seen close up should be wearing proper outdoor gear. Covers: "stunning" colour shots as above.
Text: Illustrated articles on any aspect of hill walking, backpacking and overseas trekking, including diet, fitness, etc. Only accepted from contributors who clearly understand what the magazine is about and what the readers need. Always discuss ideas with the editor in the first instance.
Overall freelance potential: Very good for high quality material.
Editor's tips: It is essential that people in pictures be wearing proper walking/climbing clothes and shoes – no jeans and trainers.
Fees: From £25–£150 (DPS). Text £140 per 1,000 words.

WALK
The Ramblers, 2nd Floor, Camelford House, 87-90 Albert Embankment, London SE1 7TW.
Tel: 020 7339 8500. Fax: 020 7339 8501. E-mail: denise.noble@ramblers.org.uk
Editor: Dominic Bates. **Picture Editor:** Denise Noble.
Quarterly journal for members of the Ramblers.
Illustrations: Scenic views of the British countryside, preferably with walkers in shot. Also pictures of difficulties encountered when walking in the countryside, eg damaged bridges, locked gates, obstructed footpaths, etc. Walking images from abroad also required.
Text: Little scope for text as most articles are commissioned from regulars.
Overall freelance potential: Limited other than by commission.
Fees: By agreement.

YORKSHIRE LIFE
Archant Life, PO Box 163, Ripon HG4 9AG.
Tel: 01423 546216. E-mail: esther.leach@yorkshirelife.co.uk
Editor: Esther Leach.
Monthly up-market county magazine for Yorkshire.
Illustrations: Pictures of the Yorkshire region, mainly to accompany features. Pictures of nationally known personalities with a Yorkshire connection, and local society events, but most by commission. Covers: top quality regional scenes.
Text: Articles and features on regional topics, from those with a truly professional approach. Always consult the editor in the first instance.
Fees: By negotiation.

Cycling & Motorcycling

BACK STREET HEROES
Ocean Media Group, One Canada Square, Canary Wharf, London E14 5AP.
Tel: 020 7772 8300. Fax: 020 7772 8585. E-mail: bsh-magazine@yahoo.com
Editor: Stu Garland.
Monthly magazine for custom bike enthusiasts.
Illustrations: Pictures of individual customised or one-off machines, and coverage of custom bike meetings and events. The style of photography must be tailored to fit the style of the magazine.
Text: Limited freelance market.
Overall freelance potential: Good for those who can capture the flavour and style of the custom bike scene.
Editor's tips: This is something of a lifestyle magazine, and it is essential that the stylistic approach be absolutely right.
Fees: By negotiation.

BIKE
Bauer Automotive Ltd, Media House, Lynchwood, Peterborough PE2 6EA.
Tel: 01733 468000. Fax: 01733 468290. E-mail: tim@bikemagazine.co.uk
Editor: Tim Thompson. **Editorial Assistant:** Sally Barker.
Monthly motorcycling magazine aimed at all enthusiasts.
Illustrations: Interesting or unusual topical pictures always required for news section. Sporting pictures for file. Top quality action pictures, "moody" statics and shots that are strong on creative effects. Reportage/documentary shots of events/people.
Text: Interesting or unusual news items. Scope for features on touring, personalities, icons etc; 1,000–3,000 words.
Overall freelance potential: Good for those with experience.
Editor's tips: Always looking for new photographers and styles.
Fees: By agreement.

CLASSIC BIKE
Bauer Automotive Ltd, Media House, Lynchwood, Peterborough PE2 6EA.
Tel: 01733 468081. Fax: 01733 468290. E-mail: hugo.wilson@bauerautomotive.co.uk
Editor: Hugo Wilson. **Editorial Assistant:** Sally Barker.
Monthly magazine dealing with thoroughbred and classic motorcycles from 1896 to 1990.
Illustrations: Pictures of rallies, races, restored motorcycles.
Text: Technical features, histories of particular motorcycles, restoration stories, profiles of famous riders, designers etc. 500–2,000 words.
Overall freelance potential: Most photography is freelance.
Editor's tips: Contact the editor before submitting.
Fees: By agreement and on merit.

CLASSIC BIKE
Bauer Automotive Ltd, Media House, Lynchwood, Peterborough PE2 6EA.
Tel: 01733 468081. Fax: 01733 468290. E-mail: hugo.wilson@bauerautomotive.co.uk
Editor: Hugo Wilson. **Editorial Assistant**: Sally Barker.
Monthly magazine dealing with thoroughbred and classic motorcycles from 1896 to 1990.
Illustrations: Pictures of rallies, races, restored motorcycles.
Text: Technical features, histories of particular motorcycles, restoration stories, profiles of famous riders, designers etc. 500–2,000 words.
Overall freelance potential: Most photography is freelance.
Editor's tips: Contact the editor before submitting.
Fees: By agreement and on merit.

THE CLASSIC MOTORCYCLE
Mortons Media Group Ltd, PO Box 99, Horncastle, Lincs LN9 6LZ.
Tel: 01507 529405. Fax: 01507 529495. E-mail: jrobinson@mortons.co.uk
Editor: James Robinson.
Monthly magazine covering veteran, vintage and post-war motor cycles and motorcycling.
Illustrations: Mostly colour. Pictures that cover interesting restoration projects, unusual machines, personalities with a background story, etc. Covers: colour pictures, usually a well-restored and technically interesting motor cycle, always related to editorial.
Text: Features on subjects detailed above. 1,500–2,500 words.
Overall freelance potential: Around 50 per cent of the magazine comes from freelances, but much of it is commissioned.
Fees: Good; on a rising scale according to size of reproduction or length of article.

CYCLE SPORT
IPC Focus Network, Leon House, 233 High Street, Croydon CR9 1HZ.
Tel: 020 8726 8000. Fax: 020 8774 0952. E-mail: robert_garbutt@ipcmedia.com
Editor: Robert Garbutt.
Monthly devoted to professional cycle sport, offering a British perspective on this essentially Continental sport.
Illustrations: High quality, topical photographs relating to professional cycle racing.
Text: Illustrated features on the professional scene, but always query the editor before submitting. 1,500–4,000 words.
Editor's tips: Most interested in "the news behind the news".
Fees: Pictures according to nature and use. Text £100–£200 per 1,000 words.

CYCLING PLUS
Future Publishing Ltd, Beauford Court, 30 Monmouth Street, Bath BA1 2BW.
Tel: 01225 442244. Fax: 01225 732310. E-mail: warren.rossiter@futurenet.co.uk
Editor: Rob Spedding. **Art/Picture Editor:** Warren Rossiter.
Monthly magazine aimed at recreational cyclists, concentrating on touring and leisure/fitness riding. Some racing coverage.
Illustrations: Photographs that capture the excitement and dynamics of cycle sport. Speculative submissions welcomed; commissions also available.
Text: Little freelance scope; most is produced by a team of regular writers.
Overall freelance potential: Good for photographers.
Fees: By negotiation.

CYCLING WEEKLY
IPC Media Ltd, Leon House, 233 High Street, Croydon CR9 1HZ.
Tel: 020 8726 8000. Fax: 020 8774 0952. E-mail: cycling@ipcmedia.com
Editor: Robert Garbutt.
News-based weekly magazine covering all aspects of cycling; aimed at the informed cyclist.
Illustrations: Digital files preferred. Good photographs of cycle racing, plus any topical photographs of interest to cyclists. Covers: striking colour photographs of cycle racing; must be current.
Text: Well-illustrated articles on racing and technical matters. Around 1,500 words.
Overall freelance potential: Fairly good.
Fees: According to use.

DIRT BIKE RIDER
L&M Newspapers. Editorial: 12 Victoria Street, Morecambe, Lancs LA4 4AG.
Tel: 01524 834077. Fax: 01524 425469. E-mail: sean.lawless@dirtbikerider.co.uk
Editor: Sean Lawless.
Monthly covering all forms of off-road motorcycle sport, aimed at competitors and those who aspire

to compete.
Illustrations: Current pictures of off-road events, bikes and riders.
Text: Illustrated features on all aspects of off-road motorcycling and racing. Contact editor with suggestions in the first instance.
Overall freelance potential: Good.
Fees: Negotiable.

MOTO MAGAZINE
Factory Media Ltd, 1 West Smithfield, London EC1A 9JU.
Tel: 020 7332 9700. E-mail: adam@motomagazine.co.uk
Editor: Ben Johnson.
Bi-monthly magazine covering motocross from an international perspective.
Illustrations: Will consider any topical and relevant images on spec. Has two regular photographers covering main events but commissions may be available.
Text: Possible scope for features on leading riders - contact editor with suggestions.
Overall freelance potential: Quite good for specialists.
Fees: By negotiation.

MOTOR CYCLE NEWS
Bauer Automotive Ltd, Media House, Lynchwood, Peterborough PE2 6EA.
Tel: 01733 468006. Fax: 01733 468028. E-mail: marc.potter@motorcyclenews.com
Editor: Marc Potter.
Weekly tabloid for all road-riding and recreational motorcyclists. Also covers motorcycle sport.
Illustrations: Rarely use on-spec material, but frequently require freelances for assignments. Seek competent photographers with keen news sense, able to work closely to a given brief yet able to incorporate their own visual ideas. Successful applicants are added to a nationwide contact list and may be approached to cover stories at any time.
Text: Illustrated news stories on all aspects of motorcycling always considered. Lively tabloid style required.
Overall freelance potential: Good.
Editor's tips: Assignments are often at short notice and to tight deadlines – photographers who can work quickly and flexibly stand the best chance of success. Commission fees include copyright assignment to MCN, though permission for re-use by the photographer is rarely denied.
Fees: Single pictures from £50; day rate £200 plus expenses.

MOUNTAIN BIKING UK
Future Publishing Ltd, Beauford Court, 30 Monmouth Street, Bath BA1 2BW.
Tel: 01225 442244. Fax: 01225 822790. E-mail: danny.walter@futurenet.co.uk
Editor: Danny Walter.
Monthly magazine devoted to the sport of mountain biking.
Illustrations: Spectacular or unusual shots of mountain biking, action pictures that convey a sense of both movement and height. General coverage of events and individual riders may be of interest.
Text: Well-illustrated articles that show good knowledge of the sport.
Overall freelance potential: Good scope for individual and original photography.
Fees: By negotiation.

PRACTICAL SPORTSBIKES
Bauer Automotive Ltd, Media House, Lynchwood, Peterborough PE2 6EA.
Tel: 01733 468043. E-mail: jim.moore@bauermedia.co.uk
Editor: Jim Moore.
Quarterly magazine focused on sports motorcycles from the mid-70s to mid-90s era.
Illustrations: Only required as part of illustrated article packages as below.
Text: Well-illustrated feature stories about individual bikes and restoration projects, but contributors must have detailed knowledge of machines from the relevant era.

Overall freelance potential: Limited, only for the specialist.
Editor's Tips: Ideas or suggestions should be submitted to the editor along with examples of work that show the contributor genuinely knows the subject.
Fees: By negotiation.

RIDE
Bauer Automotive, Media House, Lynchwood, Peterborough PE2 6EA.
Tel: 01733 468081. Fax: 01733 468092. E-mail: colin.overland@bauermedia.co.uk
Editor: Colin Overland.
Monthly magazine for the motorcycling enthusiast.
Illustrations: Always interested in expanding network of photographers, for reader shots, news pictures etc. Commissions available to produce coverage for road tests and general features, but only for those with prior experience of motor sport or similar action photography.
Text: Little scope.
Overall freelance potential: Limited.
Fees: Around £250 per day.

SCOOTERING
PO Box 99, Horncastle, Lincs LN9 6LZ.
Tel/fax: 01507 524004. E-mail: editorial@scootering.com
Editor: Andy Gillard.
Monthly magazine for motor scooter enthusiasts.
Illustrations: Pictures of motor scooters of the Lambretta/Vespa type – shows, meetings, "runs", racing, special paint jobs, "chopped" scooters, etc. Covers: usually staff-produced, but a good freelance shot might be used.
Text: Original ideas considered. Contributors should be aware of the particular lifestyle and terminology attached to the scooter scene.
Overall freelance potential: Potential scope for those who know the current scooter scene and its followers, but most is produced by staff or regular contributors.
Editor's tips: Be aware that the readers have a very good knowledge of this specialised subject.
Fees: By negotiation.

SUPERBIKE
IPC Media, Leon House, 233 High Street, Croydon CR9 1HZ.
Tel: 020 8726 8445. Fax: 020 8726 8499. E-mail: kenny_pryde@ipcmedia.com
Editor: Kenny Pryde. **Art Editor:** Huw Williams.
Monthly for sports motorcycle enthusiasts. Specialising in new model tests and old model reviews, motorcycle Grand Prix, World Superbike and UK racing scene.
Illustrations: Pictures of unusual motorcycles, road-racing, drag-racing and other sports pictures of unusual interest or impact; crash sequences; motorcycle people.
Text: Features of general or specific motorcycle interest. Editorial style is humorous, irreverent. 1,500–3,000 words.
Overall freelance potential: Around 30 per cent of the magazine is contributed from outside sources.
Fees: Dependent on size and position in magazine.

Are you working from the latest edition of The Freelance Photographer's Market Handbook? It's published on 1 October each year. Markets are constantly changing, so it pays to have the latest edition

VISORDOWN
Magicalia Media, 15-18 White Lion Street, London N1 9PG.
Tel: 020 7843 8800. E-mail: ben.cope@magicalia.com
Editor: Ben Cope.
Wide-ranging monthly for all motorcycling enthusiasts. Covers road bikes, racing, touring and scooters.
Illustrations: Any strong and interesting images connected with any aspect of motorcycling and the biking lifestyle – unusual bikes or biking situations, good race action, celebrities with bikes, etc. Most major feature photography is handled by a regular team but commissions may be available to those with experience.
Text: Limited scope, but original ideas considered.
Overall freelance potential: Good for the specialist.
Editor's tips: Images from the sidelines of the motorcycling scene may be of more interest than action or straight shots of bikes.
Fees: Negotiable, depending on what is offered.

Electronics & Computing

PRACTICAL WIRELESS
PW Publishing Ltd, Arrowsmith Court, Station Approach, Broadstone, Dorset BH18 8PW.
Tel: 0845 803 1979. Fax: 01202 659950. E-mail: steve@pwpublishing.ltd.uk
Editor: Rob Mannion. **Art Editor:** Stephen Hunt.
Monthly magazine covering all aspects of radio of interest to the radio amateur and enthusiast.
Illustrations: B&W and colour. Usually only required to illustrate specific articles or covers.
Text: Articles on amateur radio or short wave listening, or on aspects of professional radio systems of interest to the enthusiast. 1,000–5,000 words.
Overall freelance potential: Little scope for individual photographs, but complete, illustrated articles always welcome.
Fees: By negotiation.

PRO SOUND NEWS
CMP Information, 7th Floor, Ludgate House, 245 Blackfriars Road, London SE1 9UR.
Tel: 020 7921 8319. Fax: 020 7921 8302. E-mail: david.robinson@cmpinformation.com
Editor: Dave Robinson.
Monthly news magazine for professionals working in the European sound production industry. Covers recording, live sound, post-production, mastering and broadcasting.
Illustrations: News pictures on all aspects of the industry, from equipment manufacture to live sound shows and concert performances to recording studios.
Text: Illustrated news items and features (800–1,000 words) on any aspect of the industry, but always check with the editor before submitting.
Overall freelance potential: Good for those with contacts in the audio and music business.
Fees: £140 per 1,000 words for text; photographs from £25.

RADIO USER
PW Publishing Ltd, Arrowsmith Court, Station Approach, Broadstone, Dorset BH18 8PW.
Tel: 0845 803 1979. Fax: 01202 659950. E-mail: roger@pwpublishing.ltd.uk
Editor: Roger Hall. **Art Editor:** Stephen Hunt.
Monthly magazine for anyone interested in the world of radio communications.
Illustrations: Pictures connected with the world of radio and communications including ships, aircraft and vehicles, but usually only required to illustrate specific articles.
Text: Features on radio systems or on other aspects of radio of interest to the enthusiast. News and reviews of equipment, clubs, etc. 1,000–2,000 words.

Overall freelance potential: Between 50 and 75 per cent comes from freelances.
Editor's tips: The magazine is always on the lookout for features on new and novel uses for radio communications. Visual articles on all aspects of communications welcome.
Fees: £40 per published page.

WHAT SATELLITE & DIGITAL TV
Future Publishing Ltd, 2 Balcombe Street, London NW1 6NW.
Tel: 020 7042 4000. Fax: 020 7042 4471. E-mail: alex.lane@futurenet.co.uk
Editor: Alex Lane.
Monthly magazine for satellite TV system buyers and users. Contains tests on receivers and dishes, general features, programme listings, reviews and the latest satellite news.
Illustrations: Photographs of satellite systems in situ, family/people shots with equipment in use.
Text: Technical topics, plus programme reviews and personality pieces. 500–1,200 words.
Overall freelance potential: Around 50 per cent from such sources.
Fees: By agreement.

Equestrian

EQUESTRIAN TRADE NEWS
Equestrian Management Consultants Ltd, Stockeld Park, Wetherby, West Yorkshire LS22 4AW.
Tel: 01937 582111. Fax: 01937 582778. E-mail: editor@equestriantradenews.com
Editor: Liz Benwell.
Monthly publication for business people and trade in the equestrian world.
Illustrations: Pictures covering saddlery, feedstuffs, new riding schools and business in the industry. Also news pictures of people connected with the industry – people retiring, getting married, etc.
Text: Features on specialist subjects and general articles on retailing, marketing and business. 1,000 words.
Overall freelance potential: Around 50 per cent comes from freelances.
Editor's tips: Only stories with a business angle will be considered. No scope for general horsey or racing material.
Fees: Text, £25 per 1,000 words; pictures by arrangement.

HORSE
IPC Media Ltd, Blue Fin Building, 110 Southwark Street, London SE1 0SU.
Tel: 020 3148 5000. E-mail: joanna_brown@ipcmedia.com
Editor: Jo Brown. **Picture Editor:** Eve Jones.
Monthly aimed at the serious leisure rider.
Illustrations: All photography by commission only to illustrate specific features. Experienced workers should send an introductory letter with examples of previously published work.
Text: No scope.
Overall freelance potential: Limited and only for the experienced equestrian specialist.
Fees: By negotiation.

HORSE & HOUND
IPC Media, Blue Fin Building, 110 Southwark Street, London SE1 0SU.
Tel: 020 3148 4554. E-mail: hhpictures@ipcmedia.com
Editor: Lucy Higginson. **Picture Editor:** Jayne Toyne.

Weekly news magazine covering all equestrian sports.

Illustrations: News and feature pictures considered on spec for immediate use or for stock, covering racing, point-to-pointing, showjumping, eventing, polo, hunting, driving and showing. Commissions available to experienced equestrian/countryside photographers; make appointment with the picture editor to show portfolio.

Text: Possible opportunities for those with knowledge and experience of the above disciplines.

Overall freelance potential: Good for those who can show skill in this field; enquiries from photographers are encouraged.

Fees: Single pictures according to size of reproduction. Commission rates £200 per day (all rights); £135 per day (first use).

HORSE & RIDER

D. J. Murphy (Publishers) Ltd, Headley House, Headley Road, Grayshott, Surrey GU26 6TU.
Tel: 01428 601020. Fax: 01428 601030. E-mail: djm@djmurphy.co.uk
Editor: Nicky Moffatt.
Monthly magazine aimed at adult horse-riders.

Illustrations: Off-beat personality shots and pictures for photo stories illustrating equestrian subjects, eg plaiting up, clipping, etc. May also consider general yard pictures, riding pictures, people and horses, but only by prior arrangement.

Text: Illustrated instructional features on stable management, grooming, etc, from contributors with real knowledge of the subject. Submit ideas only in the first instance.

Overall freelance potential: Only for freelances who have a real understanding of the market.

Editor's tips: Material must be technically accurate – riders must be shown wearing the correct clothes, especially hats; horses must be fit and correctly tacked.

Fees: Pictures £25–£60. Text £65 per 1,000 words.

Farming

CROPS

Reed Farmers Publishing Group, Quadrant House, The Quadrant, Sutton, Surrey SM2 5AS.
Tel: 020 8652 4081. Fax: 020 8652 8928. E-mail: richard.allinson@rbi.co.uk
Editor: Richard Allinson.
Monthly magazine catering exclusively for the arable farmer.

Illustrations: News pictures depicting anything of topical, unusual or technical interest concerning crop farming and production. Captions must be precise and detailed.

Text: Limited scope for short topical articles written by specialists.

Overall freelance potential: Good for farming specialists.

Fees: By negotiation.

DAIRY FARMER

CMP Information Ltd, Riverbank House, Angel Lane, Tonbridge, Kent TN9 1SE.
Tel: 01732 377273. Fax: 01732 377543. E-mail: phollinshead@cmpibiz.com
Editor: Peter Hollinshead.
Monthly journal for dairy farmers.

Are you working from the latest edition of The Freelance Photographer's Market Handbook? It's published on 1 October each year. Markets are constantly changing, so it pays to have the latest edition

---

Illustrations: Captioned pictures, technical or possibly historical. Also humourous or unusual pictures concerning the dairy industry. Some assignments to visit farms available.
Text: In-depth, technical features to help dairy farmers run their businesses more profitably.
Overall freelance potential: Limited, but open to suggestions.
Fees: By arrangement.

FARMERS GUARDIAN

CMP Information Ltd, Unit 4, Fulwood Park, Caxton Road, Fulwood, Preston PR2 9NZ.
Tel: 01772 799445. Fax: 01772 654987. E-mail: teveson@cmpi.biz
Editor: Emma Penny. **Picture Editor:** Theresa Eveson.
Weekly news publication for all farmers, with the emphasis on commerce.
Illustrations: Current farming, rural and equestrian news pictures accompanied by story or extended captions.
Text: News items always of interest. Possible scope for articles on current agricultural and rural issues.
Overall freelance potential: Fair.
Fees: According to use.

FARMERS WEEKLY

Reed Business Information, Quadrant House, The Quadrant, Sutton, Surrey SM2 5AS.
Tel: 020 8652 4080. Fax: 020 8652 4005. E-mail: farmers.weekly@rbi.co.uk
Editor: Jane King. Group **Picture Editor:** Jodie Deakin.
Weekly publication covering all matters of interest to farmers.
Illustrations: News pictures relating to the world of farming and picture stories on technical aspects of agriculture. Also opportunities for assignments.
Text: Tight, well-written copy on farming matters and anything that will help farmers run their business more efficiently.
Overall freelance potential: Good.
Fees: News material by negotiation. Photo assignment work around £170 per day.
Editor's tips: News pages are started on Monday and close for press on Wednesday afternoon, so news material should be submitted during that period. Copy and pics can be received by e-mail.

HOME FARMER

The Good Life Press Ltd, The Old Pigsties, Clifton Fields, Lytham Road, Preston PR4 0XG.
Tel: 01772 633444. E-mail: editor@homefarmer.co.uk
Editors: Diana Sutton, Paul Peacock.
Monthly magazine aimed at anyone interested in small-scale farming and home-based food production, as well as environmental issues.
Illustrations: Will consider interesting images in their own right, but prefer to see them as part of a complete illustrated feature as below.
Text: Always interested in articles that can help readers realise their lifestyle dreams on subjects such as self-sufficiency, recycling, vegetable growing, urban poultry or pig keeping, beekeeping, caring for animals on a small acreage, etc. Initial contact by e-mail is preferred.
Overall freelance potential: Excellent for the right type of material.
Editor's Tips: Prefer to publish material on accessible and practical options that don't assume that people have a lot of land at their disposal.
Fees: By negotiation, depending upon what is on offer.

POULTRY WORLD

Reed Business Information, Quadrant House, The Quadrant, Sutton, Surrey SM2 5AS.
Tel: 020 8652 3500. Fax: 020 8652 4042. E-mail: poultry.world@rbi.co.uk
Editor: Philip Clarke.
Monthly publication aimed at the UK, EU and worldwide commercial poultry industries. Covers egg production as well as chickens, turkeys, ducks and geese. Includes Pure Breeds section.

Illustrations: News pictures and good general stock relating to the poultry industry, both in UK and overseas.

Text: News stories and ideas for features always considered; breeding, processing, packing, marketing, etc.

Overall freelance potential: Limited.

Fees: By negotiation.

Food & Drink

DECANTER

IPC Inspire, Blue Fin Building, 110 Southwark Street, London SE1 0SU.

Tel: 020 3148 5000. Fax: 020 3148 8524. E-mail: decanterpictures@decanter.com

Editor: Guy Woodward.

Monthly magazine for the serious wine enthusiast, featuring producer and regional profiles, tastings, and related food and travel features.

Illustrations: Stock images of wine-producing regions occasionally needed to illustrate features, including attractive travel images of the region, not necessarily specifically wine-related. Send details of coverage available in the first instance.

Text: Illustrated articles on topics as above; submit synopsis first.

Overall freelance potential: Limited.

Fees: By negotiation.

ITALIA UK

Italia UK Limited, 3 Brooklands Place, Brooklands Road, Sale, Manchester M33 3SD.

Tel: 0161 976 1212. Fax: 0161 976 2888. E-mail: gr@italiauk.net

Editor: Glenn Routledge.

Anglo-Italian publication distributed through catering and food retail outlets.

Illustrations: Images of Italian food, drink, restaurants. Send details of subjects available in the first instance.

Text: May consider quality restaurant reviews (with pictures) from main UK cities, and general feature suggestions.

Overall freelance potential: Limited.

Editor's tips: Bear in mind readership is pro-Italian and already has a reasonable knowledge of Italy.

Fees: By negotiation.

LIFESCAPE

Madafu Publishing Ltd, 353 Shenley Road, Borehamwood, Herts WD6 1TN.

Tel: 01707 859805. E-mail: rajasana@lifescapemag.com

Editor: Rajasana Otiende.

Magazine designed as a complete resource for vegetarians, covering not just food but also holidays, fair trade fashion/beauty and the use of organic products generally.

Illustrations: Agency pictures often used but the editor would prefer to use freelance stock or even commission images. In-house photographer produces most beauty coverage but possible opportunities for fashion work.

Text: Approaches from writers with expert knowledge of health subjects always welcomed.

Overall freelance potential: Fair.
Editor's tips: Would rather pay for something unique than rely on agencies, though it does have to be within budget.
Fees: By negotiation.

OLIVE
BBC Worldwide Publishing, Woodlands, 80 Wood Lane, London W12 0TT.
Tel: 020 8433 1769. Fax: 020 8433 3499. E-mail: elizabeth.galbraith@bbc.co.uk
Editor: Christine Hayes. **Creative Director:** Elizabeth Galbraith.
Monthly food and travel magazine for a young, upmarket readership.
Illustrations: Digital files preferred. Almost all by commission to illustrate major features. Experienced workers should make an an appointment to show portfolio to the creative director. Those with relevant stock collections should send lists.
Text: Will consider ideas from experienced contributors, especially for travel-related material, but no on spec submissions.
Overall freelance potential: Opportunities for specialists only.
Fees: By negotation.

PUBLICAN
United Business Media, Ludgate House, 245 Blackfriars Road, London SE1 9UY.
Tel: 020 7955 3711. E-mail: cnodder@cmpinformation.com
Editor: Caroline Nodder.
Weekly independent newspaper for publicans and pub companies throughout the UK.
Illustrations: Topical pictures concerning pubs and publicans, brewery and pub company management, and the drinks trade generally. Must be newsworthy or have some point of unusual interest, and preferably include people. Call before submitting.
Text: News items and picture stories about publicans – humorous, unusual, or controversial. Stories that have implications for the whole pub trade, or that illustrate a problem; original ways of increasing trade. News items up to 250 words; features around 500–800 words, but discuss proposal before submitting.
Overall freelance potential: Good for original material, especially from outside London and the South East.
Editor's tips: Forget charity bottle smashes, pub openings, and pictures of people pulling or holding pints – hundreds of these are received already.
Fees: On a rising scale according to size of reproduction or length of text.

RESTAURANT
William Reed Business Media, Broadfield Park, Crawley, West Sussex RH11 9RT.
Tel: 01293 610214. E-mail: will.drew@william-reed.co.uk
Editor: Will Drew. **Art Director:** Gary Simons.
Monthly magazine for the restaurant trade, with coverage ranging from top London restaurants to high street operations. Also designed to appeal to serious food lovers and restaurant-goers.
Illustrations: Mostly by commission to shoot food, interiors, portraiture, reportage, still life and travel. Some scope for those with in-depth stock collections on suitable subjects. On-spec opportunities for coverage of restaurant openings, events and informal shots of trade personalities.
Text: Will consider ideas on any relevant subject.
Overall freelance potential: Good for experienced freelances.
Fees: By negotiation.

SCOTTISH LICENSED TRADE NEWS
Peebles Media Group, Berguis House, 20 Clifton Street, Glasgow G3 7LA.
Tel: 0141 567 6000. Fax: 0141 331 1395. E-mail: scott.wright@peeblesmedia.com
Editor: Scott Wright.
Fortnightly publication for Scottish publicans, off-licensees, hoteliers, caterers, restaurateurs,

drinks executives, drinks companies.
Illustrations: News pictures connected with the above subjects.
Text: News and features of specific interest to the Scottish trade.
Overall freelance potential: Limited.
Fees: By agreement.

WAITROSE KITCHEN
John Brown Publishing, 136-142 Bramley Road, London W10 6SR.
Tel: 020 7565 3000. Fax: 020 7565 3076. E-mail: food@johnbrowngroup.co.uk
Editor: William Sitwell. **Art Director:** Ben Brannen. **Art Editor:** Tabitha Hawkins.
Picture-led monthly concentrating on the "culture of food" as well as recipes and cookery.
Illustrations: Colour transparencies only. Very high quality food photography, plus coverage of food producers, gourmet travel, restaurants and chefs. Much commissioned from established specialists; those with suitable skills should initally submit some examples of previous work. Limited use of top quality specialist stock; send lists to picture editor. Commissions for interior/food shots for restaurant reviews around the UK are frequently sought.
Text: Scope for well-experienced food and drink writers.
Overall freelance potential: Excellent, but only for the experienced worker in the field.
Fees: By negotiation.

Gardening

BBC GARDENERS' WORLD MAGAZINE
BBC Worldwide, Media Centre, 201 Wood Lane, London W12 7TQ.
Tel: 020 8433 3959. Fax: 020 8433 3986. E-mail: guy.bennington@bbc.com
Editor: Adam Pasco. **Art Editor:** Guy Bennington.
Monthly magazine for gardeners at all levels of expertise.
Illustrations: No speculative submissions. Photographers with specialist gardening collections should send lists of material available with all plants properly named. Commissions may be available to photograph individual gardens; the editor will always be pleased to hear from photographers who can bring potential subjects to his attention. Also photographers prepared to set up small studios with lights on location: good studio, portrait and reportage photography also commissioned.
Text: All text is commissioned.
Overall freelance potential: Mainly for specialists.
Editor's tips: Always looking for interesting "real" gardens for possible coverage. Small gardens, patios and container gardening of particular interest.
Fees: By negotiation.

THE ENGLISH GARDEN
Archant Specialist, Archant House, Oriel Road, Cheltenham GL50 1BB.
Tel: 01242 211080. E-mail: theenglishgarden@archant.co.uk
Editor: Tamsin Westhorpe.
Picture-led monthly featuring the most attractive gardens in Britain, from cottage gardens to stately homes.
Illustrations: Pictures mainly required as part of complete feature packages as below and usually commissioned. Possible scope for library shots illustrating specific types of garden, plant or tree – send lists of subjects available in the first instance.
Text: High-quality, exclusive features on individual gardens accompanied by a good selection of pictures (15-20 published within each feature). Discuss with the editor first.
Overall freelance potential: A lot of photography is used but much is produced by regular contributors.

Editor's tips: Most interested in beautiful, idyllic gardens that readers can either visit or just fantasise about.
Fees: By negotiation and according to use.

THE GARDEN
RHS Publications, 4th Floor, Churchgate, New Road, Peterborough PE1 1TT.
Tel: 0845 260 0909. Fax: 01733 341633. E-mail: thegarden@rhs.org.uk
Editor: Ian Hodgson.
Monthly Journal of the Royal Horticultural Society. Publishes articles on plants and specialist aspects and techniques of horticulture.
Illustrations: Top quality photographs of identified plants, general horticultural subjects and specific gardens.
Text: Some freelance market; submit suggestions first.
Overall freelance potential: Some potential opportunities.
Fees: £40–£165 according to size of reproduction.

GARDEN ANSWERS
Bauer Media, Media House, Lynchwood, Peterborough PE2 6EA.
Tel: 01733 468000. E-mail: geoffstebbings@bauermedia.co.uk
Editor: Geoff Stebbings.
Monthly magazine for the enthusiastic gardener.
Illustrations: Little scope for speculative submissions, but always interested in receiving lists of subjects available from photographers. Do not send transparencies unless requested.
Text: Experienced gardening writers may be able to obtain commissions.
Overall freelance potential: Limited to the experienced gardening contributor.
Editor's tips: Practical gardening pictures are required, rather than simple shots of plants. Must be accompanied by detailed and accurate captions.
Fees: By arrangement.

GARDEN NEWS
Bauer Active Ltd, Media House, Lynchwood, Peterborough PE2 6EA.
Tel: 01733 468000. E-mail: clare.foggett@bauermedia.co.uk
Editor: Clare Foggett.
Weekly consumer newspaper for gardeners.
Illustrations: Digital files or medium format transparencies. Pictures of general horticultural subjects. Practical photographs to illustrate gardening techniques, top quality colour portraits of trees, shrubs, flowers and vegetables, and coverage of quality small/medium sized gardens.
Text: Short practical features of interest to gardeners. 600–800 words.
Overall freelance potential: Fair.
Fees: By agreement.

GARDEN TRADE NEWS
The Garden Communication and Media Company, The Old School, 4 Crowland Road, Eye, Peterborough PE6 7TN.
Tel: 01733 775700. Fax: 01733 775838. E-mail: editorial@gardentradenews.co.uk
Editor: Mike Wyatt.
Monthly business publication containing news, features and advice for retailers, wholesalers, manufacturers and distributors of horticultural products.
Illustrations: Pictures to illustrate news items or features.
Text: Illustrated news stories or articles concerning garden centres, nurseries and garden shops. Maximum 600 words.
Overall freelance potential: Limited.
Fees: £12.50 per 100 words; pictures from £17.50–£50 according to size of reproduction.

GARDENS ILLUSTRATED

Bristol Magazines Ltd, 14th Floor, Tower House, Fairfax Street, Bristol BS1 3BN.
Tel: 0117 314 8770. Fax: 0117 934 9008. E-mail: davidgrenham@originpublishing.co.uk
Editor: Juliet Roberts. **Art Director:** David Grenham.
Heavily-illustrated monthly with a practical and inspirational approach.
Illustrations: Usually commissioned, but high quality submissions may be considered on spec. Photography should have a narrative and journalistic slant rather than just pretty pictures of gardens. The gardens should be depicted in relation to the landscape, houses and the people who own or work them. Coverage from outside UK welcome.
Text: Scope for experienced gardening writers – submit samples of previously published work first.
Overall freelance potential: Very good for the right material.
Editor's tips: Quality is key. Material previously published in the UK is not of interest.
Fees: By negotiation.

GARDENS MONTHLY

MyHobbyStore Ltd, Berwick House, 8-10 Knoll Rise, Orpington, Kent BR6 0EL.
Tel: 08444 122262. Fax: 01689 899266. E-mail: liz.dobbs@myhobbystore.com
Editor: Liz Dobbs.
Monthly aimed at gardeners of all levels, with an emphasis on easy to achieve success.
Illustrations: Stock images of gardening and garden subjects sometimes needed; send detailed list of subjects available in the first instance.
Text: No scope.
Overall freelance potential: Limited.
Fees: From £15, to £100 for full page or cover.

HORTICULTURE WEEK

Haymarket Media Ltd, 174 Hammersmith Road, London W6 4JP.
Tel: 020 8267 4977. Fax: 020 8267 4987. E-mail: hortweek@haymarket.com
Editor: Kate Lowe. **Art Editor:** David Grant.
Weekly news magazine for commercial growers of plants and those employed in landscape work, garden centres, public parks and gardens.
Illustrations: Captioned news and feature pictures relating to commercial horticulture, landscaping, public parks, garden centres. Stock botanical images often needed – send details of material available. Some commissions available.
Text: Short news items about happenings affecting the trade. Longer articles may be considered – discuss ideas with the editor. 500–1,500 words.
Overall freelance potential: Limited.
Fees: By arrangement.

PROFESSIONAL LANDSCAPER & GROUNDSMAN

Albatross Publications, PO Box 523, Horsham, West Sussex RH12 4WL.
Tel: 01293 871201. Fax: 01293 871301. E-mail: newsdesk123@aol.com
Editor: Carol Andrews.
Quarterly magazine for landscapers, contractors, foresters, environmental designers, groundsmen and local authorities. Covers both hard and soft landscape creation.
Illustrations: Pictures depicting subjects as below, usually only accepted as part of a complete illustrated feature.
Text: Well-illustrated articles or case histories dealing with technical or practical landscaping matters, horticulture, and general environmental and conservation issues. 1,200–1,500 words.
Overall freelance potential: Limited.
Fees: By negotiation.

General Interest

BEST OF BRITISH
Church Lane Publishing Ltd, 6 Market Gate, Market Deeping, Lincs PE6 8DL.
Tel/fax: 01778 342814. E-mail: linne@bestofbritishmag.co.uk
Editor: Linne Matthews.
Monthly magazine covering all aspects of British heritage and nostalgia, but with a strong emphasis on 1940s/1950s/1960s.
Illustrations: Mainly colour plus B&W for archive pictures from earlier eras. Top quality coverage of all British heritage subjects, from landscapes and museums to craftspeople and collectors; send details of material available in the first instance.
Text: Illustrated articles offering a positive view of aspects of Britain, past and present. Also profiles of people with unusual passions, humorous pieces about the British people and interviews with celebrities about aspects of Britain they love. Submit ideas or an outline first.
Overall freelance potential: Excellent.
Editor's tips: Pictures with good captions are always more interesting than those without. Material should always reflect a positive view of Britain. Nostalgic pictures always welcome, with a particular interest in the 1940s. See website at www.bestofbritishmag.co.uk.
Fees: By negotiation with editor.

BIZARRE
Dennis Publishing Ltd, 30 Cleveland Street, London W1T 4JD.
Tel: 020 7907 6000. Fax: 020 7907 6020. E-mail: bizarre.pictures@dennis.co.uk
Editor: David McComb. **Picture Editor:** Tom Broadbent.
Monthly magazine specialising in alternative (fetish and subversive) lifestyles. Heavily illustrated, including special 14-page photo section.
Illustrations: Will consider pictures depicting anything that broadly falls within the above parameters, with a heavy emphasis on shocking reportage photography. "Weird, disturbing and downright bizarre photos from around the world, the more unique the better." Prefer material that has not been previously published.
Text: Little freelance scope unless the contributor is a genuine expert in a specific subject.
Overall freelance potential: Very good.
Editor's tips: Always call first with details of what you have to offer. Please no "ghost" photos.
Fees: By negotiation and dependent on what is being offered.

COAST
The National Magazine Company Ltd, 72 Broadwick Street, London W1F 9EP.
Tel: 020 7439 5000. Fax: 7439 6880. E-mail: suzy.koo@natmags.co.uk
Editor: Clare Gogerty. **Art Director:** Joe McIntyre. **Picture Editor:** Suzy Koo.
Monthly glossy that celebrates the best of British coastal and seaside living.
Illustrations: High-quality seaside imagery, including coastal landscapes, seascapes, marine wildlife, etc, either for use in their own right with captions or to illustrate features. Mainly interested in hearing from photographers who can offer good coverage of specific coastal locations or subjects. Initial approach should be by e-mail with a small selection of low-res images. Also some opportunities for commissions, mainly for homes and interiors work – contact art editor in the first instance.
Text: Illustrated articles and features on suitable subjects always considered.
Overall freelance potential: Excellent for quality material.
Editor's tips: Keep in mind that requirements vary from month to month according to what features and locations are being included in each issue.
Fees: By negotiation.

CONDÉ NAST CUSTOMER PUBLISHING
6-8 Bond Street, London W1S 0AD.
Tel: 020 7152 3954. E-mail: michael.harrison@condenast.co.uk
Creative Director: Michael Harrison. **Group Picture Editor:** Victoria Lukens.
Contract publishing division of Condé Nast. Produces upmarket titles for corporate clients such as major store and hotel groups.
Illustrations: Opportunities for experienced photographers to obtain commissions in the fields of fashion, portraiture, travel, lifestyle and still life. Contact creative director by e-mail with details of previous experience and examples of work.
Text: N/A.
Overall freelance potential: Scope for photographers producing the highest quality work.
Fees: By negotiation.

READER'S DIGEST
Vivat Direct Ltd (T/A Reader's Digest) 11 Westferry Circus, Canary Wharf, London E14 4HE.
Tel: 020 7715 8029. Fax: 020 7715 8716. E-mail: theeditor@readersdigest.co.uk
Editor-in-Chief: Gill Hudson. **Picture Researcher:** Roberta Mitchell.
British edition of the monthly magazine for a general interest readership.
Illustrations: Pictures to illustrate specific general interest features. Some commission possibilities for experienced specialist workers.
Text: High quality features on all topics.
Overall freelance potential: Limited opportunities for new freelance contributors.
Fees: By agreement.

SAGA MAGAZINE
Saga Publishing Ltd, The Saga Pavilion, Enbrook Park, Sandgate, Folkestone CT20 3SE.
Tel: 01303 771523. Fax: 01303 776699.
Editor: Katy Bravery. **Art Director:** Paul Hayes-Watkins.
Monthly, subscription-only, general interest magazine aimed at readers over 50.
Illustrations: Photography is mainly by commission only, but some top quality photo features occasionally accepted.
Text: Will consider wide range of articles – human interest, "real life" stories, intriguing overseas interest (not travel), celebrity interviews, some natural history – all relevant to 50+ readership.
Overall freelance potential: Limited, but some possiblities for carefully-targeted ideas exclusive to UK.
Fees: Good, but by negotiation.

THE TRAVEL & LEISURE MAGAZINE
Travel & Leisure Magazines Limited, 103 Cranbrook Road, Ilford, Essex IG1 4PU.
Tel: 020 8477 1529. E-mail: peter@ellegard.co.uk
Editor: Peter Ellegard.
Family-oriented quarterly, covering not just travel but also motoring, health, interiors, gardens, food and drink.
Illustrations: Always interested in seeing potential front cover shots. These are always seasonal in nature and most frequently feature happy families in a seasonal setting.
Text: Some scope for illustrated articles, mainly on the travel side and for the magazine's regular sections – intending contributors should ask for a copy of the magazine so that they can see the usual format of the sections. Rarely take speculative pieces but often ask freelances to write on specific locations or topics.
Overall freelance potential: Limited.
Fees: By negotiation.

WORLD ILLUSTRATED
HotShoe International Ltd, 29-31 Saffron Hill, London EC1N 8SW.
Tel: 020 7421 6009. E-mail: ctaylor@photoshot.com
Editor: Melissa DeWitt.
Showcase magazine for established and up-and-coming photographic talent.
Illustrations: As above, photographic work across a wide range of styles and genres.
Text: No scope.
Overall freelance potential: Good for really top-quality material.
Editor's tips: Sets of images need to tell a story and have contemporary relevance.
Fees: By negotiation.

YOURS
Bauer Consumer Media, Media House, Lynchwood, Peterborough PE2 6EA.
Tel: 01733 468000. E-mail: yours@bauerconsumer.co.uk
Editor: Valery McConnell. **Picture Editor:** Davina Dunn.
Fortnightly publication aimed at 50-plus women.
Illustrations: Good stock shots of mature people engaged in a variety of activities, or depicted in varying moods (happy, worried, thoughtful, etc), always needed for general illustration purposes. The latter should be model-released. Send list of subjects and a few samples first. Experienced photographers required for commissions around the country, able to take strong, sympathetic shots to accompany news items and real life stories.
Text: Positive stories about older people's achievements and general features likely to be of particular interest to an older readership. 600–1,000 words.
Overall freelance potential: Very good.
Fees: By negotiation.

Health & Medical

GP
Haymarket Medical Ltd, 174 Hammersmith Road, London W6 7JP.
Tel: 020 8267 4849. Fax: 020 8267 4859. E-mail: pauline.lock@haymarket.com
Editor: Emma Bower. **Group Art Editor:** Pauline Lock.
Weekly newspaper for family doctors.
Illustrations: Pictures of general practitioners involved in news stories, and clinical/scientific pictures for features. Commissions frequently available to shoot portraits of GPs or practice nurses.
Text: News stories, up to 400 words, preferably by prior arrangement. Features considered, by prior arrangement with the features editor.
Overall freelance potential: The paper uses a lot of pictures from freelances.
Fees: By negotiation, but around £200-£300 per 1,000 words, and £100 for half-day photographic session.

H&E NATURIST
New Freedom Publications Ltd, Burlington Court, Carlisle Street, Goole, East Yorkshire DN14 5EG.
Tel: 01405 760298. Fax: 01405 763815. E-mail: editor@henaturist.net
Editor: Sam Hawcroft.
Monthly naturist/nudist magazine.
Illustrations: Attractive photos of naturists in landscapes, on beaches, in countryside. Couples and singles, male and female, any age from 18 upwards. Also travel and scenic shots used.
Text: Illustrated articles up to 1,200 words about naturist lives and resorts, and off the beaten track naturism.
Overall freelance potential: Excellent.
Editor's tips: Contributors' guidelines are available on request.
Fees: Cover £150; £20 per quarter page inside.

HEALTH & FITNESS
Dennis Publishing, 30 Cleveland Street, London W1T 4JD.
Tel: 020 7907 6000. E-mail: victoria_hill@dennis.co.uk
Editor: Mary Comber. **Deputy Art Editor:** Victoria Hill.
Glossy monthly covering all aspects of fitness, health and nutrition, aimed at women.
Illustrations: Photographs for use in illustrating articles and features on topics as above. Covers: outstanding and striking shots featuring an obviously fit and healthy young female model.
Text: Articles and features on suitable topics, with an appeal to women. Always query the editor before submitting.
Overall freelance potential: Good.
Fees: By negotiation.

PULSE
UBM Medica, Ludgate House, 245 Blackfriars Road, London SE1 9UY.
Tel: 020 7921 8102. Fax: 020 7921 8248. E-mail: mcollard@cmpmedica.com
Editor: Jo Haynes. Group **Picture Editor:** Marie Louise Collard.
Weekly newspaper for family doctors covering all aspects of general practice medicine.
Illustrations: Topical pictures with captions, involving GPs or illustrating relevant news stories. Commissions available for high quality portraiture, especially outside the London area. Pictures are also commissioned for the Pulse Picture Library, a specialist collection of life and medicine in general practice.
Text: News and topical features about general practice and GPs.
Overall freelance potential: Good, especially for portrait specialists.
Editor's tips: Most interested in photographers who can produce original and creative portrait work.
Fees: Negotiable. £100 per half day for commissions.

Hobbies & Craft

CLASSIC STITCHES
D C Thomson & Company Ltd, 80 Kingsway East, Dundee DD4 8SL.
Tel: 01382 575120. Fax: 01382 452491. E-mail: editorial@classicstitches.com
Editor: Bea Neilson.
Bi-monthly embroidery magazine which looks at the work of designers and their lifestyles. Includes project-based features.
Illustrations: Photography generally required only to accompany features, though feature ideas are often generated by photographs. Commissions available to experienced workers to shoot still life material.
Text: Illustrated embroidery-related articles and specific projects, up to 1,500 words. Look at previous issues for style.
Overall freelance potential: Good; 70% of content is freelance.
Editor's tips: Make sure any submissions are relevant. For photographs, lighting and focus are paramount.
Fees: By negotiation.

CLOCKS
Splat Publishing Ltd, 141B Lower Granton Road, Edinburgh EH5 1EX.
Tel: 0131 331 3200. Fax: 0131 331 3213. E-mail: editor@clocksmagazine.com
Editor: John Hunter.
Monthly magazine for clock enthusiasts generally, those interested in building, repairing, restoring and collecting clocks and watches.
Illustrations: Pictures of anything concerned with clocks, e.g. public clocks, clocks in private

collections or museums, clock movements and parts, people involved in clock making, repairing or restoration. Detailed captions essential.

Text: Features on clockmakers, repairers or restorers; museums and collections; clock companies. 1,000–2,000 words.

Overall freelance potential: Around 90 per cent of the magazine is contributed by freelances.

Editor's tips: Pictures unaccompanied by textual descriptions of the clocks, or articles about them, are rarely used.

Fees: By arrangement.

ENGINEERING IN MINIATURE

TEE Publishing Ltd, The Fosse, Fosse Way, Radford Semele, Leamington Spa, CV31 1XN.
Tel: 01926 614101. Fax: 01926 614293. E-mail: info@teepublishing.com
Managing Editor: Chris Deith.
Monthly magazine concerned with model engineering and working steam models.

Illustrations: B&W and colour. Photographs only used in conjunction with specific news items or articles. No stock photos required. Covers: colour of model steam locomotives, engines or other model engineering subjects. A4 portrait format.

Text: Well-illustrated articles and features on all aspects of model engineering and serious modelling, and on full size railways and steam road vehicles. Must be of a serious and technical nature.

Overall freelance potential: Some 80 per cent of contributions come from freelances.

Editor's tips: Ideally engines depicted should be true steam-operated, not electric steam outline. There is no coverage of model railways below "0" gauge, or of plastic models. Telephone contact is preferred in the first instance.

Fees: Negotiable.

FURNITURE & CABINETMAKING

GMC Publications Ltd, 86 High Street, Lewes, East Sussex BN7 1XN.
Tel: 01273 402843. Fax: 01273 402849. E-mail: derekj@thegmcgroup.com
Editor: Derek Jones.
Monthly magazine for the serious furniture maker.

Illustrations: Mostly by commission to illustrate step-by-step projects and features on individual craftsmen – write with details of experience and samples of work. Good stock shots of fine furniture often required to illustrate specific styles. Topical single pictures may be considered if accompanied by detailed supporting text.

Text: Ideas for illustrated features always welcome. Submit a synopsis and one sample picture in the first instance.

Overall freelance potential: Good for experienced workers.

Fees: £25 per single picture inside; illustrated articles £50–£70 per page.

GIBBONS STAMP MONTHLY

Stanley Gibbons Publications, 7 Parkside, Christchurch Road, Ringwood, Hampshire BH24 3SH.
Tel: 01425 472363. Fax: 01425 470247. E-mail: hjefferies@stanleygibbons.co.uk
Editor: Hugh Jefferies.
Monthly magazine for stamp collectors.

Illustrations: Pictures inside only as illustrations for articles. Covers: pictures of interesting or unusual stamps relating to editorial features.

Text: Features on stamp collecting. 500–3,000 words.

Overall freelance potential: Most of the editorial comes from freelance contributors.

Fees: From £50 per 1,000 words.

GOOD WOODWORKING

MyHobbyStore Ltd, Berwick House, 8-10 Knoll Rise, Orpington, Kent BR6 0EL.
Tel: 0844 412 2262. E-mail: dave.roberts@magicalia.com

Editor: Darren Louciades.
Four weekly magazine for the serious amateur woodworker.
Illustrations: By commission only. Assignments available to cover specific projects.
Text: Ideas and suggestions welcome, but writers must have good technical knowledge of the subject. Commissions available to interview individual woodworkers.
Overall freelance potential: Good for those with experience of the subject.
Fees: Photography by negotiation. Text around £150 per 1,000 words.

KNITTING

Guild of Master Craftsman Publications Ltd, 86 High Street, Lewes, East Sussex BN8 4TH.
Tel: 01273 402824. Fax: 01273 487692. E-mail emmak@thegmcgroup.com
Editor: Emma Kennedy.
Monthly magazine for hand knitting enthusiasts.
Illustrations: Seek interesting, unusual and colourful images of people knitting from around the world. Must be accompanied by detailed captions, up to 500 words. Images of celebrities knitting welcomed.
Text: Will consider features on knitting events, stitch 'n' bitch groups, new wool shops, and how-to articles about knitting and crochet. Up to 1500 words with about 10 pictures. Ideas always welcomed.
Overall freelance potential: Good.
Fees: By negotiation.

MODEL ENGINEER

MyHobbyStore Ltd, Berwick House, 8-10 Knoll Rise, Orpington, Kent BR6 0EL.
Tel: 01689 899200. Fax: 01689 876438. E-mail: david.clark@myhobbystore.com
Editor: David Clark.
Fortnightly magazine aimed at the serious model engineering enthusiast.
Illustrations: No stock shots required; all pictures must be part of an article. Covers: photographs depicting models of steam locomotives and traction engines; metalworking equipment and home workshop scenes; some full size vintage vehicles.
Text: Well-illustrated articles from specialists.
Overall freelance potential: Considerable for the specialist.
Fees: Negotiable.

PARROTS

Imax Visual Ltd, The Old Cart House, Applesham Farm, Coombes, West Sussex BN15 0RP.
Tel: 01273 464777. Fax: 01273 463999. E-mail: editorial@imaxweb.co.uk
Editor: John Catchpole.
Monthly magazine for the parrot enthusiast.
Illustrations: High quality photographs of specific types of parrots and parakeets. Must be well-posed and well lit, showing clear details of plumage. Full and accurate caption information (preferably including scientific names) also essential. Amusing pictures involving parrots considered if accompanied by a good story.
Text: Articles aimed at the parrot enthusiast.
Editor's tips: Do not submit unidentified generic pictures of the "parrot on a branch" variety, or shots taken from long distances in zoos or bird parks.
Fees: Dependent on quality.

Are you working from the latest edition of The Freelance Photographer's Market Handbook? It's published on 1 October each year. Markets are constantly changing, so it pays to have the latest edition

---

PRACTICAL FISHKEEPING
Bauer Active Ltd, Media House, Lynchwood, Peterborough PE2 6EA.
Tel: 01733 468000. E-mail: matt.clarke@bauermedia.co.uk
Editor-in-Chief: Matt Clarke.
Monthly magazine for all tropical freshwater, marine, pond and coldwater fishkeepers, aimed at every level from hobbyist to expert.
Illustrations: Pictures of all species of tropical, marine and coldwater fish, plants, tanks, ponds and water gardens. Fish diseases, pond and tank maintenance, and pictures of things that have "gone wrong" are especially welcome. Prefer to hold material on file for possible future use.
Text: Emphasis on instructional articles on the subject. 1,000–2,000 words.
Overall freelance potential: Most is supplied by contributors with a specific knowledge of the hobby, but freelance material is considered on its merit at all times.
Editor's tips: Telephone first to give a brief on the intended copy and/or photographs available. Caption all fish clearly and get names right.
Fees: Negotiable.

TREASURE HUNTING
Greenlight Publishing, The Publishing House, 119 Newland Street, Witham, Essex CM8 1NF.
Tel: 01376 521900. Fax: 01376 521901. E-mail: greg@acguk.com
Editor: Greg Payne.
Monthly magazine for metal detecting and local history enthusiasts.
Illustrations: Colour prints or digital files. Usually only as illustrations for features detailed below, but captioned news pictures may be of interest. Covers: colour pictures of people using metal detectors in a countryside or seaside setting.
Text: Illustrated stories and features on individual finds, club treasure hunts, lost property recovery, local history, etc. However, fees nominal.
Overall freelance potential: Approximately 50 per cent of the magazine comes from freelances.
Editor's tips: Advisable to telephone the magazine before attempting a cover.
Fees: Covers, £50; features £20 per 1,000 words.

WOODCARVING
Guild of Master Craftsman Publications Ltd, 86 High Street, Lewes, East Sussex BN7 1XN.
Tel: 01273 477374. Fax: 01273 487692. E-mail: michelle@thegmcgroup.com
Editor: Michelle Robertson.
Magazine published six times per year and aimed at both amateur and professional woodcarvers.
Illustrations: Mostly to illustrate specific articles, but some scope for news pictures and shots of interesting pieces of work accompanied by detailed captions. Covers: striking colour shots of exceptional woodcarvings or woodcarvers in action, relating to article inside.
Text: Illustrated articles on all aspects of serious woodcarving, including profiles of individual craftsmen.
Overall freelance potential: Good for the right material.
Fees: Negotiable for one-off reproductions inside. £70 per published page for articles, including photos.

WOODTURNING
Guild of Master Craftsman Publications Ltd, 86 High Street, Lewes, East Sussex BN7 1XN.
Tel: 01273 477374. Fax: 01273 486300. E-mail: markb@thegmcgroup.com
Editor: Mark Baker.
Monthly magazine aimed at both amateur and professional woodturners.
Illustrations: Mostly to illustrate specific articles, but some scope for unusual or interesting single pictures with full captions. Covers: striking colour shots of turned items, relating to article inside.

Text: Illustrated articles on all aspects of woodturning, including profiles of individual craftsmen.
Overall freelance potential: Good for the right material.
Fees: £25 for one-off reproductions inside. £50 per published page for articles, including photos.

THE WOODWORKER

MyHobbyStore Ltd, Berwick House, 8-10 Knoll Rise, Orpington, Kent BR6 0EL.
Tel: 0844 412 2262. E-mail: mike.lawrence@myhobbystore.com
Editor: Mike Lawrence.
Monthly magazine for all craftspeople in wood. Readership includes schools and woodworking businesses, as well as individual hobbyists.
Illustrations: Pictures relating to wood and wood crafts, mostly as illustrations for features. Covers: pictures of fine furniture.
Text: Illustrated features on all facets of woodworking crafts, including profiles of individual woodworkers, how-to articles and material on period furniture and woodworking through the ages.
Overall freelance potential: Excellent; most content bought from outside contributors.
Editor's tips: Clear, concise authoritative writing in readable, modern style essential.
Fees: By negotiation.

Home Interest

COUNTRY HOMES & INTERIORS

Southbank Publishing Group, Blue Fin Building, 110 Southwark Street, London SE1 0SU.
Tel: 020 3148 7642. E-mail: petra_manley-leach@ipcmedia.com
Editor: Rhoda Parry. **Art Director:** Petra Manley-Leach.
Monthly magazine concerning up-market country homes, interiors and gardens.
Illustrations: Top quality coverage of architecture, interiors, gardens and landscapes. Mostly by commission, but speculative submissions of picture features on specific country houses or gardens, or other country-based topics, may be considered if of the highest quality. Covers: always related to a major feature inside.
Text: Top level coverage of country home and lifestyle subjects, only by commission.
Overall freelance potential: Excellent for photographers who can provide the right sort of material.
Fees: Negotiable from a minimum of £100.

ELLE DECORATION

Hachette Filipacchi (UK) Ltd, 64 North Row, London W1K 7LL.
Tel: 020 7150 7000. Fax: 020 7150 7001. E-mail: elledecopictures@hf-uk.com
Editor: Michelle Ogundehin. **Picture Editor:** Flora Bathurst.
Monthly interior decoration magazine aimed at a trend-setting readership.
Illustrations: By commission only, but always interested in hearing from photographers experienced in this field.
Text: Ideas for features always of interest.
Overall freelance potential: Plenty of scope for the experienced freelance.
Editor's tips: Particular projects must always be discussed in detail beforehand to ensure that the magazine's specific styling requirements are observed.
Fees: Photography according to commission.

THE ENGLISH HOME

Archant Specialist, Archant House, 3 Oriel Road, Cheltenham GL50 1BB.
Tel: 01242 211080. E-mail: englishhome@archant.co.uk
Editor: Kerryn Harper-Cuss.

Bi-monthly home interest title emphasising classic, elegant and country English style.
Illustrations: Mainly by commission. Opportunities for experienced architectural and interiors photographers to obtain assignments. Suggestions, with sample pictures, of suitable homes or beautiful regional localities to feature always welcome.
Text: Illustrated features on elegantly classic English homes, decoration, UK travel and events. Submit ideas in the first instance.
Overall freelance potential: Good.
Fees: By negotiation.

GOOD HOMES
Kelsey Publishing Group, Cudham Tithe Barn, Berry's Hill, Cudham, Kent TN16 3AG.
Tel: 01959 541444. Fax: 01959 541400. E-mail: x.x@kelsey.co.uk
Editor: Emma Dublin. **Art Director:** Natalie Williams.
Glossy monthly aimed at people who love their homes and love to decorate. Maintains some links with BBC TV programmes on home topics.
Illustrations: Top quality photography of interiors, gardens, home products, etc, all by commission. Photographers who have previously worked on top quality homes publications should write with details of their experience.
Text: No scope.
Overall freelance potential: Limited to those experienced in producing the highest standard of work.
Editor's tips: Not interested in hearing from photographers who have not done editorial interiors work before, no matter how skilled in other fields.
Fees: Standard day rate £450.

HOMES & GARDENS
IPC Media Ltd, Blue Fin Building, 110 Southwark Street, London SE1 0SU.
Tel: 020 3148 5000. E-mail: caroline_harrington@ipcmedia.com
Editor: Deborah Barker. **Art Director:** Caroline Harrington.
Monthly glossy magazine devoted to quality interior design and related matters.
Illustrations: High quality commissioned coverage of interior decoration, design, architecture, gardens, furnishings, food and travel. Emphasis on homes decorated in a tasteful style, up-market and attractive rather than wacky. Ideas for coverage always welcome.
Text: Heavily-illustrated features as above.
Overall freelance potential: Good for really top quality work.
Editor's tips: Out of London material particularly welcome.
Fees: By negotiation.

HOUSE BEAUTIFUL
National Magazine Company Ltd, 72 Broadwick Street, London W1F 9EP.
Tel: 020 7439 5642. Fax: 020 7437 6886. E-mail: chris.thurston@natmags.co.uk
Editor: Julia Goodwin. **Art Director:** Chris Thurston. **Picture Researcher:** Pascale Rowan.
Monthly magazine with the emphasis on practical home decorating ideas.
Illustrations: Usually by commission. Photographs of houses, interior decoration, furnishings, cookery and gardens. Complete picture features depicting houses and interiors of interest.
Text: Features on subjects as above, invariably commissioned, but possible scope for speculative features on suitable subjects.
Overall freelance potential: Quite good for experienced contributors in the home interest and interiors field.
Fees: By negotiation.

IDEAL HOME
IPC Media Ltd, Blue Fin Building, 110 Southwark Street, London SE1 0SU.
Tel: 020 3148 5000. E-mail: warren_filmer@ipcmedia.com

Editor: Isobel McKenzie-Price.
Monthly devoted to interiors and decorating.
Illustrations: Major feature photography always by commission; make appointment to show portfolio. Some scope for good general home style and decorating images for stock and general illustration.
Text: No scope.
Overall freelance potential: Very good for experienced workers.
Editor's tips: Research past issues to see what subjects have already been covered and to anticipate the types of issues likely to be covered in the future.
Fees: By negotiation.

PERIOD LIVING

Centaur Special Interest Media, St Giles House, 50 Poland Street, London W1V 4AX.
Tel: 020 7970 4433. Fax: 020 7970 4438. E-mail: period.living@centaur.co.uk
Editor: Sarah Whelan. **Art Editor:** Puishun Li.
Monthly magazine covering traditional homes and gardens, antiques and renovation.
Illustrations: Commissions available to experienced architectural and interiors photographers, who should make appointment to show portfolios in the first instance.
Text: No scope.
Overall freelance potential: Good.
Fees: By negotiation.

REAL HOMES

Ascent Publishing Ltd, 2 Sugarbrook Court, Aston, Birmingham B60 3EX.
Tel: 01527 834454. E-mail: firstname.lastname@centaur.co.uk
Editor: Caron Bronson. Deputy **Editor:** Helena Fulford.
Monthly aiming to help homeowners make the most of the home they have.
Illustrations: By commission only, but always interested in hearing from photographers experienced in this field. For those seeking house shoots, contact homes editor; for other images contact deputy editor.
Text: Ideas for features always considered, mainly practical, accessible solution-focused ideas.
Overall freelance potential: Good scope for the experienced freelance.
Editor's tips: Feature ideas must always be discussed in detail beforehand to ensure that the magazine's specific styling requirements are observed.
Fees: By negotiation.

25 BEAUTIFUL HOMES

IPC Media Ltd, Blue Fin Building, 110 Southwark Street, London SE1 0SU.
Tel: 020 3148 7290. E-mail: penny_botting@ipcmedia.com
Editor: Deborah Barker. **Commissioning Editor:** Penny Botting.
Interior design magazine featuring 25 individual homes per issue.
Illustrations: High-res digital files or medium format transparencies. Top quality interiors photography illustrating specific homes. Always looking for homes to feature: initially send a selection of recce snaps showing each room, plus an exterior shot, with brief details about the home and its owners; a commission to produce a full feature may follow.
Text: Features as above.
Overall freelance potential: Very good for the experienced interiors photographer.
Fees: Fee for complete feature package of words and pictures normally around £1,000.

THE WORLD OF INTERIORS

The Condé Nast Publications Ltd, Vogue House, Hanover Square, London W1S 1JU.
Tel: 020 7152 3831. Fax: 020 7493 4013. E-mail: mark.lazenby@condenast.co.uk
Editor-in-Chief: Rupert Thomas. **Art Director:** Mark Lazenby.
Monthly magazine showing the best interior decoration of all periods and in all countries.

Illustrations: Mainly colour, occasional B&W. Subjects as above. Extra high standard of work required.
Text: Complete coverage of interesting houses; occasionally public buildings, churches, shops, etc. 1,000–2,000 words.
Overall freelance potential: Much of the work in the magazine comes from freelances.
Fees: Negotiable.

YOUR HOME
Hubert Burda Media UK, The Tower, Phoenix Square, Colchester, Essex CO4 9HU.
Tel: 01206 851117. Fax: 01206 849078. E-mail: yourhome@burdamagazines.co.uk
Editor: Anna-Lisa De'ath.
Monthly home interest magazine concerned with real homes, makeovers, decorating, home improvements, DIY and creative projects.
Illustrations: Only as part of complete packages as detailed below.
Text: Scope for experienced interiors writers and photographers who can supply words/picture packages on a First Rights basis, for budget room makeovers and affordable real reader homes.
Overall freelance potential: Limited and only for the experienced contributor.
Fees: By negotiation.

Industry

CLASSIC PLANT & MACHINERY
Kelsey Publishing Group, Cudham Tithe Barn, Berry's Hill, Cudham, Kent TN16 3AG.
Tel: 01959 541444. Fax: 01959 541400. E-mail: cpm.ed@kelsey.co.uk
Editor: George Bowstead.
Monthly magazine covering vintage construction and mining plant and ancillary equipment.
Illustrations: Pictures of collectable, classic and vintage machinery, including dumptrucks, excavators, forklifts, road making and mining machinery. Must be accompanied by detailed and accurate captions. Contact editor before preparing a submission.
Text: Suggestions from those with suitable knowledge of these subjects always welcomed.
Overall freelance potential: Good.
Fees: By arrangement.

ENERGY IN BUILDINGS & INDUSTRY
Pinede Publishing Ltd, PO Box 825, Guildford, Surrey GU4 8WQ.
Tel/fax: 01483 452854. E-mail: mark.thrower@btinternet.com
Editor: Mark Thrower.
Monthly magazine concerned with the use and conservation of energy in large buildings and the industrial environment.
Illustrations: Pictures of relevant and interesting installations.
Text: Some scope for writer/photographers who have good knowledge of the energy business.
Overall freelance potential: Limited unless contributors have connections within the field.
Fees: £30–£40 per picture; £140 per 1,000 words for text.

ENGINEERING
Gillard Welch Ltd, 6a New Street, Warwick CV34 4RX.
Tel: 01926 408244. Fax: 01926 408206. E-mail: steve@engineeringnet.co.uk

As a member of the Bureau of Freelance Photographers, you'll be kept up-to-date with markets through the BFP Market Newsletter, published monthly. For details of membership, turn to page 9

Managing Editor: Steve Welch.
Monthly magazine dealing with all areas of manufacturing engineering from a design viewpoint.
Illustrations: Photographs depicting all aspects of design in industrial engineering, from aerospace and computers to energy management and waste disposal. Much from manufacturers but some by commission. Covers: Abstract and "artistic" photography.
Text: Short illustrated news items up to major design features. 250–2,000 words.
Overall freelance potential: Good for commissioned work.
Fees: £100 per published page for text. Covers £300–£400. Other commissioned photography around £120 per day.

INDUSTRIAL DIAMOND REVIEW

Odeon House, 146 College Road, Harrow, Middlesex HA1 1BH.
Tel: 020 8863 2767. E-mail: martin.jennings@idr-online.com
Editor: Martin Jennings.
Quarterly publication designed to promote a wider and more efficient use of diamond tools, i.e. grinding wheels, drill bits, saw blades, etc. in all branches of engineering.
Illustrations: Will consider pictures of any type of diamond tool in action.
Text: Case histories on the use of diamond tools in engineering, mining, etc. Up to 2,000 words for finished feature.
Overall freelance potential: Excellent but highly specialised.
Editor's tips: Technical case histories are welcome, but check acceptance with editor before submitting material. Potential contributors are requested to consult the editor before pursuing any possible editorial leads.
Fees: Excellent; by arrangement.

INDUSTRIAL FIRE JOURNAL

Hemming Information Services, No 8, The Old Yarn Mills, Westbury, Sherborne, Dorset DT9 3RG.
Tel: 01935 816030. Fax: 01935 817200. E-mail: am.knegt@hisdorset.com
Editor: Ann-Marie Knegt.
Quarterly magazine concerning firefighting in the industrial sector.
Illustrations: Pictures of anything concerning or involving firefighting services in an industrial context, including firefighting personnel in action. Covers: powerful colour images of the same.
Text: No scope for non-specialists.
Overall freelance potential: Fair.
Editor's tips: Seek editor's agreement before submitting. No photos of ordinary car fires or firefighters/engines at domestic home/high street fires. Look for racy, exciting and explicit shots to interest and educate a readership of fire professionals who've "seen it all before".
Fees: Negotiable, but generally good. Up to £200 for a really good cover picture.

MANUFACTURING CHEMIST

HPCI Ltd, Paulton House, 8 Shepherdess Walk, London N1 7LB.
Tel: 020 7549 2566. Fax: 020 7549 8622. E-mail: hilarya@hpcimedia.com
Editor: Hilary Ayshford.
Monthly journal for the pharmaceutical industry. Read by senior management involved in research, development, manufacturing and marketing of pharmaceuticals.
Illustrations: Pictures of any aspect of the pharmaceutical industry.
Text: Features on any aspect of the pharmaceutical industry as detailed above. 1,000–2,000 words.
Overall freelance potential: Approximately 30 per cent is contributed by freelances.
Fees: Text, £170 per 1,000 words for features, £15 per 100 words for news stories; pictures by agreement.

MARINE ENGINEERS REVIEW

Institute of Marine Engineering, Science & Technology, 80 Coleman Street, London EC2R 5BJ.
Tel: 020 7382 2600. Fax: 020 7382 2670. E-mail: mer@imarest.org

Editor: John Barnes.
Monthly publications for marine engineers.
Illustrations: Interesting topical photographs of ships and marine machinery.
Text: Articles on shipping and marine engineering, including naval and offshore topics.
Overall freelance potential: Good, but enquire before submitting.
Fees: By negotiation.

NEW CIVIL ENGINEER
EMAP Construct, Greater London House, Hampstead Road, London NW1 7EJ.
Tel: 020 7728 4541. Fax: 020 7728 4666. E-mail: anthony.oliver@emap.com
Editor: Anthony Oliver.
Weekly news magazine for professional civil engineers.
Illustrations: Up-to-date pictures depicting any civil engineering project. Must be well captioned and newsworthy.
Text: By commission only.
Overall freelance potential: Limited.
Fees: On a rising scale according to size of reproduction or length of text.

NEW DESIGN
Gillard Welch Ltd, 6a New Street, Warwick CV34 4RX.
Tel: 01926 408244. Fax: 01926 408206. E-mail: info@newdesignmagazine.co.uk
Managing Editor: Steve Welch.
Monthly for professional designers and manufacturers, covering developments in industrial and product design.
Illustrations: Photographs depicting new or current product, industrial and interior design, including architecture, theatre, textile, medical and transport design. Pictures should either have a news angle or be particularly strong images in their own right that might be used for covers.
Text: Illustrated news stories or features on any aspect of contemporary commercial design.
Overall freelance potential: Good.
Fees: Dependent on use, up to £300–£400 for covers.

PROFESSIONAL ENGINEERING
Caspian Publishing, 198 Kings Road, London, SW3 5XP.
Tel: 020 7973 1299. Fax: 020 7973 0462. E-mail: pe@pepublishing.com
Editor: Lee Hibbert.
Fortnightly publication for members of the Institution of Mechanical Engineers and decision-makers in industry.
Illustrations: Digital files preferred. Pictures of relevant people, locations, factories, processes and specific industries.
Text: Features with a general engineering bias at a fairly high management level, eg management techniques, new processes, materials applications, etc. 1,500 words maximum.
Overall freelance potential: Limited, and usually commissioned specifically.
Fees: Not less than around £200 per 1,000 words; pictures by agreement.

URETHANES TECHNOLOGIES INTERNATIONAL
Crain Communications Ltd, 3rd Floor, 21 St Thomas Street, London SE1 9RY.
Tel/fax: 020 7457 1400. E-mail: lwhite@crain.co.uk
Editor: Liz White.
Bi-monthly publication for the polyurethane producing, processing, and using industries.
Illustrations: Pictures of production, equipment, and application of polyurethane materials. Also news pictures and shots of trade personalities. Covers: top quality and graphically striking medium format colour of polyurethane-related subjects.
Text: Features on new applications of polyurethanes; new products; new equipment and processing. Business, marketing, personnel and technical news items. Up to 2,000 words.

Overall freelance potential: Good scope for those with access to the industries involved.
Fees: By arrangement.

UTILITY WEEK
Faversham House Group, 232A, Addington Road, South Croydon, Surrey, CR2 8LE
Tel: 020 8651 7103. Fax: 020 8651 7100. E-mail: steve.hobson@rbi.co.uk
Editor: Janet Wood.
Weekly business magazine for the three major supply utilities: electricity, gas and water.
Illustrations: News pictures concerning the major utilities. Possible scope for good stock coverage of industry subjects. Commissions often available to experienced portrait and business/industry workers.
Text: Contributors with expert knowledge always welcomed. Submit details of experience in the first instance.
Overall freelance potential: Very good for industrial specialists.
Fees: By negotiation.

WORKS MANAGEMENT
Findlay Publications Ltd, Hawley Mill, Hawley Road, Dartford, Kent DA2 7TJ.
Tel: 01322 221144. Fax: 01322 221188. E-mail: khurst@findlay.co.uk
Editor: Ken Hurst. **Art Editor:** Neil Young.
Monthly publication for managers and engineers who directly control or perform the works management function in selected manufacturing concerns.
Illustrations: Occasional need for regional coverage of managers and workers in realistic work situations in factories. Mostly pictures are used only to illustrate features.
Text: Illustrated features of interest to management, eg productivity, automation in factories, industrial relations, employment law, finance, energy, maintenance, handling and storage, safety and welfare. Around 1,500 words.
Overall freelance potential: Up to 30 per cent is contributed by freelances.
Fees: By agreement.

Local Government & Services

CHILDREN & YOUNG PEOPLE NOW
Haymarket Publishing Ltd, 174 Hammersmith Road, London W6 7JP.
Tel: 020 8267 4707. Fax: 020 8267 4728. E-mail: cypnow.editorial@haymarket.com
Editor: Ravi Chandiramani. **Art Editor:** David McCullough.
Weekly publication for youth workers, social workers, careers officers, teachers, counsellors and others working in the the children's service and youth affairs sectors.
Illustrations: Mainly commissioned shoots to cover youth work and youth workers around the country. Contact art editor with details and samples in the first instance.
Text: Small proportion of copy is from freelance contributors.
Overall freelance potential: Occasional news pictures and one or two features using freelance photos per issue.
Fees: According to use.

FIRE RISK MANAGEMENT
Fire Protection Association, London Road, Moreton in Marsh, Gloucestershire GL56 0RH.
Tel: 01608 812518. Fax: 01608 812501. E-mail: rgilbey@thefpa.co.uk

Editor: Rupert Gilbey.
Monthly technical publication on fire safety. Aimed at fire brigades, fire equipment manufacturers, architects, insurance companies, and those with responsibility for fire safety in public sector bodies, commerce and industry.
Illustrations: Pictures of large and small fires to illustrate reports. Also pictures showing different types of building design and occupancy (offices, commercial premises, warehouses, etc), and of emergency services at work.
Text: Technical articles and news items on fire prevention and protection. Features 1,000–2,000 words.
Overall freelance potential: Good pictures of fires and unusual fire safety experiences are always welcome.
Fees: Pictures, negotiable from £15. Text, negotiable from £110 per 1,000 words.

JANE'S POLICE REVIEW
IHS Jane's, 2nd Floor, 133 Houndsditch, London EC3A 7BX.
Tel: 020 3159 3579. Fax: 020 3159 3276. E-mail: chris.herbert@ihsjanes.com
Editor: Chris Herbert. **Art Editor:** David Playford.
Weekly news magazine for the police service.
Illustrations: All aspects of the police service. Particular interest in up-to-date news pictures covering the previous seven days (e-mail policereviewnews@janes.com). Some commissioned work available, with a need for more photographers to carry out regional work. Contact art editor first to show portfolio.
Text: Limited scope because of specialist subject matter, but will consider any subject of contemporary interest to police officers, 1,000–1,500 words.
Overall freelance potential: Good.
Editor's tips: The magazine is published on Friday with a Tuesday morning deadline for news pictures. Photographs for features should be good photojournalism and reportage; not interested in "publicity-style" photos.
Fees: Negotiable, minimum £50.

LEGAL ACTION
The Legal Action Group, 242 Pentonville Road, London N1 9UN.
Tel: 020 7833 2931. Fax: 020 7837 6094. E-mail: vwilliams@lag.org.uk
Editor: Valerie Williams.
Monthly publication for lawyers, advice workers, law students and academics.
Illustrations: Pictures of lawyers and judges, especially other than the standard head and shoulders shot. Plus stock pictures to illustrate features covering a wide range of subjects (e.g. housing, police, immigration, advice services).
Text: Features on legal services and professional issues, including the courts. High technical detail required. Also information for news and feature material that can be written in-house.
Overall freelance potential: Always interested in hearing from photographers holding suitable material.
Fees: By negotiation.

MUNICIPAL JOURNAL
Hemming Group Ltd, 32 Vauxhall Bridge Road, London SW1V 2SS.
Tel: 020 7973 6400. Fax: 020 7233 5051.
Editor: Michael Burton.
Weekly publication for senior local government officers, councillors, Whitehall departments and academic and other institutions.
Illustrations: B&W and colour. News pictures; relevant personalities, vehicles, buildings, etc;

general stock shots of local government subjects and situations to illustrate features.
Text: Features on local government issues. 750–1,000 words.
Overall freelance potential: Very good.
Fees: Good; on a rising scale according to the size of reproduction or length of feature.

PLANNING

Haymarket Business Publications Ltd, 174 Hammersmith Road, London W6 7JP
Tel: 020 8267 4469. Fax: 020 8267 4013. E-mail: planning@haymarket.com
Editor: Huw Morris.
Weekly news magazine for all involved with town and country planning and related issues. Official journal of the Royal Town Planning Institute.
Illustrations: News pictures always of interest, on specific planning issues. Also good generic shots of subjects planning touches on, e.g. conservation, transport, rivers, waste disposal, housing, energy, industry, retailing, etc. Some commissions available to illustrate major features.
Text: Illustrated news stories and longer features from contributors with good knowledge of planning issues, up to 1,500 words. Must be relevant to planners.
Overall freelance potential: Good for genuinely relevant topical material.
Editor's tips: Photos can be of general or specific interest.
Fees: Photography according to use or assignment; text £100 per 1,000 words.

SCHOLASTIC MAGAZINES

Scholastic Ltd, Villiers House, Clarendon Avenue, Leamington Spa CV32 5PR.
Tel: 01926 887799. Fax: 01926 883331.
Design Manager: Sarah Garbett.
Range of monthly publications for teachers in primary and nursery education.
Illustrations: Digital files preferred. News pictures and good, unposed pictures of school children from 3-12 years, in classrooms and other school situations. Cover pictures as above often commissioned. Pictures are retained within a large in-house library.
Text: No scope.
Fees: By agreement.

THE TEACHER

National Union of Teachers, Hamilton House, Mabledon Place, London WC1H 9BD.
Tel: 020 7380 4708. Fax: 020 7387 8458. E-mail: teacher@nut.org.uk
Editor: Ellie Campbell-Barr.
Official magazine of the National Union of Teachers.
Illustrations: News pictures concerning any educational topic, especially those taken in schools and colleges. Coverage of union activities, personalities, demonstrations, etc.
Text: Short articles and news items on educational matters.
Overall freelance potential: Limited; interested in good pictures though.
Editor's tips: Consult the editor before submitting.
Fees: According to use.

As a member of the Bureau of Freelance Photographers, you'll be kept up-to-date with markets through the BFP Market Newsletter, published monthly. For details of membership, turn to page 9

Male Interest

ATTITUDE
Third Floor, 207 Old Street, London EC1V 9NR.
Tel: 020 7608 6300. E-mail: matthew.todd@attitudemag.co.uk
Editor: Matthew Todd. Deputy **Editor:** Daniel Fulvio.
Monthly style magazine aimed primarily, but not exclusively, at gay men.
Illustrations: Mostly by commission to illustrate specific features. Some opportunities for experienced fashion and style workers (contact fashion editor). Also some scope for travel, reportage and popular culture material.
Text: Ideas for features – human interest, travel, celebrities – always considered; submit an outline first. Should appeal to a gay readership even if written from a "straight" perspective.
Overall freelance potential: Fair.
Fees: £100 per page for photography; text £150 per 1,000 words.

BOYS TOYS
Freestyle Publications Ltd, Alexander House, Ling Road, Poole, Dorset BH12 4NZ.
Tel: 01202 735090. Fax: 01202 733969. E-mail: tperkins@freestyle-group.com
Editor: Tom Perkins.
Monthly for young men, covering all lifestyle topics but with an emphasis on desirable products and technology.
Illustrations: Mostly commissioned in the fields of sport, fashion, motoring, technology and portraiture. Portfolios can be viewed in London. On spec material also considered if it fits the magazine's style.
Text: Ideas always considered.
Overall freelance potential: Excellent.
Fees: By negotiation.

CLUB INTERNATIONAL
Paul Raymond Publications, 3rd Floor, 207 Old Street, London EC1V 9NR.
Tel: 020 7608 6300. E-mail: mattb@paulraymond.com
Editor: Matt Berry.
Popular glamour monthly for men.
Illustrations: Requires top quality glamour sets of very attractive girls (aged 18 – 25).
Text: Articles on sexual or humorous topics, or factual/investigative pieces. 1,000–2,000 words.
Overall freelance potential: Most of the published glamour material comes from freelances, but they are normally experienced glamour photographers.
Editor's tips: Study the magazine to appreciate style. As well as being very attractive, girls featured must look contemporary and fashionable.
Fees: £600 for glamour sets. Text up to £200 per 1,000 words.

ESCORT
Paul Raymond Publications, 3rd Floor, 207 Old Street, London EC1V 9NR.
Tel: 020 7608 6300. E-mail: escort@paulraymond.com
Editor: James Hundleby.
Monthly glamour magazine; less sophisticated than the other Paul Raymond publications, Men Only and Club International.
Illustrations: Transparency or digital. Looks for glamour sets of "normal, healthy, girl-next-door" types. Each issue contains about 10 glamour sets running to 2–5 pages each.
Text: Purely "readers' contributions".
Overall freelance potential: Good.
Fees: £400+ for glamour sets, or from £25 per picture.

ESQUIRE

The National Magazine Company Ltd, 72 Broadwick Street, London W1F 9EP.
Tel: 020 7439 5000. Fax: 020 7439 5675. E-mail: henny.manley@natmags.co.uk
Editor: Jeremy Langmead. **Art Director:** David McKendrick. **Picture Editor:** Henny Manley.
Up-market general interest monthly for intelligent and affluent men in the 25–44 age group.
Illustrations: Top-quality material only, invariably by commission. Mostly portraiture, fashion and photojournalism.
Text: Scope for "name" writers only.
Overall freelance potential: Good for photographers, but restricted to those experienced at the highest level of magazine work.
Fees: By negotiation.

FHM

Bauer Media, Endeavour House, 189 Shaftesbury Avenue, London WC2H 8JG.
Tel: 020 7295 8534. E-mail: simon.everitt@bauerconsumer.co.uk
Editor: Colin Kennedy. **Photo Director:** Simon Everitt. **Picture Editor:** Samantha Webster.
Monthly lifestyle and fashion magazine for young men.
Illustrations: Mainly colour. Main feature and fashion photography always by commission. Stock images relating to subjects of major interest (sports, travel, adventure, cars, sex) often required – send details of coverage available.
Text: Will consider interesting short items of interest to a young male readership, and feature ideas from experienced workers.
Overall freelance potential: Good for the experienced contributor.
Fees: By negotiation.

FRONT

The Kane Corporation Ltd, 2nd Floor, 2–4 Noel Street, London W1F 8GB.
Tel: 020 3141 9840. E-mail: adam.gordon@frontarmy.co.uk
Editor: Joe Barnes. **Picture Editor:** Adam Gordon.
Alternative lifestyle monthly for 18-24 year old men.
Illustrations: Mostly commissioned. Opportunities for portrait photographers who can capture the energy of the magazine in a portrait, alternative scene music photographers for live and posed shots, and glamour photographers with a fashion background and plenty of new ideas.
Text: Little scope.
Overall freelance potential: Good.
Editor's tips: Always looking for new, keen photographers.
Fees: By negotiation.

GQ

Condé Nast Publications Ltd, Vogue House, Hanover Square, London W1S 1JU.
Tel: 020 7499 9080. Fax: 020 7629 2093. E-mail: james.mullinger@condenast.co.uk
Editor: Dylan Jones. Photo **Editor:** James Mullinger.
Up-market general interest magazine for men in the 20–45 age group.
Illustrations: Mainly colour. Top-quality illustrations for articles on a range of topics, invariably by commission.
Text: Top level investigative, personality, fashion and style features, plus articles on other subjects likely to be of interest to successful and affluent men.

Are you working from the latest edition of The Freelance Photographer's Market Handbook? It's published on 1 October each year. Markets are constantly changing, so it pays to have the latest edition

---

Overall freelance potential: Only for the contributor experienced at the top level of magazine work.
Editor's tips: See from the magazine itself what sort of style and quality is required.
Fees: By negotiation.

LOADED
IPC Media Ltd, Blue Fin Building, 110 Southwark Street, London SE1 0SU.
Tel: 020 3148 6818. E-mail: joel_gilgallon@ipcmedia.com
Editor: Martin Daubney. **Picture Editor:** Joel Gilgallon.
General interest monthly for men in their 20s. Covers music, sport, humour, fashion and popular culture in a down-to-earth and irreverent manner.
Illustrations: Mostly by commission to accompany features, but speculative submissions always considered.
Text: Fashion features, reportage (clubs, drugs, crime, etc), interviews, humour and "anything off the wall".
Overall freelance potential: Always open to fresh and original photography and ideas.
Fees: By negotiation.

MAYFAIR
Paul Raymond Publications, 3rd Floor, 207 Old Street, London EC1V 9NR.
Tel: 020 7608 6300. E-mail: mayfair@paulraymond.com
Editor: Matt Berry. **Art Editor:** Matt Hampson.
Glamour-based monthly for men.
Illustrations: Only top quality material will be considered. Glamour sets taken in up-market surroundings and real-life locations, such as a luxury furnished flat. Outdoor material needs strong sunlight.
Text: No scope.
Overall freelance potential: Only for high-quality material; much is produced by regular contributors.
Editor's tips: For glamour thought should be given to the erotic use of clothing and suggestion of sex appeal or sexual situation, together with striking but simple colour co-ordination. Always call before submitting.
Fees: £250–£1,000 for glamour sets, or dependent on use. Covers: from £50.

MEN ONLY
Paul Raymond Publications, 3rd Floor, 207 Old Street, London EC1V 9NR.
Tel: 020 7608 6300. E-mail: mattb@paulraymond.com
Editor: Matt Berry.
Sophisticated erotic monthly for men.
Illustrations: Imaginative glamour sets featuring "the most beautiful women". Models must be young, fresh, athletic and natural. Sets welcomed from new photographers as well as established contributors. Also picture-led supporting features.
Text: Laid-back humour, sport, male interests etc.
Overall freelance potential: Excellent.
Editor's tips: Attention to detail in clothes and make-up, a wide variety of poses, and imaginative locations will always set you apart. New ideas and faces always welcome.
Fees: £350-£750 for glamour sets. Other pictures by negotiation.

MEN'S HEALTH
NatMag Rodale Ltd, 72 Broadwick Street, London W1F 9EP.
Tel: 020 7339 4400. Fax: 020 7339 4444. E-mail: ash.gibson@natmag-rodale.co.uk
Editor: Morgan Rees. **Art Director:** Ash Gibson.

Magazine published 10 times per year and covering sports, fitness, grooming and other aspects of male lifestyle.
Illustrations: Mainly colour. Mostly by commission, though possible scope for good generic stock shots of fitness etc. subjects.
Text: Articles on male lifestyle subjects, especially health and fitness. Write with ideas and details of experience in the first instance.
Overall freelance potential: Only for the experienced contributor.
Fees: By negotiation.

NUTS

IPC Inspire, Blue Fin Building, 110 Southwark Street, London SE1 0SU.
Tel: 020 3148 6937. Fax: 020 3148 8107. E-mail: nutspictures@ipcmedia.com
Editor: Dominic Smith. **Picture Editor:** John Gooch.
Weekly general interest magazine for young men.
Illustrations: Always interested in "amazing, spectacular and extreme" images – single pictures or series of pictures often used over double-page spreads, usually 4–5 per issue. Must have obvious appeal to the target market, anything from spectacular sports shots through sensational photojournalism to unusual animal pics. Also relevant news pictures (sport, celebrities) which have not been seen elsewhere. Limited opportunities for commissioned work, but will consider approaches from experienced photographers working in suitable areas.
Text: Little scope.
Overall freelance potential: Excellent.
Fees: Dependent on the individual image and how it is used, as well as on level of exclusivity.

REFRESH

reFRESH Magazines Ltd, 3rd Floor, 207 Old Street, London EC1V 9NR.
Tel: 020 7608 6509. E-mail: editorial@refreshmag.co.uk
Editor: David Tickner.
Monthly magazine for affluent gay men.
Illustrations: Mostly by commission, but opportunities often available. Main scope is for fashion shoots, both studio and location. Some portraiture, interiors and travel. E-mail samples with a CV in the first instance.
Text: Ideas for features always considered.
Overall freelance potential: Good – always looking to broaden the range of photographers used.
Fees: By negotiation.

ZOO

Bauer Media, Endeavour House, 189 Shaftesbury Avenue, London WC2H 8JG.
Tel: 020 7437 9011. E-mail: zoopictures@zootoday.com
Editor: Tom Etherington. Features **Editor:** Richard Innes. Associate Editor (Pictures): Matt Velazquez. **Picture Editor**: Gemma Parker.
Weekly general interest magazine for young men.
Illustrations: Always need topical, unusual and visually striking images for the magazine's news section – several double-page spreads per issue displaying spectacular or unusual images of all kinds. Also unusual or exclusive sports images. Commissions in relevant areas may be available.
Text: Will consider ideas for topical features and real life stories. Material should have a laddish/humorous approach but be backed with genuine knowledge of the subject. Submit suggestions to features editor in the first instance.
Fees: Negotiable, dependent on the nature of images and their exclusivity.

As a member of the Bureau of Freelance Photographers, you'll be kept up-to-date with markets through the BFP Market Newsletter, published monthly. For details of membership, turn to page 9

Motoring

AMERICAN CAR WORLD
Shut Up and Drive Publishing Ltd, 321 Broadstone Mill, Stockport, Cheshire SK5 7DL..
Tel: 0161 443 4122. E-mail: andy.craig@shutupanddrivepublishing.com
Editor: Andy Craig.
Monthly magazine covering custom cars and hot rods based on pre-1975 vehicles, British or American; and American cars, standard and modified, up to present day.
Illustrations: Newsy and well-captioned single pictures depicting happenings on the UK custom and American car scene. Other pictures usually as part of a story/picture package on subjects detailed below. Prefers British-sourced material.
Text: Well-illustrated features on completed cars, step-by-step illustrated material on how to do it, track tests of modified cars and coverage of shows and events. Always phone or write first to discuss ideas.
Overall freelance potential: Good for the right sort of material.
Editor's tips: Not interested in front-wheel drive or post-1980 vehicles.
Fees: £50 for news items; text £125 per 1,000 words.

AUTO EXPRESS
Dennis Publishing, 30 Cleveland Street, London W1T 4JD.
Tel: 020 7907 6000. Picture library: 020 7907 6132. Fax: 020 7917 5556. E-mail: editorial@autoexpress.co.uk
Editor-in-Chief: David Johns. **News/Features Editor:** Julie Sinclair. **Picture Editor:** Dawn Tennant.
Popular weekly magazine, aimed at the average motorist rather than the car enthusiast.
Illustrations: Hard news pictures and topical motoring subjects with impact may be considered on spec, but most is by commission.
Text: Features on any motoring topic, to appeal to a general readership. May be practical but should not be too technical. 1,000–2,000 words. Always submit a synopsis in the first instance.
Overall freelance potential: Limited for the non-specialist.
Editor's tips: Although a popular non-technical title, accuracy is essential.
Fees: Photographs according to size of reproduction. Text usually £200 per 1,000 words.

AUTOCAR
Haymarket Publishing Ltd, Teddington Studios, Broom Road, Teddington, Middlesex TW11 9BE.
Tel: 020 8267 5630. Fax: 020 8267 5759. E-mail: peter.charles@haymarket.com
Editor: Chas Hallett. **Art Editor:** Peter Charles.
High quality general interest motoring weekly. Includes road tests, new car descriptions, international motor sport, motor shows, etc.
Illustrations: Mostly by commission for top quality general car coverage, test reports, performance cars, industry picture stories and portraits – submit CV/portfolio to the Art Editor. Always interested in scoop pictures of pre-production models under test or any other exclusive motor industry photo items.
Text: Illustrated features on motoring subjects, by prior arrangement with the editor. 1,000–2,000 words.
Overall freelance potential: Good for those with experience.
Editor's tips: Technical accuracy and full information on the cars featured is essential. Familiarise yourself with the magazine first; too much material received is unsuitable.
Fees: Features by negotiation.

THE AUTOMOBILE
Enthusiast Publishing Ltd. Editorial: PO Box 153, Cranleigh, Surrey, GU6 8ZL
Tel: 01483 268818 Fax: 01483 268993. E-mail: jonathanrishton@hotmail.com

Editor: Jonathan Rishton.
Monthly publication featuring veteran, vintage, and pre-1960s motor vehicles.
Illustrations: Not much scope for single pictures unless of particular interest. Main requirement is for well-illustrated articles concerning any pre-1960s motor vehicle; not only cars but also commercial vehicles. Also limited room for coverage of race meetings, exhibitions or other events at which old motor vehicles are present. All images must be accompanied by detailed captions.
Text: Informative illustrated articles as above. Of particular interest are good restoration features, with both "before" and "after" pictures showing what can be achieved.
Overall freelance potential: Although limited there is scope for illustrated features – consult the editor before starting on feature.
Editor's tips: Do not submit material concerning post-1960s vehicles.
Fees: By negotiation.

CAR & ACCESSORY TRADER

Haymarket Publishing Ltd, Teddington Studios, Broom Road, Teddington, Middlesex TW11 9BE.
Tel: 020 8267 5992. Fax: 020 8267 5993. E-mail: cat.eds@haymarket.com
Editor: Emma Butcher.
Monthly magazine for traders involved in the selling of car parts and accessories.
Illustrations: Captioned news pictures concerning new products, openings of new premises, handover of sales awards, etc. Much is commissioned. Covers: excellent relevant photographs considered.
Text: Varied subjects of interest to the trade, by commission only.
Overall freelance potential: About 50 per cent of contributions are from freelance sources.
Fees: £100 per £1,000 words. Photographs negotiable.

CLASSIC AMERICAN

Mortons Media Group Ltd, Media Centre, Morton Way, Horncastle, Lincs LN9 6JR.
Tel: 01507 529503. E-mail: bklemenszon@mortons.co.uk
Editor: Ben Klemenzson.
Monthly magazine concerning American cars mainly of the '50s, '60s and '70s.
Illustrations: Striking or unusual pictures of classic US vehicles. However, much of the photography is commissioned from regulars or staff-produced.
Text: Illustrated articles on specific cars or bikes and their owners, plus features on other aspects of American-style youth culture such as clothing, music, sport, etc. 1,000–2,000 words. Always check with the editor before submitting.
Overall freelance potential: Car coverage welcome, but best scope is for lifestyle features.
Fees: Pictures by negotiation. £150 per 1,000 words for text.

CLASSIC CARS

Bauer Automotive Ltd, Media House, Lynchwood, Peterborough PE2 6EA.
Tel: 01733 468000. Fax: 01733 468888. E-mail:
classic.cars@bauermedia.co.uk/tony.turner@bauermedia.co.uk
Editor: Phil Bell. Deputy **Editor:** Mike Goodbun. **Picture Researcher:** Tony Turner.
Glossy, heavily-illustrated monthly covering classic cars of all eras.
Illustrations: Will consider on-spec reportage-style coverage of classic car gatherings around the country. Major feature photography mostly handled by a team of regulars. E-mail picture researcher in the first instance.
Text: Limited scope, but suggestions considered.

Are you working from the latest edition of The Freelance Photographer's Market Handbook? It's published on 1 October each year. Markets are constantly changing, so it pays to have the latest edition

---

Overall freelance potential: Very good for the right sort of material.
Editor's tips: Detailed captions and a contact number for each car's owner are essential.
Fees: On a rising scale according to size of reproduction, up to £150 for a full-bleed page.

CLASSIC & SPORTS CAR
Haymarket Publishing Ltd, Teddington Studios, Broom Road, Teddington, Middlesex TW11 9BE.
Tel: 020 8267 5399. Fax: 020 8267 5318. E-mail: james.elliott@haymarket.com
Editor: James Elliott.
Monthly magazine covering mainly post-1945 classic cars, generally of a sporting nature. Strong coverage of the owners' scene.
Illustrations: Colour; B&W archive material. Mainly interested in coverage of club or historic car gatherings, unless staff photographer is present. Feature photography always commissioned.
Text: Articles of interest to the classic car enthusiast and collector, up to 2,500 words.
Overall freelance potential: Small, as much material is staff produced.
Editor's tips: Always get in touch before submitting.
Fees: According to merit.

CLASSICS MONTHLY
Future Publishing Ltd, Beauford Court, 30 Monmouth Street, Bath BA1 2BW.
Tel: 01225 442244. E-mail: classicsmonthly@futurenet.co.uk
Editor: Gary Stretton.
Practical monthly for classic car owners.
Illustrations: Captioned pictures of newsworthy cars and events, including relevant motorsport coverage, always considered on spec. Also scope for commissions to do photo shoots of featured cars; send samples of previous work in the first instance.
Text: Well-illustrated features about restoring classic cars; reports from events.
Overall freelance potential: Good.
Editor's tips: Look at mag carefully before submitting work, particularly the editorial profile and style. Always interested in hearing about cars which might make a good feature subject. Send a sample shot with some details about the car and a commission to shoot may be offered.
Fees: Pictures, typically £100 per feature; £120 per 1,000 words; commissioned photography, £200 per day.

DRIVING MAGAZINE
Safety House, Beddington Farm Road, Croydon CR0 4XZ.
Tel: 020 8665 5151. Fax: 020 8665 5565. E-mail: dia@driving.org
Editor: Stephen Picton.
Bi-monthly road safety publication for advanced drivers, road safety educationists and driving instructors.
Illustrations: Pictures of home or overseas motorists/driving school vehicles in unusual surroundings or circumstances. Humorous incidents, traffic accidents of an unusual nature, unusual road signs, humorous signs or those in extraordinary positions.
Text: Features on road safety, driver training occasionally accepted. 500–2,000 words.
Overall freelance potential: Modest.
Fees: Photographs from £15–£20, variable according to subject and quality.

EVO
Evo Publications Ltd, 5 Tower Court, Irchester Road, Wollaston, Wellingborough NN29 7PJ.
Tel: 020 7907 6310. E-mail: eds@evo.co.uk
Editorial Director: Harry Metcalfe. **Art Director:** Paul Lang.

Glossy monthly covering the high-performance end of the car market.
Illustrations: Digital files preferred. All by commission. Will consider approaches from freelances who can produce good action photography of cars on the move.
Text: No scope.
Overall freelance potential: Good for the experienced car photographer.
Fees: By negotiation.

FLEET NEWS

Bauer Automotive Ltd, Media House, Lynchwood, Peterborough Business Park, Peterborough PE2 6EA.
Tel: 01733 468000. Fax: 01733 468296. E-mail: fleetnews@bauermedia.co.uk
Editor: Stephen Briers. News **Editor:** Daniel Attwood.
Weekly newspaper aimed at those responsible for running company car and light commercial vehicle fleets.
Illustrations: Captioned news pictures concerning company car operations, handover of car fleets to companies, appointments in the trade, etc.
Text: News, articles on business car management and related subjects.
Overall freelance potential: Excellent.
Editor's tips: Always write or e-mail first.
Fees: Negotiable.

4X4

Kelsey Publishing Group, Cudham Tithe Barn, Berry's Hill, Cudham, Kent TN16 3AG.
Tel: 01959 541444. Fax: 01959 541400. E-mail: 4x4.ed@kelsey.co.uk
Editor: Hils Everett.
Monthly magazine devoted to four-wheel-drive vehicles.
Illustrations: Pictures of new vehicles, travel and other "off road" events. Must be captioned with full details of driver, event and location.
Text: Illustrated articles concerning four-wheel-drive vehicles and off-road activities. 1,000–2,000 words.
Overall freelance potential: Limited, but there is room for new contributors.
Fees: By negotiation.

JAGUAR

Haymarket Publishing Ltd, Teddington Studios, Broom Road, Teddington, Middlesex TW11 9BE.
Tel: 020 8267 5331. Fax: 020 8267 5872. E-mail: jaguar-magazine@haymarket.com
Editor: Richard Robinson.
Glossy general interest quarterly for owners of Jaguar cars.
Illustrations: High quality commissioned photography of Jaguar cars, travel and general lifestyle subjects. Opportunities only for experienced workers with medium format equipment.
Text: Strongly-illustrated articles on travel and lifestyle subjects. All work is by commission, no unsolicited work is accepted.
Overall freelance potential: Good for experienced workers, though limited by the publishing frequency.
Fees: Photography by negotiation. Articles around £400; pictures, £600.

LAND ROVER MONTHLY

Dennis Publishing Ltd, 5 Tower Court, Irchester Road, Wollaston, Wellingborough NN29 7PJ.
Tel: 020 7907 6878. E-mail: editorial@lrm.co.uk
Editor: Richard Howell-Thomas.
Monthly magazine for Land Rover enthusiasts.
Illustrations: Little scope for individual photographs unless accompanied by extended captions or background text.
Text: Well-illustrated articles on all matters relating to Land Rover, Range Rover, Discovery and

Freelander vehicles; travel/adventure stories, features on interesting individual vehicles and off-roading personalities, competition and club event reports. Limited scope for vehicle test reports.
Overall freelance potential: Excellent for those who can add words to their pictures, and have good knowledge of Land Rover products.
Fees: By negotiation.

LAND ROVER OWNER INTERNATIONAL

Bauer Automotive Ltd, Media House, Lynchwood, Peterborough PE2 6EA.
Tel: 01733 468000. Fax: 01733 468238. E-mail: info@lro.com
Editor-in-Chief: John Pearson.
Magazine for Land Rover owners and enthusiasts. 13 issues a year.
Illustrations: Interesting or unusual pictures of Land Rovers, Range Rovers, Freelanders, Defenders and Discoverys. Celebrities pictured with such vehicles.
Text: Illustrated articles on overland expeditions using Land Rovers. Length 1,000 words, plus around six pictures.
Overall freelance potential: Good.
Fees: Text, £100 per 1,000 words; pictures by negotiation.

MAX POWER

Bauer Automotive Ltd, Media House, Lynchwood, Peterborough PE2 6EA.
Tel: 01733 468000. Fax: 01733 468001. E-mail: mark.guest@bauermedia.co.uk
Editor: Mark Guest.
Monthly for young men heavily involved with fast cars and modifying them.
Illustrations: Pictures of smart and well-modified cars; also "sheds" (particularly badly modified cars). Also picture stories of likely interest to the target readership, including coverage of car gatherings.
Text: Ideas for features of interest to "lads" in their twenties always considered.
Overall freelance potential: Good for those in touch with this scene.
Editor's tips: Freelances need to be able to recognise the particular type of "cool" car that is featured here, and be aware of the general mood of the magazine.
Fees: Picture stories around £200–£300; single pictures according to use.

MOTOR SPORT

38 Chelsea Wharf, 15 Lots Road, London SW10 0QJ.
Tel: 020 7349 8484. Fax: 020 7349 8494. E-mail: editorial@motorsportmagazine.co.uk
Editor: Damien Smith. Deputy **Editor:** Gordon Cruickshank. **Picture Editor:** Ian Marshall.
Monthly devoted to motor sport and sports cars, both old and new.
Illustrations: Colour; B&W archive material. Will always consider coverage of classic or vintage sports car meetings and racing. Archive collections always of interest.
Text: No scope.
Overall freelance potential: Fair.
Fees: From around £35 upwards.

MOTOR TRADER

Metropolis Business Publishing, 6th Floor, Davis House, Robert Street, Croydon CR0 1QQ.
Tel: 020 8253 8711. Fax: 020 8253 8727. E-mail: curtis.hutchinson@metropolis.co.uk
Editor: Curtis Hutchinson.
Weekly trade newspaper and website read by dealers & manufacturers in the car and component industries, garage owners, body shop workers.
Illustrations: News pictures on anything connected with the motor trade.
Text: News and features relevant to the motor trade and industry. 300–1,000 words.
Overall freelance potential: Good for those in touch with the trade.
Fees: Negotiable.

MOTORING & LEISURE
CSMA Club, Britannia House, 21 Station Street, Brighton BN1 4DE.
Tel: 01273 744744. Fax: 01273 744761. E-mail: jeremy.whittle@csmaclub.co.uk
Editor: Jeremy Whittle.
Monthly journal of the Civil Service Motoring Association, covering motoring, travel and leisure activities.
Illustrations: General car-related subjects and Continental travel.
Text: Illustrated articles on motoring, travel, camping and caravanning. 750–1,000 words.
Overall freelance potential: Fair.
Fees: By arrangement.

911 & PORSCHE WORLD
CH Publications Ltd, Nimax House, 20 Ullswater Crescent, Ullswater Business Park, Coulsdon, Surrey CR5 2HR.
Tel: 020 8655 6400. Fax: 020 8763 1001. E-mail: chp@chpltd.com
Editor: Steve Bennett.
Magazine published nine times a year and devoted to Porsche or Porsche-derived cars.
Illustrations: All commissioned, with opportunities for those who have original ideas and can produce top quality car photography.
Text: Ideas for articles always of interest; write with details in the first instance.
Overall freelance potential: Very good for specialist coverage.
Fees: Photography by arrangement; around £100 per 1,000 words.

OCTANE
Dennis Publishing Ltd, Tower Court, Irchester Road, Wollaston, Northants NN29 7PJ.
Tel: 020 7907 6585. E-mail: rob@octane-magazine.co.uk
Editor: Robert Coucher. **Art Editor:** Robert Gould.
Monthly covering both contemporary high-performance cars and prestige classics from all eras.
Illustrations: Colour and historic B&W. Mostly by commission with good opportunities for experienced car photographers. Possible on-spec scope for picture stories covering specific events such as meets, rallies, races, etc. Relevant archive material also of interest.
Text: Suggestions always considered.
Overall freelance potential: Good.
Fees: By negotiation.

PERFORMANCE FORD
Unity Media Communications Ltd, Becket House, Vestry Road, Sevenoaks, Kent TN14 5EJ.
Tel: 01732 748000. Fax: 01732 748001. E-mail: performanceford@unity-media.com
Editor: Luke Wood. **Features Editor:** Alex Robbins.
Monthly magazine devoted to Ford and Ford-based vehicles, with the emphasis on high-performance road use.
Illustrations: Pictures commissioned to illustrate features, or topical single pictures of particular quality, i.e. prototypes, one-offs, etc.
Text: Illustrated articles on maintenance and modification of Ford-based cars. Personality profiles with a direct relevance to Ford products.
Overall freelance potential: Fair.
Editor's tips: Always raise ideas with the editor before submitting material.
Fees: Pictures according to size of reproduction or day rate by arrangement; text £120 per 1,000 words.

REDLINE
Future Publishing Ltd, Beauford Court, 30 Monmouth Street, Bath BA1 2BW.
Tel: 01225 442244. Fax: 01225 822793. E-mail: tim.durant@futurenet.co.uk
Editor: Davy Lewis. **Art Editor:** Tim Durant.

Motoring monthly for young men who want to get the best out of their modified cars.
Illustrations: Exciting and dramatic pictures of modified cars, sporting and speed events, unusual vehicles and fast lifestyles. Commissions available for car shoots, also some glamour; make appointment with the art editor.
Text: Will always consider suggestions for illustrated articles on suitable subjects, such as touring trips, unusual events, weird car-based experiences, etc.
Overall freelance potential: Moderate.
Editor's tips: Although photographers should know how to light and shoot cars, non-specialists are welcome if they can produce something exciting and different.
Fees: Single pictures £25–£250; page rate £50–£125; day rate £150–£300.

TOP GEAR MAGAZINE

BBC Magazines, 2nd Floor A, Energy Centre, Media Village, 201 Wood Lane, London W12 0TT.
Tel: 020 8433 2313. Fax: 020 8576 3754. E-mail: queries.tgmag@bbc.co.uk
Editor: Charlie Turner.
General interest motoring magazine designed to complement the BBC TV programme of the same name.
Illustrations: All by commission and much from known specialists, but photographers with a fresh approach and a good portfolio are welcomed. Send samples and details of previous experience in the first instance, or call for appointment. Stock images of pre-1990 cars often needed to illustrate articles.
Text: Motoring-related features considered, preferably out of the ordinary.
Overall freelance potential: Good opportunities for talented car photographers.
Fees: By negotiation.

TOTAL 911

9 Publishing, PO Box 6815, Matlock, Derbyshire DE4 4WZ.
Tel: 0845 450 6964. E-mail: phil@9publishing.co.uk
Editor: Philip Raby.
Monthly for Porsche 911 car enthusiasts, covering both classic and modern models.
Illustrations: All by commission only. Interested in hearing from professional car photographers who can offer something different. Write first enclosing samples of work.
Text: Ideas from professional motoring writers always welcome – apply in writing only.
Overall freelance potential: Good.
Editor's tips: Study the magazine before getting in touch.
Fees: Negotiable, but from around £150 for photo assignments, £100 per 1,000 words for text.

TRIUMPH WORLD

Kelsey Publishing Group, PO Box 13, Westerham, Kent TN16 3WT.
Tel: 01895 623612. E-mail: tw.ed@kelsey.co.uk
Editor: Simon Goldsworthy.
Monthly magazine for Triumph car (not motorcycle) enthusiasts.
Illustrations: Photographs of newsworthy or unusual Triumph cars, especially the "classics" such as Heralds, TRs, Spitfires and Stags. Some opportunities for experienced photographers to produce commissioned work for major features.
Text: Illustrated articles likely to appeal to the dedicated enthusiast. Phone first to discuss ideas.
Overall freelance potential: Good.
Fees: By negotiation.

> *As a member of the Bureau of Freelance Photographers, you'll be kept up-to-date with markets through the BFP Market Newsletter, published monthly. For details of membership, turn to page 9*

Music

BLUES & SOUL
Blues & Soul Ltd, 153 Praed Street, London W2 1RL.
Tel: 020 3174 8020. E-mail: editorial@bluesandsoul.com
Editor: Lee Tyler.
Online publication with quarterly print edition, covering soul, R&B, funk, fusion, jazz, house, garage, dance – all forms of black music.
Illustrations: Will always consider original and exclusive pictures of relevant performers in the above fields.
Text: Small amount of scope for exclusive articles or interviews.
Overall freelance potential: Limited.
Editor's tips: Think of the readership, and the format, in order to produce something really striking and eye-catching.
Fees: By negotiation.

CLASSICAL MUSIC
Rhinegold Publishing Ltd, 241 Shaftesbury Avenue, London WC2H 8TF.
Tel: 020 7333 1742. Fax: 020 7333 1769. E-mail: classical.music@rhinegold.co.uk
Editor: Keith Clarke.
Fortnightly news and feature magazine for classical music professionals and the interested general public.
Illustrations: Digital files preferred. Very limited scope as most pictures are supplied by promoters, etc, but always happy to look at portfolios, subject to appointment. Occasional urgent need for a musician or group in the news – most easily met if freelances can supply lists of photographs they hold.
Text: Short news items and news stories about events in the music/arts world, including politics and performance, up to 800 words. Longer background features about musicians, usually relating to a forthcoming event, up to 2,000 words. All work is commissioned.
Overall freelance potential: Limited for photographers, but most text is from commissioned freelance sources.
Fees: Pictures by negotiation; text from £125 per 1,000 words.

FROOTS
Southern Rag Ltd, PO Box 337, London N4 1TW.
Tel: 020 8340 9651. Fax: 020 8348 5626. E-mail: froots@frootsmag.com
Editor: Ian Anderson.
Monthly publication concerned with folk and world roots music.
Illustrations: Pictures to be used in conjunction with interviews, reviews of records or reports on events. Mostly commissioned.
Text: Interviews and reviews concerned with folk and world music.
Overall freelance potential: Limited for the contributor unknown in this field. The magazine favours its regular contributors.
Fees: By agreement.

KERRANG!
Bauer Media, Endeavour House, 189 Shaftesbury Avenue, London WC2H 8JG.
Tel: 020 7295 5000. E-mail: kerrang@bauerconsumer.co.uk
Editor: Nichola Brown. News **Editor:** Simon Young.
Weekly magazine covering a wide range of hard rock.
Illustrations: Pictures of relevant bands. On-stage performance shots preferred, with the emphasis on action. Some posed shots and portraits of top performers also used.
Text: Little freelance market.

Overall freelance potential: Very good. The magazine is heavily illustrated.
Fees: According to size of reproduction.

KEYBOARD PLAYER
Bookrose Ltd, 100 Birkbeck Road, Enfield, Middlesex EN2 0ED.
Tel: 020 8245 5840. E-mail: steve@keyboardplayer.com
Editor: Steve Miller.
Monthly magazine for players of all types of keyboard instrument. Covers pianos, organs, keyboards and synthesisers; and all forms of music, from pop to classical.
Illustrations: Photographs of keyboard instruments and their players, preferably accompanied by a newsy caption. Covers: striking colour pictures of keyboard instruments.
Text: Articles of around 1,000 words on any topic of interest to keyboard players.
Overall freelance potential: Fairly limited, but scope is there for the right type of material.
Editor's tips: Run-of-the-mill pictures of players seated at their instruments will not be met with much enthusiasm – a strikingly different approach is required.
Fees: By negotiation.

METAL HAMMER
Future Publishing Ltd, 2 Balcombe Street, London NW1 6NW.
Tel: 020 7042 4000. Fax: 020 7042 4471. E-mail: amilas@futurenet.co.uk
Editor: Alexander Milas. **Art Editor:** James Isaacs.
Monthly for heavy metal and hard rock fans.
Illustrations: Good action and group portrait photographs of hard rock or heavy metal performers – send lists of subjects available. Commissions available to experienced rock photographers.
Text: Illustrated articles, interviews and reviews. Submit suggestions only in the first instance.
Overall freelance potential: Excellent for those in touch with this scene.
Fees: By negotiation.

MIXMAG
Development Hell, 90-92 Pentonville Road, London N1 9HS.
Tel: 020 7078 8400. Fax: 020 7833 9900. E-mail: mixmag@mixmag.net
Editor: Nick de Cosemo.
Monthly covering the dance music and clubbing scene.
Illustrations: Photographs of clubs and clubbers throughout the country; portraits of musicians; photo features. Fresh young photographers always welcome.
Text: Reports from clubs nationwide; young writers welcome.
Overall freelance potential: Very good.
Editor's tips: Contributors don't have to have experience, just a good sense of what the dance scene is about.
Fees: By negotiation.

MOJO
Bauer Media, Mappin House, 4 Winsley Street, London W1W 8HF.
Tel: 020 7295 5000. E-mail: matt.turner@bauerconsumer.co.uk
Editor-in-Chief: Phil Alexander. **Picture Editor:** Matt Turner.
Monthly rock music magazine aimed at fans of all ages.
Illustrations: Colour and archive B&W. Photographs of leading rock artists, both contemporary and from earlier eras. Archive material from the '50s, '60s and '70s always of interest. Good opportunities for commissioned work.
Text: In-depth profiles of individual artists and bands, but scope mainly for established writers.
Overall freelance potential: Good.
Editor's tips: Previously unpublished or unseen photographs, or those that have not been used for some years, are of particular interest.
Fees: According to use.

NEW MUSICAL EXPRESS
IPC Media Ltd, Blue Fin Building, 110 Southwark Street, London SE1 0SU.
Tel: 020 3148 6864. Fax: 020 3148 8107. E-mail: nmepics@ipcmedia.com
Editor: Krissi Murison. **Art Director:** Joe Frost. **Picture Director:** Marian Paterson.
Weekly magazine covering all aspects of popular music and allied youth culture.
Illustrations: All aspects of contemporary popular music, but see below.
Text: Scope for exclusive news stories or interviews with rock musicians, film stars, or other personalities of interest to a young and aware readership. Always write or phone with suggestions first.
Overall freelance potential: Good, but very dependent on subject matter.
Editor's tips: NME only covers those parts of the music scene considered worthwhile by the editorial team – study recent issues.
Fees: On a rising scale according to size of reproduction.

Q
Bauer Media, Mappin House, 4 Winsley Street, London W1W 8HF.
Tel: 020 7295 5000. Fax: 020 7182 8547. E-mail: russ.o'connell@qthemusic.com
Editor: Paul Rees. **Picture Director:** Russ O'Connell.
Monthly rock music magazine aimed at the 18–35 age group.
Illustrations: Most pictures staff-produced or commissioned from a pool of regular contributors, but suitable stock pictures of relevant personalities will always be considered.
Text: Top quality profiles, interviews and feature articles of interest to a rock-oriented readership, invariably by commission.
Overall freelance potential: 50 per cent is commissions; good for library/stock shots.
Fees: Set rates.

RHYTHM
Future Publishing Ltd, Beauford Court, 30 Monmouth Street, Bath BA1 2BW.
Tel: 01225 442244. Fax: 01225 732285. E-mail: chris.barnes@futurenet.co.uk
Editor: Chris Barnes.
Monthly magazine for drummers and percussionists in the rock and pop music field.
Illustrations: Mostly colour. Interesting photographs relating to contemporary percussion instruments and their players, including the use of electronic and computer-aided equipment.
Text: Illustrated profiles, interviews and features about leading contemporary drummers and percussionists. Articles on technique and programming from knowledgeable contributors.
Overall freelance potential: Limited.
Fees: £110 per 1,000 words for text; photographs according to use.

TOTAL GUITAR
Future Publishing Ltd, Beauford Court, 30 Monmouth Street, Bath BA1 2BW.
Tel: 01225 442244. Fax: 01225 462986. E-mail: totalguitar@futurenet.co.uk
Editor: Stephen Lawson. **Art Editor:** John Blackshaw.
Monthly magazine for guitar players at all levels, concentrating on practical advice.
Illustrations: Mostly commissioned to accompany features and reviews. Stock shots of well-known players and individual instruments always of interest; send lists first.
Text: Profiles and interviews with leading guitarists, and practical articles. Submit ideas only in the first instance.
Overall freelance potential: Limited.
Fees: By negotiation.

Are you working from the latest edition of The Freelance Photographer's Market Handbook? It's published on 1 October each year. Markets are constantly changing, so it pays to have the latest edition

---

Parenting

MOTHER & BABY
Bauer Consumer Media, Endeavour House, 189 Shaftesbury Avenue, London WC2H 8JG.
Tel: 020 7295 5560. E-mail: mother&baby@bauermedia.co.uk
Editor: Miranda Levy. **Art Editor:** Ruth Hulbert.
Monthly aimed at pregnant women and mothers of young children.
Illustrations: May consider high quality photographs of mothers with babies, or babies (under one year) on their own, but the magazine is closely linked with the Mother & Baby Picture Library so has ready access to stock images. Experienced child photographers may be able to obtain commissions for editorial features and real life stories.
Text: Articles on all subjects related to pregnancy, birth, baby care and the early years.
Overall freelance potential: Limited.
Editor's tips: Looking for top quality pictures with a fresh eye on parenting.
Fees: From £30 upwards for stock shots, negotiable for commissions.

NURSERY WORLD
Haymarket Publishing Ltd, 22 Bute Gardens, London W6 7HN.
Tel: 020 8267 8410. E-mail: calvin.mckenzie@haymarket.com
Editor: Liz Roberts. **Picture Editor:** Calvin McKenzie.
Weekly publication on child care. Aimed at professional baby and child care workers such as teachers, nursery nurses and nannies.
Illustrations: Pictures of babies and young children (up to five years old) involved in various activities in childcare settings. Covers: Location shots of children, always linked to a feature inside.
Text: Features on child care, education, health, and any aspect of bringing up children, e.g. physical, intellectual, emotional etc. Ideas for nurseries and playgroups.
Overall freelance potential: Many features come from freelance contributors.
Fees: By arrangement.

PREGNANCY & BIRTH
Bauer Media, Endeavour House, 189 Shaftesbury Avenue, London WC2H 8JG.
Tel: 020 7295 5563. E-mail: jo.elston@bauermedia.co.uk
Editor: Ellie Hughes. **Art Editor:** Jo Elston.
Monthly covering pregnancy from conception to birth.
Illustrations: Mostly by commission. Opportunities for experienced photographers to produce cover shots, pregnancy fashion, interior shoots of nurseries, and "real life" material; contact art editor in the first instance. Always interested in hearing of good specialist stock collections.
Text: No scope.
Overall freelance potential: Good for experienced workers.
Editor's tips: Photographers need to be capable of working with real people rather than models.
Fees: By negotiation.

PRIMA BABY & PREGNANCY
National Magazine Company, 72 Broadwick Street, London W1F 9EP.
Tel: 020 7439 5000. Fax: 020 7312 3744. E-mail: lisa.mcsorley@natmags.co.uk
Editor: Elaine Griffiths. **Art Director:** Lisa McSorley.
Glossy monthly covering pregnancy, babies and toddlers up to three years.
Illustrations: Top quality pictures of babies and toddlers, with/without parents, in situations, engaged in activities, etc. Also pictures relating to aspects of childcare, health, fashion and home life. Must be warm, natural lifestyle images rather than posed "stock" shots. Write with details in the first instance. Some commissions available, mainly for reportage and studio photographers; call first to discuss possibilities.
Text: Limited freelance scope.

Overall freelance potential: Very good for quality material.
Fees: Variable; day rate around £400.

RIGHT START
Ten Alps Publishing, 9 Savoy Street, London WC2E 7HR.
Tel: 020 7878 2338. Fax: 020 7379 6261. E-mail: lynette.lowthian@tenalpspublishing.com
Editor: Lynette Lowthian.
Bi-monthly magazine for parents of pre-school and primary school age children, covering health, behaviour, education and family life.
Illustrations: Mostly by commission but some scope for good stock coverage of children in educational and learning situations; send only lists or details of coverage available in the first instance.
Text: Opportunities for education and child care specialists. Approach with details of ideas and previous experience.
Overall freelance potential: Limited.
Fees: By negotiation.

Photography & Video

AV
Haymarket Specialist, 174 Hammersmith Road, London W6 7NH.
Tel: 020 8267 8005. E-mail: bhavna.mistry@haymarket.com
Editor: Bhavna Mistry. Assistant **Editor:** Paul Milligan.
Monthly magazine for managers in industry and commerce, public services, government etc who use audiovisual communication techniques, eg slides, film, video, overhead projection and filmstrips, plus the new technologies of computer graphics and telecommunication.
Illustrations: Pictures of programmes being shown to audiences, preferably supported by case history details; relevant news; new products or location shooting pictures. All must be backed with solid information. Covers: colour pictures of same, but check before submitting.
Text: Case histories of either shows, conferences or studies of a particular company's use of AV techniques. Good location/conference stories always welcome. 1,000–2,500 words.
Overall freelance potential: Up to 25 per cent comes from freelances.
Fees: Text, £180-£200 per 1,000 words; pictures by agreement.

AMATEUR PHOTOGRAPHER
IPC Inspire, Blue Fin Building, 110 Southwark Street, London SE1 0SU.
Tel: 020 3148 4138. Fax: 020 3148 8130. E-mail: amateurphotographer@ipcmedia.com
Editor: Damien Demolder.
Weekly magazine for all photographers, from beginners to experienced enthusiasts.
Illustrations: B&W and colour. Pictures to illustrate specific photo techniques and general photo features. General portfolios in B&W and colour. Send no more than 10 pictures, prints unmounted, slides in a plastic slide wallet. Digital files on CD should be saved as JPEG or TIFF and accompanied by contact sheet.
Text: No scope.
Overall freelance potential: Good.
Fees: £50 per published page, pictures and text, except "Reader Spotlight".

Are you working from the latest edition of The Freelance Photographer's Market Handbook? It's published on 1 October each year. Markets are constantly changing, so it pays to have the latest edition

---

BLACK & WHITE PHOTOGRAPHY
GMC Publications Ltd, 86 High Street, Lewes, East Sussex BN7 1XN.
Tel: 01273 477374. Fax: 01273 402849. E-mail: lizr@thegmcgroup.com
Editor: Elizabeth Roberts.
Published 13 times a year, the magazine is devoted to showcasing the best in black and white photography.
Illustrations: B&W only. Features and portfolios showcasing the work of individual photographers, usually a cohesive body of work on a specific subject or theme. Regular "Reader Gallery" feature devotes up to two pages per reader/contributor. Photojournalistic work of particular interest, especially long-term projects produced over an extended period. Also step by step features showing all stages from a straight print to the final print. Digital techniques also covered. Little scope for single images. Also runs annual Black & White Photographer of the Year competition.
Text: Illustrated articles on printing techniques, film/paper combinations, equipment choices, etc. Submit sample prints and synopsis in the first instance.
Overall freelance potential: Excellent for the dedicated B&W worker.
Fees: According to subject and use.

THE BRITISH JOURNAL OF PHOTOGRAPHY
Incisive Media, 32–34 Broadwick Street, London W1A 2HG.
Tel: 020 7316 9658. Fax: 020 7316 9003. E-mail: bjp.features@bjphoto.co.uk
Editor: Simon Bainbridge. **Deputy Editor:** Diane Smyth.
Monthly magazine for professional and semi-professional photographers, students, advanced amateurs and all those engaged in professional photography.
Illustrations: B&W and colour. Portfolios along with some biographical notes about the photographer concerned. Contact deputy editor in the first instance.
Text: Interested in anything related to professional photography, particularly the more unusual and technical aspects.
Overall freelance potential: Good for bringing freelances to the attention of potential clients.
Editor's tips: Contributors do need to offer something special. Remember the magazine is aimed at those engaged in professional and semi-professional photography – technical features must therefore be of the highest calibre.
Fees: Portfolios not normally paid for; exposure in the magazine frequently leads to commissions elsewhere. Negotiable for text.

CAMCORDER BUYER HD READY MAGAZINE
Bright Publishing Ltd, Bright House, 82 High Street, Sawston, Cambridge CB2 4HJ.
Tel: 01223 499450. Fax: 01223 839953. E-mail: editorial@bright-publishing.com
Editor: Adam Scorey.
Bi-monthly buyers' guide aimed at the camcorder beginner. Concentrates primarily on high definition models but includes standard definition models too.
Illustrations: Always interested in hearing from new photographers.
Text: Looking for feature ideas, camcorder and gear reviewers, technical bods and general writers.
Overall freelance potential: Excellent.
Fees: By negotiation.

DIGITAL CAMERA
Future Publishing Ltd, Beauford Court, 30 Monmouth Street, Bath BA1 2BW.
Tel: 01225 442244. Fax: 01225 732295. E-mail: editor.dcm@futurenet.co.uk
Editor: Geoff Harris.
Monthly for the mid-market of digital camera users, those mainly using digital SLRs in the £600–£1400 price range.
Illustrations: Good single images required to illustrate seasonal subjects and topical events, and as examples of creative digital manipulations/compositions. Should be accompanied by detailed captions.

Text: Well-illustrated "how to" articles on digital photography and image editing. Contributors need to have some prior experience of producing such material.

Overall freelance potential: Good.

Editor's tips: Contributors should supply as much background detail about their images as they can.

Fees: Single images by negotiation and according to use; features £80 per published page.

DIGITAL PHOTO

Bauer Active Ltd, Media House, Lynchwood, Peterborough PE2 6EA.

Tel: 01733 468000. E-mail: jon.adams@bauermedia.co.uk

Editor: Jon Adams.

Monthly aimed at photographers keen to use their computer to enhance their pictures.

Illustrations: B&W and colour. Need for high-quality – technically and pictorially – original images that inspire readers to produce similar work. Ideally submissions should be accompanied by step-by-step screengrabs and words illustrating the thought processes and the stages involved in producing the work. Creative work always needed for the portfolio pages; require ten outstanding digitally manipulated images.

Text: Good potential for quality, step-by-step tutorials, but the final image must be outstanding and relevant. Contact editor in the first instance.

Overall freelance potential: Excellent for step-by-step tutorials.

Editor's tips: Look at and read the magazine first, then e-mail ideas and low-resolution JPEGs to illustrate. If submitting on CD always enclose high-quality inkjet prints too.

Fees: Negotiable, but typically £60 per page or £120 per 1,000 words.

DIGITAL PHOTOGRAPHER

Imagine Publishing Ltd, Richmond House, 33 Richmond Hill, Bournemouth BH2 6EZ.

Tel: 01202 586218. Fax: 01202 299955. E-mail: rosie.tanner@imagine-publishing.co.uk

Editor: Rosie Tanner.

Digital photography magazine for the more advanced user, aimed at serious enthusiasts and professionals.

Illustrations: Pictures mainly required to illustrate features on contemporary digital photography. Opportunities best for photographers using digital for specialist subjects (landscape, wildlife, portraiture, etc) or those experienced in Photoshop techniques.

Text: Practical illustrated articles and features on topics as above.

Overall freelance potential: Good for those with well-developed skills in digital work.

Fees: Negotiable, depending on what is on offer.

DIGITAL SLR PHOTOGRAPHY

Dennis Publishing, 6 Swan Court, Cygnet Park, Hampton, Peterborough PE7 8GX.

Tel: 01733 567401. Fax: 01733 352650. E-mail: jo_lezano@dennis.co.uk

Editor: Daniel Lezano. Editorial Co-ordinater: Jo Lezano.

Monthly for all photographers who use digital SLRs.

Illustrations: Regular requirement for high-quality images produced on digital SLRs. Most interested in seeing portfolios of between 20-100 images. For all submissions, supply TIFFs or maximum-quality JPEGs on CD/DVD, with thumbnail printouts (maximum 20 images per A4 sheet).

Text: Mostly produced by regulars, but ideas always considered.

Overall freelance potential: Excellent.

Editor's tips: See website at www.digitalslrphoto.com for a flavour of the content of the magazine along with details of picture requirements and submission guidelines.

Fees: On a standard scale according to use.

DIGITAL SLR USER

Bright Publishing Ltd, Bright House, 82 High Street, Sawston, Cambridge CB2 4HJ.

Tel: 01223 499450. Fax: 01223 839953. E-mail: editorial@bright-publishing.com
Editor-in-Chief: Terry Hope. **Deputy Editor:** Adam Scorey.
Monthly magazine for owners of digital SLR cameras, aimed at beginners and semi-proficient users. Emphasis on photographic technique, digital workflow and all things digital.
Illustrations: Normally images and articles as a package, but always interested in hearing from new photographers.
Text: Ideas, suggestions or draft articles on all aspects of digital SLR photography – technique, software reviews, location guides etc – are always welcome. Check with the editor before submitting.
Overall freelance potential: Excellent.
Fees: By negotiation.

EOS MAGAZINE

Robert Scott Publishing Ltd, The Old Barn, Ball Lane, Tackley, Kidlington, Oxon OX5 3AG.
Tel: 01869 331741. Fax: 01869 331641. E-mail: editorial@eos-magazine.com
Editor: Angela August.
Quarterly magazine for users of Canon EOS cameras.
Illustrations: Digital files only. Top quality photographs of any subject taken with Canon EOS cameras. Should demonstrate some aspect of photographic technique or the use of equipment. Comparison shots always of interest.
Text: Contributions are welcomed, but always phone or e-mail first to discuss.
Overall freelance potential: Very good.
Editor's tips: For photo requirements e-mail request with "Notes for Contributors" in subject box.
Fees: Minimum fee for pictures is £15, but most are paid at between £20 and £60 depending on usage. Cover and dps, £100-£250. Text £90–£150 per 1,000 words (higher rates are for technique material which is comprehensive and well researched).

HOTSHOE INTERNATIONAL

Hotshoe International Ltd, 29-31 Saffron Hill, London EC1N 8SW.
Tel: 020 7421 6009. Fax: 020 7421 6006. E-mail: melissa.dewitt@photoshot.com
Editor: Melissa De Witt.
Bi-monthly contemporary photography magazine covering all genres.
Illustrations: High-quality photography and portfolios of all kinds, including fine art, documentary, reportage, photojournalism and creative photography.
Text: Only in support of material as above.
Overall freelance potential: Very good for high-quality, original material.
Editor's tips: Contributions need to be of real interest to other working photographers.
Fees: By negotiation.

MARKET NEWSLETTER

Bureau of Freelance Photographers, Focus House, 497 Green Lanes, London N13 4BP.
Tel: 020 8882 3315. E-mail: eds@thebfp.com
Editor: John Tracy.
Monthly journal of the BFP, mainly devoted to detailing markets for photography. For members only.
Illustrations: Photographs required for "Pictures that Sell" feature – photographs taken by BFP members that have proven commercial success, having earned high fees and/or having sold to a wide range of markets.
Text: Photographer profiles in which a successful photographer outlines his or her freelance

---

As a member of the Bureau of Freelance Photographers, you'll be kept up-to-date with markets through the BFP Market Newsletter, published monthly. For details of membership, turn to page 9

activities, or general features on aspects of selling photography, backed up with examples of successful pictures and hints and tips to encourage others. Around 1,000 words.
Overall freelance potential: Limited.
Fees: £40 for "Pictures that Sell", £150 for photographer profile.

MASTER PHOTOGRAPHY
Icon Publications Ltd, Maxwell Lane, Kelso, Roxburghshire TD5 7BB.
Tel: 01573 226032. Fax: 01573 26000. E-mail: iconmags@btconnect.com
Editor: David Kilpatrick.
Magazine for the UK's commercial and studio photographers, with the emphasis on photographing people for profit. Official journal of the Master Photographers Association (MPA). Ten issues per year.
Illustrations: Images only required to accompany and illustrate specific articles mainly relating to commercial studio or events photography.
Text: Illustrated articles and features on topics as above, mainly profiles/interviews with successful practitioners. Some technical articles.
Overall freelance potential: Limited; most material is contributed on a voluntarary basis by MPA members.
Fees: Interviews and technical material, £60-£90 per published page.

OUTDOOR PHOTOGRAPHY
GMC Publications, 86 High Street, Lewes, East Sussex BN7 1XN.
Tel: 01273 477374. Fax: 01273 478606. E-mail: stevew@thegmcgroup.com
Editor: Steve Watkins.
Monthly devoted to the photography of all types of outdoor subject matter.
Illustrations: Mainly colour, digital or transparencies. Top-quality photographs of British landscapes, countryside, wildlife, gardens and architecture. Scope for good single images in the portfolio gallery section, but prefer packages of both words and pictures.
Text: Well-illustrated articles on all aspects of outdoor photography, accompanied by full background details on location or subject.
Overall freelance potential: Excellent; the magazine relies on freelances contributors.
Editor's tips: The magazine is seasonally-led, so subject matter needs to be relevant to the month of publication. Don't send on-spec pictures by e-mail.
Fees: By negotiation.

PENTAX USER
The Turbine, Shireoaks Business Park, Coach Close, Shireoaks S81 8AP.
Tel: 01909 512147. Fax: 01909 512147. E-mail: info@pentaxuser.co.uk
Editor: Peter Bargh.
Exclusive magazine for members of the Pentax User club. Features techniques reviews and how-to articles on all areas of photography with an emphasis on Pentax camera equipment.
Illustrations: B&W and colour. Images mainly required for cover – any image that is taken on a Pentax, with space available to allow logo to appear top right and tasters bottom left. Other images usually only as part of a complete package of words and pictures.
Text: Well-illustrated articles on all aspects of photography with an emphasis on Pentax camera equipment. How-to articles on using modes of compacts and SLRs particularly sought after, along with techniques on using flash, lenses, filters etc. Please submit suggestions in writing in first instance. The editor will then phone or reply to discuss commission.
Overall freelance potential: Most of the magazine is based on articles from club members or freelances.
Fees: £50 per published page.

PHOTO PRO MAGAZINE
Bright Publishing Ltd, Bright House, 82 High Street, Sawston, Cambridge CB2 4HJ.
Tel: 01223 499450. Fax: 01223 839953. E-mail: editorial@bright-publishing.com
Editor: Terry Hope. **Deputy Editor:** Charlotte Griffiths, **Web, News & Features Editor:**
Charlotte Griffiths.
Monthly magazine dedicated to aspiring professional photographers and established pros. Strong
emphasis on business, technique and the life of a modern professional.
Illustrations: Normally images and articles submitted as a package, but always interested in
brilliant one-offs or portfolios of images.
Text: Ideas, suggestions or draft articles on all aspects of professional photography – equipment,
workflow, technique – are always welcome. Check with the editor before submitting.
Overall freelance potential: Excellent.
Fees: By negotiation.

PHOTOGRAPHY MONTHLY
Archant Specialist, Archant House, Oriel Road, Cheltenham GL50 1BB.
Tel: 01242 211080. E-mail: pm@photographymonthly.co.uk
Editor: Grant Scott.
Magazine for the beginner and enthusiast, with the emphasis on helping readers improve their
images using the latest imaging techniques and equipment.
Illustrations: High quality photography of all types, especially images that illustrate specific points
of camera and computing technique. All subjects welcome but in particular landscapes, nature and
people. Step-by-step digital tutorials are also of interest.
Text: Much is produced by regular writers but the magazine is always on the lookout for new
contributors and ideas.
Overall freelance potential: Excellent.
Editor's tips: Best scope is for well-conceived ideas that tie in with the existing style of the title.
Fees: According to use.

PHOTOPLUS
Future Publishing Limited, 30 Monmouth Street, Bath BA1 2BW.
Tel: 01225 442244. E-mail: chris.george@futurenet.com
Editor: Chris George.
Photography magazine aimed at users of Canon digital SLRs. 13 issues a year.
Illustrations: Always happy to consider good images taken with Canon DSLR cameras. Subjects
should be those of general appeal to the keen photo enthusiast, such as landscapes, nature,
portraiture, etc. Send a few low-res samples via e-mail, weblink or on CD/DVD in the first instance.
Text: Mostly staff-produced.
Overall freelance potential: Good for strong enthusiast-type material.
Fees: According to use, but typically around £60 half page, £120 full page, £200 dps or cover.

PRACTICAL PHOTOGRAPHY
Bauer Media, Media House, Lynchwood, Peterborough PE2 6EA.
Tel: 01733 468000. E-mail: practical.photography@bauermedia.co.uk
Editor-in-Chief: Andrew James. **Deputy Editor:** Ben Hawkins.
Monthly magazine aimed at all photographers, with news, interviews and equipment tests, with
emphasis on digital SLRs and imaging techniques.
Illustrations: Colour and B&W. Photographs of any subject considered for general illustration and

---

*Are you working from the latest edition of The Freelance Photographer's
Market Handbook? It's published on 1 October each year. Markets are
constantly changing, so it pays to have the latest edition*

for the magazine's files. Images should have strong impact and be original, also illustrating some aspect of photographic technique – use of filters, shooting at the right time of day, camera viewpoint, etc. Colour and B&W portfolios regularly featured.

Text: Some potential, but contact editor in the first instance. Will use writers who can offer something the staff writers can't.

Overall freelance potential: Excellent for pictures and digital techniques; fewer opportunities for words but ideas still welcome.

Editor's tips: Read the magazine and study the pictures; if you can produce comparable work, send it in.

Fees: Negotiable but typically £80 per page and £120–£140 per 1,000 words.

PROFESSIONAL PHOTOGRAPHER

Archant Specialist, Archant House, Oriel Road, Cheltenham GL50 1BB.
Tel: 01242 211080. E-mail: grant.scott@archant.co.uk
Editor: Grant Scott.
Monthly magazine for professional photographers.
Illustrations: B&W and colour. Images only used as part of features as below.
Text: Check with the editor before submitting ideas.
Overall freelance potential: Only for the right material appropriately written.
Editor's tips: The magazine appeals to readers who find other magazines too superficial. It is therefore more important than ever that potential contributors study recent issues.
Fees: By negotiation.

WHAT DIGITAL CAMERA

IPC Inspire, Blue Fin Building, 110 Southwark Street, London SE1 0SU.
Tel: 020 3148 4796. Fax: 020 3148 8123. E-mail: wdc@ipcmedia.com
Editor: Nigel Atherton.
Monthly consumer magazine for digital photography enthusiasts.
Illustrations: Will consider original, creative, digital images and portfolios, either digitally originated or manipulations from conventional film.
Text: Illustrated features about the techniques and applications of digital cameras. Contact editor with suggestions first.
Overall freelance potential: Good.
Fees: Pictures by negotiation and according to use. Text £100 per 1,000 words.

Politics & Current Affairs

THE BIG ISSUE

1-5 Wandsworth Road, London SW8 2LN.
Tel: 020 7526 3200. Fax: 020 7526 3241. E-mail: sam.price@bigissue.com
Editor: Charles Howgego. **Art Director:** Sam Price.
Current affairs weekly sold in support of the homeless.
Illustrations: B&W and colour. Broad range of mainly news-based images covering politics, social issues and the arts. For hard news pictures contact the news desk; for general feature photography contact the art director.
Text: Suitable reportage-type features always considered. usually around 1,200 with with 2-3 illustrations.
Overall freelance potential: Very good for the right sort of material.
Fees: By negotiation.

THE ECOLOGIST
Unit 102D, Lana House Studios, 116-118 Commercial Street, London E1 6NF.
Tel: 020 7422 8100. E-mail: editorial@theecologist.org
Editor: Mark Anslow.
Online magazine covering all ecological and environmental topics.
Illustrations: News pictures and images to illustrate features on current environmental or ethical concerns.
Text: News items and articles on relevant topical issues. Contributors must have good, in-depth knowledge of their subject.
Overall freelance potential: Fair.
Fees: According to use.

THE ECONOMIST
The Economist Newspaper Ltd, 25 St James's Street, London SW1A 1HG.
Tel: 020 7830 7000. Fax: 020 7830 7130. E-mail: celinadunlop@economist.com
Editor: John Micklethwait. **Picture Editor:** Celina Dunlop.
Weekly publication covering world political, business and scientific affairs.
Illustrations: Pictures of politicians, businessmen, social conditions (housing, health service, etc), major industries (coal, steel, oil, motor, agriculture, etc). Always prepared to keep digital images for stock.
Text: All staff-produced.
Overall freelance potential: Only for serious and experienced photojournalists. Commissions not available.
Editor's tips: Telephone picture editor in the first instance.
Fees: On a rising scale according to size of reproduction inside.

JANE'S DEFENCE WEEKLY
IHS Jane's, Sentinel House, 163 Brighton Road, Coulsdon, Surrey CR5 2YH.
Tel: 020 8700 3700. Fax: 020 8763 1007. E-mail: jdw@janes.com
Editor: Peter Felstead.
News magazine concentrating on developments in all military fields.
Illustrations: News pictures of defence subjects worldwide – exercises, deployments, equipment, etc. Contact the editor initially.
Text: News items and informed articles on the military, industrial and political aspects of global defence.
Overall freelance potential: Limited for those without contacts in the forces or defence industry, but work submitted here may also be published in the various annuals produced by the Jane's Information Group.
Fees: Photographs £40 inside; covers negotiable; text from £200 per 1,000 words.

THE JEWISH CHRONICLE
Jewish Chronicle Newspapers Ltd, 25 Furnival Street, London EC4A 1JT.
Tel: 020 7415 1500 Fax: 020 7405 9040. E-mail: editorial@thejc.com
Editor: Stephen Pollard.
Weekly newspaper publishing news and features concerning, and of interest to, the British Jewish community.
Illustrations: Any topical pictures related to the purpose stated above. Also material for the paper's wide range of supplements that deal with subjects such as holidays, fashion, interior decoration, regional development, etc.
Text: Features on topics detailed above. 600–2,500 words.
Overall freelance potential: At least 30 per cent of the content comes from freelance sources.
Fees: By negotiation.

LIBERAL DEMOCRAT NEWS
Liberal Democrats, 4 Cowley Street, London SW1P 3NB.
Tel: 020 7227 1361. Fax: 020 7222 7904. E-mail: ldn@libdems.org.uk
Editor: Deirdre Razzall.
Weekly tabloid newspaper of the Liberal Democrats.
Illustrations: Prints or digital files accepted. Pictures of Liberal Democrat activities around the country and general political news pictures.
Text: News and features: politics, current affairs.
Overall freelance potential: Limited.
Fees: By negotiation.

THE MIDDLE EAST
IC Publications Ltd, 7 Coldbath Square, London EC1R 4LQ.
Tel: 020 7713 7711. Fax: 020 7713 7970. E-mail: p.lancaster@africasia.com
Editor: Pat Lancaster.
Monthly publication directed at senior management, governmental personnel and universities. Covers Middle Eastern current affairs of a political, cultural and economic nature.
Illustrations: B&W and colour. Pictures of all topical Middle Eastern subjects, personalities and scenes.
Text: Features on Middle Eastern subjects or world subjects that relate to the area. 1,000–3,000 words.
Overall freelance potential: Most of the pictures come from freelances.
Fees: B&W pictures £15–£35; covers by agreement. Text, from £80 per 1,000 words.

NEW INTERNATIONALIST
55 Rectory Road, Oxford OX4 1BW.
Tel: 01865 811400. Fax: 01865 793152. E-mail: ni_ed@newint.org
Co-Editors: (UK) Vanessa Baird, Dinyar Godrej, Jess Worth
Monthly magazine covering global issues from a mainly Southern (Africa, Asia, Latin American) perspective.
Illustrations: Pictures to illustrate news stories and topical features on subjects such as social justice, human rights, environmental issues, poverty, sustainable development, etc.
Text: Illustrated stories and features on relevant topics as above.
Overall freelance potential: Good.
Editor's tips: Each editor edits individually themed issues and is responsible for his/her own picture research.
Fees: Pictures, from a minimum of £40 to £250 for front cover.

PCS VIEW
The Public & Commercial Services Union, 160 Falcon Road, Clapham, London SW11 2LN.
Tel: 020 7924 2727 Fax: 020 7801 2822. E-mail: editor@pcs.org.uk
Editor: Sharon Breen.
Monthly publication for members of the PCS Union, the biggest civil service union. Also has large private sector membership.
Illustrations: News pictures of trade union activity, especially involving members of PCS. Other topical pictures of current affairs that may impinge on Union members may also be of interest.
Text: No scope.
Overall freelance potential: Good, 75 per cent of pictures come from outside contributors.
Fees: Good; on a rising scale according to size of reproduction.

As a member of the Bureau of Freelance Photographers, you'll be kept up-to-date with markets through the BFP Market Newsletter, published monthly. For details of membership, turn to page 9

Railways

HERITAGE RAILWAY

Mortons Media Group Ltd, Media Centre, Morton Way, Horncastle, Lincs LN9 6JR.
Tel: 01507 529300. Fax: 01507 529301. E-mail: rjones@mortons.co.uk
Editor: Robin Jones.
Monthly magazine devoted to railway preservation – steam, diesel and electric.
Illustrations: Mainly colour. Captioned news pictures depicting restoration projects, restored locomotives on their first runs, special events etc, especially from less well-known lines and museums. Mainly UK-based but will also consider overseas coverage of locomotives with a British connection, especially really "stunning and attractive" pictures.
Text: Well-illustrated features on preservation and restoration topics; write with suggestions first.
Overall freelance potential: Very good.
Fees: By negotiation.

INTERNATIONAL RAILWAY JOURNAL

Simmons-Boardman Publishing Corporation, 46 Killigrew Street, Falmouth, Cornwall TR11 3PP.
Tel: 01326 313945. Fax: 01326 211576. E-mail: irj@railjournal.co.uk
Editor: David Briginshaw. **Associate Editor:** Keith Barrow.
Monthly publication for the principal officers of the railways of the world (including metro and light rail systems), ministers and commissioners of transport, railway equipment manufacturers and suppliers.
Illustrations: Pictures of new line construction projects, electrification projects, track or signalling improvements, new locomotives, passenger coaches and freight wagons. Interesting pictures of railway operations from far-flung corners of the world. No steam or nostalgia material. Covers: colour shots tied in with the theme of a particular issue.
Text: Features on any sizeable contracts for railway equipment; plans for railway developments, eg new line construction, track or signalling improvements; almost anything which involves a railway spending money or making improvements and techniques. No padding or speculation.
Overall freelance potential: Quite good for the right business-oriented material.
Fees: Rising scale according to size of pictures; text, £120 per 1,000 words.

RAIL

Bauer Media Ltd, Media House, Lynchwood, Peterborough PE2 6EA.
Tel: 01733 468000. Fax: 01733 468586. E-mail: rail@bauermedia.co.uk
Managing Editor: Nigel Harris.
Fortnightly magazine dealing with modern railways.
Illustrations: Mostly colour, some B&W. Single photographs and up-to-date news pictures on any interesting railway topic in Britain, particularly accidents and incidents of all kinds. Covers: Colour shots with strong impact.
Text: Illustrated articles of up to 1,500 words on any railway topic. Check recent issues for style.
Overall freelance potential: Excellent.
Editor's tips: Topicality is everything for news coverage. For other pictures try to get away from straightforward shots of trains; be imaginative. Always looking for something different.
Fees: Pictures range from £25–£70; illustrated articles around £90–£150. Will pay more for high-impact special pics that give the magazine a commercial advantage.

RAIL EXPRESS

Mortons Media Group Ltd, Media Centre, Morton Way, Horncastle, Lincs LN9 6JR.
Tel: 01507 529529. E-mail: gbayer@mortons.co.uk
Editor: Gareth Bayer.
Monthly magazine for modern railway enthusiasts.
Illustrations: Any good or unusual photographs of the contemporary railway scene, but really need

to be of current and newsworthy interest (new locomotives, new colour schemes, etc). Some scope for historic diesel/electric coverage.

Text: Suggestions for articles welcome, from anyone with good background knowledge of the subject, especially traction. Consult with the editor first.

Overall freelance potential: The magazine features lots of photography and always needs more.

Editor's tips: Topicality is the key, and images should always be taken in sunshine.

Fees: From basic rate of £20 per picture.

RAILNEWS

Railnews Ltd, Business & Technology Centre, Bessemer Drive, Stevenage, Herts, SG1 2D.
Tel: 01438 310011. Fax: 0844 443 2700. E-mail: newsdesk@railnews.co.uk
Managing Editor: Sim Harris.

Monthly newspaper for people in the rail industry, covering the modern railway scene in the UK.

Illustrations: Digital files preferred, B&W and colour prints accepted. Railway news pictures, unusual pictures of events, operations, activities, with good captions.

Text: No scope.

Overall freelance potential: Good.

Editor's tips: Approach before submitting.

Fees: By negotiation.

THE RAILWAY MAGAZINE

IPC Media Ltd, Blue Fin Building, 110 Southwark Street, London SE1 0SU.
Tel: 020 3148 4683. Fax: 020 3148 8521. E-mail: railway@ipcmedia.com
Editor: Nick Pigott.

Monthly for all rail enthusiasts, covering both main line and heritage railways, modern and historic.

Illustrations: News pictures concerning the current rail network, as well as images from recent heritage events, galas or rail tours. Also pictures of new liveries, new trains on test, accidents/derailments, and rare or unusual workings. Previously unpublished material from the 1940s onwards always of interest for historical features. Top quality non-news pictures may be used for spreads and/or occasional calendars. For digital, e-mail thumbnails (10 images max) in first instance; CDs (50 images max) must have thumbnail sheet. For film submissions, captions should be supplied on individual slide mounts or prints, not on separate caption sheet.

Text: Well-researched illustrated articles on any British railway topic, current or historic; discuss ideas with the editor first.

Overall freelance potential: Excellent.

Editor's tips: News pictures must be recent – no more than six weeks old.

Fees: From £15 minimum for news pictures, to £50+ for larger reproductions.

STEAM RAILWAY

Bauer Active Ltd, Media House, Lynchwood, Peterborough PE2 6EA.
Tel: 01733 468000. E-mail: steam.railway@bauermedia.co.uk
Editor: Danny Hopkins.

Four-weekly magazine for the steam railway enthusiast. Closely concerned with railway preservation.

Illustrations: Mostly colour; archive B&W. Accurately captioned photographs depicting steam trains and railways past and present, preserved railway lines, and railway museums (topical subjects especially welcomed).

Text: Illustrated articles on relevant subjects.

Overall freelance potential: Most of the photographic content is contributed by freelances.

Editor's tips: Material should be lively, topical and newsworthy, although some nostalgic or historic material is accepted. Always query the editorial team before submitting.

Fees: By arrangement.

TODAY'S RAILWAYS UK
Platform 5 Publishing, 3 Wyvern House, Sark Road, Sheffield S2 4HG.
Tel: 0114 255 2625. Fax: 0114 255 2471. E-mail: editorial@platform5.com
Editor: Paul Abell.
Monthly covering the contemporary British railway scene, aimed at both rail professionals and enthusiasts.
Illustrations: News pictures relating to current or planned UK rail operations, accompanied by detailed captions or stories. Stock material may be of interest – send detailed lists in the first instance.
Text: Feature suggestions always considered, but only from writers who have in-depth knowledge of their subject.
Overall freelance potential: Limited, as much is obtained from industry sources.
Editor's tips: Always contact editor before submitting as many stories may already be covered.
Fees: Pictures from £12.50; text £50 per page.

TRACTION
Warners Group Publications plc, The Maltings, West Street, Bourne, Lincs PE10 9PH.
Tel: 01778 392455. Fax: 01778 425437. E-mail: richardw@warnersgroup.co.uk
Editor: Richard Wilson.
Monthly magazine dedicated to classic diesel and electric locomotives.
Illustrations: Mostly colour; B&W archive material. Photographs of classic diesels and electrics operating on British railways from the 1940s to the present day. Particular interest in archive shots from the earlier eras up to the early 1980s.
Text: Limited scope at present.
Overall freelance potential: Good.
Fees: From £15–£50 according to size of reproduction.

Religion

THE CATHOLIC HERALD
Herald House, 15 Lamb's Passage, Bunhill Row, London EC1Y 8TQ.
Tel: 020 7448 3602. Fax: 020 7256 9728. E-mail: editorial@catholicherald.co.uk
Editor: Luke Coppen.
Weekly newspaper reflecting on Catholicism/Christianity and its place in the wider world, plus church news.
Illustrations: Principal need for news photographs of events involving churches, clerics or prominent Catholics.
Text: Articles of up to 1,200 words on the social, economic and political significance of the church domestically and internationally, plus spiritual and reflective writings.
Overall freelance potential: Better for features than other material.
Fees: By arrangement but not high.

THE CATHOLIC TIMES
Gabriel Communications Ltd, Fourth Floor, Landmark House, Station Road, Cheadle Hulme SK8 7JH.
Tel: 0161 488 1753. Fax: 0161 237 6690. E-mail: kevin.flaherty@totalcatholic.com
Editor: Kevin Flaherty.
Weekly newspaper covering Catholic affairs.
Illustrations: Topical news pictures of Catholic interest. Also off-beat devotional shots.
Text: News stories and short features. 900 words maximum.
Overall freelance potential: Very good.
Fees: Text around £40 per 1,000 words; pictures by negotiation.

CHURCH OF ENGLAND NEWSPAPER
Religious Intelligence Ltd, 14 Great College Street, London SW1P 3RX.
Tel: 020 7878 1002. Fax: 020 7878 1031. E-mail: colin.blakely@churchnewspaper.com
Editor: Colin Blakely.
Weekly newspaper covering Anglican news and views.
Illustrations: Colour print and digital accepted. Will consider any news pictures that relate to the Church of England.
Text: News stories, plus features that relate Christian faith to politics, the arts and everyday life. Up to 1,000 words, but submit ideas only in the first instance.
Overall freelance potential: Good for those with Church connections.
Fees: £20 – £40 per published picture; text about £40 per 1,000 words.

CHURCH TIMES
G.J.Palmer & Sons Ltd, 13-17 Long Lane, London EC1A 9PN.
Tel: 020 7776 1064. E-mail: news@churchtimes.co.uk
Editor: Paul Handley.
Weekly newspaper covering Church of England affairs.
Illustrations: Up-to-the-minute news pictures of Anglican events and personalities. Detailed captions essential.
Text: Short articles on current religious topics; up to 1,000 words.
Overall freelance potential: Fair.
Editor's tips: It is preferred that people in pictures are engaged in activities rather than just looking at the camera.
Fees: Photographs according to use, average £70; text £100 per 1,000 words.

Science & Technology

BBC FOCUS
Bristol Magazines Ltd, 14th Floor, Tower House, Fairfax Street, Bristol BS1 3BN.
Tel: 0117 927 9009. Fax: 0117 934 9008. E-mail: jamescutmore@originpublishing.co.uk
Editor: Jheni Osman. **Art Editor:** Steve Sayers. **Picture Editor:** James Cutmore.
Popular science monthly relating to all BBC science content. Aimed at both adults and teenagers.
Illustrations: Will consider colour photo essays on popular science, technology, space exploration, medicine and the environment. Contact art editor in the first instance.
Text: Interesting features on subjects above always considered. Submit a synopsis first.
Overall freelance potential: Fair.
Editor's tips: Only top quality material is considered; study the magazine before submitting.
Fees: Negotiable; generally good.

EDUCATION IN CHEMISTRY
The Royal Society of Chemistry, Thomas Graham House, Science Park, Cambridge, CB4 0WF.
Tel: 01223 420066. E-mail: eic@rsc.org
Editor: Laura Howes.
Bi-monthly publication for teachers, lecturers in schools and universities, concerning all aspects of chemical education.
Illustrations: Pictures that deal with chemistry in the classroom, laboratories or the chemical industry.
Text: Features concerned with chemistry or the teaching of it. Under 2,500 words.
Overall freelance potential: Limited.
Fees: By agreement.

HOW IT WORKS
Imagine Publishing Ltd, Richmond House, 33 Richmond Hill, Bournemouth BH2 6EZ.
Tel: 01202 586200. E-mail: dave.harfield@imagine-publishing.co.uk
Editor-in-Chief: Dave Harfield.
Heavily-illustrated popular science and technology monthly for the general reader.
Illustrations: Images of any subject that broadly falls within the magazine's remit, including science, technology, transportation, space, history and the environment, but usually tied-in with specific articles or features.
Text: Illustrated articles on any up-to-date science and technology topic, with the emphasis on explaining "how it works" to the lay reader.
Overall freelance potential: Very good for the right kind of material.
Editor's Tips: Ensure all facts are fully checked and correct before submitting.
Fees: By negotiation, dependent on what is being offered.

NEW SCIENTIST
Reed Business Information, Lacon House, 84 Theobalds Road, London WC1X 8RR.
Tel: 020 7611 1200. Fax: 020 7611 1280. E-mail: adam.goff@rbi.co.uk
Editor: Roger Highfield. **Picture Editor:** Adam Goff.
Weekly magazine about science and technology for people with some scientific or technical education and also for the intelligent layman.
Illustrations: Pictures on any topic that can be loosely allied to science and technology. Particularly interested in news photographs related to scientific phenomena and events. Covers: usually connected with a feature inside.
Text: News and features on scientific/technical subjects that might appeal to a wide audience.
Overall freelance potential: A lot of freelance work used, but consult the magazine before submitting.
Fees: Photographs on a rising scale according to size of reproduction. Text £150 per 1,000 words.

T3
Future Publishing Ltd, 2 Balcombe Street, London NW1 6NW.
Tel: 020 7042 4000. Fax: 020 7042 4471. E-mail: stuart.james@futurenet.co.uk
Editor: Luke Peters. **Art Editor:** Stuart James.
Monthly technology and gadget magazine aimed primarily at young men.
Illustrations: Always interested in pictures of new technology and new designs for consumer durables, especially exclusive shots of latest developments, pre-production models, new releases etc. Also general stock of any technology-related subject.
Text: Mainly staff produced but exclusive news items on new products always of interest.
Overall freelance potential: Fair
Fees: By negotiation. Will pay top rates for exclusives.

Sport

AIR GUNNER
Archant Specialist, 3 The Courtyard, Denmark Street, Wokingham, Berkshire RG40 2AZ.
Tel: 0118 989 7203. Fax: 01189 772903. E-mail: matthew.clark@archant.co.uk
Editor: Matt Clark.
Monthly magazine for all airgun enthusiasts.
Illustrations: Illustrated news items, and stock shots of small field animals (rats, rabbits) and pest species of birds (pigeons, magpies, crows). Covers: Usually commissioned, but a speculative picture might be used.
Text: Articles on any aspect of airgun use, 700–1,000 words, and accompanied by a good selection of images.

Overall freelance potential: Good for file photos and well illustrated articles.
Fees: In the region of £60 per published page.

ALL OUT CRICKET
Unit 3.23, Canterbury Court, Kennington Park Business Centre, 1-3 Brixton Road, London SE11 5SS.
Tel: 020 7820 4190. E-mail: aff@alloutcricket.co.uk
Editor: Andy Afford.
Official magazine of the Professional Cricketer's Association. Published 10 times a year.
Illustrations: Assignments available to shoot individual cricketers or teams for profiles – submit details of experience and areas covered by e-mail in the first instance. No scope for stock images, which are supplied via agency contract.
Text: Suggestions for profiles and features always considered.
Overall freelance potential: Fair.
Fees: By negotiation.

ATHLETICS WEEKLY
Athletics Weekly Ltd, PO Box 614, Farnham, Surrey GU9 1GR.
Tel: 01733 808550. Fax: 01733 808530.
E-mail: jason.henderson@athletics-weekly.com
Editor: Jason Henderson.
Weekly news magazine for the competitive and aspiring athlete. Focuses on events and results.
Illustrations: Coverage of athletics events at grass roots level, such as area championships, rather than top events (the latter are supplied by agency photographers). Always interested in anything out of the ordinary, such as well-known athletes off the track or in unusual situations.
Text: No scope.
Overall freelance potential: Fair.
Editor's tips: Freelances aware of what is happening locally can often obtain coverage missed by the nationals and agencies – top athletes "dropping in" to take part in local events etc.
Fees: According to size of reproduction, from £10 – £30. Published pictures frequently gain extra sales via reader requests.

BADMINTON
iSPORTgroup, No.4 The Spinney, Chester Road, Poynton, Cheshire SK12 1HB.
Tel: 07973 544719. E-mail: rachel.pullan@isportgroup.com
Editor: Rachel Pullan.
The only magazine in the UK devoted to badminton. Published quarterly.
Illustrations: Will consider good action coverage, sports fashion, health material.
Text: Little scope for writing on the sport itself, but may consider articles on sports fashion, health, fitness and diet. 750–1,000 words.
Overall freelance potential: Limited.
Fees: By agreement.

BOXING MONTHLY
Topwave Ltd, 40 Morpeth Road, London E9 7LD.
Tel: 020 8986 4141. Fax: 020 8986 4145. E-mail: mail@boxing-monthly.co.uk
Editor: Glyn Leach.
Heavily illustrated publication for boxing enthusiasts, covering both professional and amateur boxing.
Illustrations: B&W and colour. Coverage of boxing at all levels, including the amateur scene.
Text: Knowledgeable articles, features, interviews, etc. on any aspect of the boxing scene. Always contact the editor in the first instance.
Fees: By negotiation.

CLIMBER
Warners Group Publications plc, The Maltings, West Street, Bourne, Lincs PE10 9PH.
Tel: 01778 392425. Fax: 01778 394748. E-mail: andym@warnersgroup.co.uk
Editor: Andy McCue.
Monthly magazine dealing with world-wide climbing from Lakeland fells to Everest. Highly literate readership. Contributors range from "unknowns" to top climbers like Chris Bonington.
Illustrations: First ascents and newsworthy events but, in the main, used only with text. Covers: action shots of climbers or dramatic mountain pictures.
Text: Features on rock climbing, Alpinism, high altitude climbing, mountain skiing (not downhill racing). 1,500–2,000 words.
Overall freelance potential: Good; 90 per cent of articles and 100 per cent of pictures come from freelances, but many are regulars.
Editor's tips: This is a specialist field and is full of good writer/photographers. There is potential for the freelance to break in, but the magazine is heavily commissioned and usually well stocked with material.
Fees: Variable.

DARTS WORLD
World Magazines Ltd, 25 Orleston View, Ham Street, Ashford, Kent TN26 2LB.
Tel: 01233 733558. E-mail: mb.graphics@virgin.net
Editor: Michael Beeken.
Monthly magazine for darts players and organisers.
Illustrations: Pictures on any darts theme, action shots and portraits of leading players. Good material also required for the annual Darts Player.
Text: Features on all darts subjects.
Overall freelance potential: Most of the copy and pictures comes from freelances.
Editor's tips: The darts-playing environment is often dim and smoky, which can make it difficult to produce bright, interesting pictures. Photographers who can come up with colourful shots that catch the eye are welcomed.
Fees: Good, on a rising scale according to size of reproduction or length of feature.

DIVE
Dive International, 1 Victoria Villas, Richmond, Surrey TW9 2GW.
Tel: 020 8332 8401. Fax: 020 8332 9307. E-mail: simon@dive.uk.com
Editor: Simon Rogerson. **Art Editor:** Angela Finnegan.
Monthly magazine for divers and underwater enthusiasts.
Illustrations: Top-quality underwater photography, usually published within photojournalistic features. Most interested in material that tells a story and involves people, with images showing divers in action.
Text: Features as above.
Overall freelance potential: Excellent for underwater specialists.
Editor's tips: Good quality material from British waters stands a good chance of being published, as this is harder to find than that from clearer waters abroad.
Fees: £150 per published page.

F1 RACING
Haymarket Publishing Ltd, Teddington Studios, Broom Road, Teddington TW11 9BE.
Tel: 020 8267 5163. Fax: 020 8267 5022. E-mail: ross.stonefeld@haymarket.com
Editor: Hans Seeberg. **Picture Editor:** Ross Stonefeld.
Glossy monthly devoted to Formula One motor racing.
Illustrations: All coverage of Formula One, past and present; professionals with collections of

relevant material should send lists. Commissions available to experienced portrait and reportage photographers who can deliver high quality whatever the circumstances – contact picture editor by email .

Text: Will always consider ideas for any F1 related material, which should always be discussed with the editor before submission.

Overall freelance potential: Fair.

Editor's tips: Write or e-mail first, don't phone.

Fees: Set rates, from £60 minimum to £230 full page, £320 dps, £400 cover.

FIELDSPORTS

BPG (Stamford) Ltd, Roebuck House, 33 Broad Street, Stamford, Lincs PE9 1RB.

Tel: 01780 766199. Fax: 01780 754774. E-mail: m.barnes@bournepublishinggroup.co.uk

Editor: Mike Barnes.

Heavily-illustrated quarterly for the serious game shooter who also enjoys a spot of fishing in the summer months.

Illustrations: High-quality images depicting all aspects of game shooting and fishing, for general illustration purposes. Commissioned photography generally handled by regulars.

Text: Will consider illustrated articles from contributors who really know their subject and can write in depth with real enthusiasm.

Overall freelance potential: Fair.

Editor's tips: Readers are not casual sportsmen but people who spend heavily on the sport and have a real passion for it.

Fees: By negotiation.

FIGHTING FIT

Newsquest Specialist Media Ltd, 30 Cannon Street, London EC4M 6YJ.

Tel: 020 7618 3072. E-mail: tris.dixon@fightingfitmagazine.co.uk

Editor: Tris Dixon.

Monthly magazine covering boxing, martial arts, judo, taekwondo, karate and Thai boxing, focusing on health, nutrition and training techniques.

Illustrations: The magazine obtains most pictures from specialist agencies, but will always consider original material from freelance photographers.

Text: Will consider illustrated profiles and interviews with leading fighters. Also expert articles on strength, power, nutrition, fitness and psychology. Also gyms, product reviews and articles on trends in the industry. Submit suggestions via e-mail in the first instance.

Overall freelance potential: Good for those with the right connections or expertise.

Editor's tips:

Fees: Dependent on subject matter and the specialist expertise of the contributor.

FOURFOURTWO

Haymarket Publishing, Teddington Studios, Broom Road, Teddington, Middlesex TW11 9BE.

Tel: 020 8267 5339. Fax: 020 8267 5354. E-mail: jeff.beasley@haymarket.com

Editor: David Hall. **Picture Editor:** Jeff Beasley.

Monthly magazine aimed at the adult soccer fan.

Illustrations: Especially interested in exclusive or unusual shots of footballers and football people. Always interested to know of good stock collections, both current and historic. Commissions possible for photographers with at least some sports experience – submit samples of work via e-mail in the first instance.

Text: Some scope for specialists.

Overall freelance potential: Quite good but best for specialists.

Fees: According to size of reproduction. Text £100–£175 per 1,000 words.

GOLF MONTHLY
IPC Media Ltd, Blue Fin Building, 110 Southwark Street, London SE1 0SU.
Tel: 020 3148 5000. Fax: 020 3148 8130. E-mail: golfmonthly@ipcmedia.com
Editor: Michael Harris. **Art Editor:** Paul Duggan.
Monthly international consumer magazine for golfers.
Illustrations: Mainly for use as illustrations to articles. Small market for one-off pictures from golf tournaments of golf-related events.
Text: Illustrated features on instruction and other golf-related topics. Also in-depth profiles of leading world players. Around 2,000 words, but not critical.
Overall freelance potential: Most of the magazine is commissioned. Room for more material of the right type from freelances.
Editor's tips: This is an international magazine so material must have a wide appeal. No features of a parochial nature.
Fees: By agreement.

GOLF WORLD
Bauer Active Ltd, Media House, Lynchwood, Peterborough PE2 6EA.
Tel: 01733 468243. Fax: 01733 468001. E-mail: paul.ridley@bauermedia.co.uk
Editor: Chris Jones. **Art Director:** Paul Ridley.
Monthly publication for golfers, covering all aspects of the sport.
Illustrations: Unusual golfing pictures always of interest.
Text: Profiles of leading golfers and general or instructional features. 1,500–2,000 words.
Overall freelance potential: Around 20 per cent comes from freelance sources.
Fees: By agreement.

MARTIAL ARTS ILLUSTRATED
Martial Arts Ltd, Revenue Chambers, St Peter Street, Huddersfield, West Yorkshire HD1 1EL.
Tel: 01484 435011. Fax: 01484 422177. E-mail: martialartsltd@btconnect.com
Editor: Bob Sykes.
Monthly magazine covering all forms of Oriental fighting and self-defence techniques.
Illustrations: Will always consider single pictures or sets depicting well-known martial artists, club events, tournament action and aspects of technique.
Text: Well-illustrated articles on any relevant subject – profiles of leading figures and individual clubs, interviews, technique sequences and self-defence features.
Overall freelance potential: Excellent for those with access to the martial arts scene.
Editor's tips: Always write in the first instance with suggestions.
Fees: Should be negotiated before submission, as many contributions are supplied free of charge.

MATCH
Bauer Media, Media House, Lynchwood, Peterborough PE2 6EA.
Tel: 01733 468000. E-mail: james.bandy@bauermedia.co.uk
Editor: James Bandy.
Weekly publication for younger readers, looking at the whole spectrum of soccer. Aimed at the 8–16 age group.
Illustrations: Action shots all agency-supplied, but will consider unusual non-action images featuring top players. Usually bought only after consultation with the editor.
Text: Profiles and interviews concerning personalities in the soccer field. Length by arrangement.
Overall freelance potential: Limited – most is staff or agency produced.
Fees: By agreement.

Are you working from the latest edition of The Freelance Photographer's Market Handbook? It's published on 1 October each year. Markets are constantly changing, so it pays to have the latest edition

---

THE NON-LEAGUE PAPER
The Football Paper Ltd, Tuition House, St George's Road, Wimbledon, London SW19 4DS.
Tel: 020 8971 4333. Fax: 020 8971 4366. ISDN: 020 8605 2391.
E-mail: leaguenewsdesk@bhtmedia.com
Editor: David Emery. **News Editor:** John Lyons. **Picture Editor:** Sam Emery.
Weekly tabloid covering the non-League soccer scene, published every Sunday.
Illustrations: Digital files required. Always interested in hearing from capable football
photographers able to produce regular coverage of their local teams, but must have the
ability/facilities to send material direct via modem on the Saturday night. Submit details of
experience and area covered in the first instance.
Text: No scope – all staff or agency produced.
Overall freelance potential: Much is produced by freelance regulars but replacements are often
needed.
Fees: According to assignment and/or use.

RACING PIGEON PICTORIAL INTERNATIONAL
The Racing Pigeon Co Ltd, Unit G5, The Seedbed Centre, Wyncolls Road, Colchester, Essex
CO4 9HT.
Tel: 01206 843456. E-mail: racing123@btconnect.co.uk
Editor: Lee Fribbins.
Monthly magazine for pigeon fanciers. Provides in-depth articles on methods, successful fanciers,
scientific information, etc.
Illustrations: Pictures to illustrate features, plus some one-off pictures of pigeons, pigeon lofts,
pigeon fanciers and related subjects.
Text: Features on subjects as above, from contributors with serious knowledge of the sport. 1,500
words.
Overall freelance potential: Around 10–15 per cent of the pictures come from freelance
photographers. Articles are mostly by specialist writers.
Editor's tips: Short, colourful, exotic articles with good illustrations stand a reasonable chance.
Fees: £20 per published page minimum.

RUGBY WORLD
IPC Media Ltd, Blue Fin Building, 110 Southwark Street, London SE1 0SU.
Tel: 020 3148 4702. E-mail: kevin_eason@ipcmedia.com
Editor: Paul Morgan. **Art Editor:** Kevin Eason.
Britain's biggest selling monthly rugby magazine giving general coverage of Rugby Union.
Illustrations: Main scope is for regional/local coverage, since the top level matches are covered by
regulars. Photographs of Cup matches, County championships, personalities, off-beat shots, etc.
Covers: Good action shots of top players.
Text: Good articles with different angles are always of interest.
Overall freelance potential: Dependent on quality and appeal.
Fees: On a rising scale according to size of reproduction or length of text.

RUNNER'S WORLD
Natmag-Rodale, 6th Floor, 33 Broadwick Street, London W1F 0DQ.
Tel: 020 7339 4409. Fax: 020 7339 4420. E-mail: russell.fairbrother@natmag-rodale.co.uk
Editor: Andy Dixon. **Art Editor:** Russell Fairbrother.
Monthly publication for running enthusiasts.
Illustrations: Pictures relating to sports, recreational and fitness running. Consult art editor before
submitting.
Text: Feature material considered, but only by prior consultation with the editor.
Overall freelance potential: Fair.
Fees: By agreement.

RUNNING FITNESS

Kelsey Publishing, 14 Priestgate, Peterborough PE1 1JA.
Tel: 01733 347559. Fax: 01733 891342. E-mail: rf.ed@kelseypb.co.uk
Editor: David Castle.
Monthly magazine for active running enthusiasts, those who run for health or recreation.
Illustrations: Coverage of competitions and running events at local or regional level, off-beat pictures, and general stock shots of runners. Both racing and training pictures are welcome. Some scope for general atmospheric pictures incorporating runners and athletic-looking subjects in picturesque and inspirational settings. Possible commission scope for "fashion" features. Covers: usually by commission – interested in hearing from photographers who can bring a creative approach to the subject.
Text: Illustrated articles of a practical nature, giving advice on training, diet, etc., and on unusual or exciting running events worldwide 1,000–1,500 words. Features of an inspirational nature also welcome – well-written and illustrated pieces on elite athletes, or other sportspeople who run as part of their training. Discuss ideas with the editor first.
Overall freelance potential: Good.
Fees: From a minimum of £20 up to £80 for a full page; text £70 per 1,000 words.

SGB UK

Datateam Publishing Ltd, London Road, Maidstone ME16 8LY.
Tel: 01622 699140. Fax: 01622 757646. E-mail: rknowles@datateam.co.uk
Editor: Rebecca Knowles.
Monthly magazine for the UK sports retail trade.
Illustrations: Topical pictures concerning the retail trade, usually to illustrate specific news stories, features and new products.
Text: Illustrated features and news stories on anything to do with the sports retail industry, including manufacturer and retailer profiles etc.
Overall freelance potential: Limited.
Fees: Text, £150 per 1,000 words; pictures by negotiation.

THE SCOTTISH SPORTING GAZETTE

BPG (Stamford) Ltd, Roebuck House, 33 Broad Street, Stamford, Lincs PE9 1RB.
Tel: 01780 766199. Fax: 01780 766416. E-mail: m.barnes@bournepublishinggroup.co.uk
Editor: Mike Barnes.
Annual publication to market Scottish shooting, fishing, stalking and allied services. Aimed at the upper income bracket in the UK, Europe and America.
Illustrations: Digital files preferred. High quality scenic photography, plus pictures of shooting, fishing, stalking, live game animals, whisky production, antique Scottish weapons, tartans, castles and hunting lodges. Covers: exceptional colour pictures of game animals or action sporting shots.
Text: Features on shooting, fishing and stalking in Scotland or articles on other topics that are particularly Scottish, as above. 600–2,000 words.
Overall freelance potential: Good.
Editor's tips: Pictures and text must be unusual, not the normal anecdotes associated with this field. Material should have a good Scottish flavour. It does not have to be essentially sporting, but should be allied in some way.
Fees: Open to negotiation.

THE SHOOTING GAZETTE

IPC Country & Leisure Media. Editorial: PO Box 225, Stamford, Lincolnshire PE9 2HS.
Tel: 01780 485350. Fax: 01780 754774. E-mail: will_hetherington@ipcmedia.com
Editor: Will Hetherington.

Britain's only monthly magazine covering exclusively game and rough shooting, wildlife, countryside.

Illustrations: Pictures for general illustration, including countryside scenes, hunting, shooting, fishing, farming, birds and animals – quarry and non-quarry species.

Text: Well-illustrated articles from those with specialist knowledge, and profiles or interviews. Up to 2,000 words.

Overall freelance potential: Good.

Fees: By negotiation.

SHOOTING TIMES AND COUNTRY MAGAZINE

IPC Media Ltd, Blue Fin Building, 110 Southwark Street, London SE1 0SU.

Tel: 020 3148 4741. Fax: 020 3148 8104. E-mail: steditorial@ipcmedia.com

Editor: Alastair Balmain .

Weekly magazine concentrating on all aspects of quarry shooting (game, pigeon, rough shooting, wildfowling and stalking). Also covers clay shooting, other fieldsports and general country topics.

Illustrations: Good photographs of shooting subjects plus gundogs, wildlife, rural crafts, country food. Some scope for good generic photographs of British counties, showing known landmarks. Covers: shots should be vertical in shape with room for title at the top.

Text: Illustrated features on all aspects of quarry shooting and general country topics as above. In the region of 900 words.

Overall freelance potential: Excellent; plenty of scope for new contributors.

Editor's tips: The magazine likes to keep pictures on file as it is not always possible to know in advance when a picture can be used. For features, remember that the readers are real country people.

Fees: Pictures £10–£60 according to size; covers £70–£90. Features £40 per 500 words.

SKI + BOARD

Ski Club of Great Britain Ltd, The White House, 57-63 Church Road, Wimbledon Village, London SW19 5SB.

Tel: 0845 4580780. Fax: 0845 4580781. E-mail: editor@skiclub.co.uk

Editor: Arnie Wilson.

Published four times a year. Official magazine of Ski Club of Great Britain, covering the sport at all levels.

Illustrations: Pictures for general illustration and for special gallery section, including holiday skiing, ski-touring, racing and equipment, good adventure/action shots, shots illustrating snowcraft and particular techniques. Also good, attractive pictures of specific ski resorts and ski slopes in season.

Text: Very interested in adventure skiing articles, especially with a good selection of images.

Overall freelance potential: Fair.

Fees: By arrangement.

THE SKIER & SNOWBOARDER MAGAZINE

Mountain Marketing Ltd, PO Box 386, Sevenoaks, Kent TN13 1AQ.

Tel: 0845 310 8303. E-mail: frank.baldwin@skierandsnowboarder.co.uk

Editor: Frank Baldwin.

Published five times a year: July, Sep/Oct, Nov/Dec, Jan/Feb, Mar/Apr. Covers all aspects of skiing and snowboarding.

Illustrations: Good action pictures and anything spectacular, odd or humorous that summons up the spirit of skiing. Also a special "Photo File" section in which photographers can submit up to three favourite shots backed by text which tells the reader about the set-ups/techniques used, linked with a short biog of the photographer.

Text: Original ideas for illustrated features always welcome. Possible scope for resort reports and news items.
Overall freelance potential: Very good.
Fees: By negotiation.

SNOOKER SCENE
Hayley Green Court, 130 Hagley Road, Hayley Green, Halesowen B63 1DY.
Tel: 0121 585 9188. Fax: 0121 585 7117. E-mail: clive.everton@talk21.com
Editor: Clive Everton.
Monthly publication for snooker players and enthusiasts.
Illustrations: Snooker action pictures and coverage related to tournaments, or material of historical interest.
Text: Features on snooker and billiards. 250–1,000 words.
Overall freelance potential: Small.
Fees: By arrangement.

SPIN
WW Magazines Ltd. Editorial: Sunnyhill House, 3/7 Sunnyhill Road, London SW16 2UG.
Tel: 020 8696 6200. E-mail: editors@spincricket.com
Editor: Duncan Steer.
Monthly cricket magazine focusing on the game at international level. Aims for a modern and youthful approach to the sport.
Illustrations: No scope for match coverage, but keen to see material documenting the lifestyle and culture that exists around the game, especially anything exotic or unusual that is rarely seen. Also interested in hearing from freelances who can supply top quality photo essays and stories on other aspects of the sport.
Text: Text with pictures is welcomed, but should be kept short and snappy in tabloid style.
Overall freelance potential: Good opportunities for unusual cricket coverage.
Fees: By negotiation.

SPORTING SHOOTER
Archant Specialist, Jubilee House, 2 Jubilee Place, London SW3 3TQ.
Tel: 020 7751 4917. E-mail: james@sportingshooter.co.uk
Editor: James Marchington.
Monthly aimed at sports shooters and gamekeepers.
Illustrations: Will consider good stock images depicting pigeon, clay and pheasant shooting, deer stalking, gun dogs, gamekeeping and relevant wildlife. Some commissions possible to photograph specific features.
Text: also very interested in illustrated articles on shooting topics
Overall freelance potential: Good.
Editor's tips: The magazine has a very specific style so always call to discuss ideas first.
Fees: By negotiation.

SWIMMING TIMES
Pavilion 3, SportPark, 3 Oakwood Drive, Loughborough, Leics LE11 3QF.
Tel: 01509 640230. Fax: 01509 640191. E-mail: swimmingtimes@swimming.org
Editor: Peter Hassall.
Official monthly magazine of the Amateur Swimming Association and Institute of Swimming. Covers all aspects of swimming including diving, synchro-swimming, water polo, etc.
Illustrations: News pictures of swimmers at major events and any off-beat or particularly

interesting shots of swimming-related activity.
Text: Human interest stories about individual swimmers.
Overall freelance potential: Limited.
Fees: Negotiable.

TODAY'S GOLFER
Bauer Media, Media House, Lynchwood, Peterborough PE2 6EA.
Tel: 01733 468000. Fax: 01733 468843. E-mail: andy.calton@bauermedia.co.uk
Editor-in-Chief: Andy Calton.
Monthly for golfing enthusiasts.
Illustrations: Stock shots of leading players and courses, and anything off-beat, considered on spec.
Text: Instructional material; player profiles; equipment features; course tests.
Overall freelance potential: Limited.
Fees: By negotiation.

THE WISDEN CRICKETER
Wisden Cricketer Publishing Ltd, 2nd Floor, 123 Buckingham Palace Road, London SW1W 9SL.
Tel: 020 7705 4911. E-mail: twc@wisdencricketer.com
Editor: John Stern. **Art Director:** Nigel Davies.
Monthly publication aimed at all cricket lovers. Concentrates on the game at first-class and especially international level.
Illustrations: Exceptional photographs of the above always considered.
Text: Scope for exclusive news stories and features. But check first before submitting. 400–2,500 words.
Overall freelance potential: Fair.
Fees: On a rising scale according to size of pictures or length and significance of article.

Trade

AM
Bauer Automotive Ltd, Media House, Lynchwood, Peterborough PE2 6EA.
Tel: 01733 468261. Fax: 01733 468350. E-mail: jeremy.bennett@bauermedia.co.uk
Editor: Jeremy Bennett.
Fortnightly publication for the motor industry, mainly franchised dealers.
Illustrations: News photographs covering the motor trade generally. Some scope for commissions to photograph industry figures and premises.
Text: News items and news features of interest to industry executives.
Overall freelance potential: Good for those with contacts in the trade and local freelances.
Fees: By negotiation.

THE BOOKSELLER
The Bookseller Media Ltd, 5th Floor, Endeavour House, 189 Shaftesbury Avenue, London WC2H 8TJ.
Tel: 020 7420 6006. Fax: 020 7420 6103. E-mail: neill.denny@bookseller.co.uk
Editor-in-Chief: Neill Denny.
Weekly trade magazine for booksellers, publishers, librarians and anyone involved in the book industry. Covers trade trends and events, authors, etc.
Illustrations: Pictures of bookshops and book-related activities outside London. Busy book fairs, busy book shops, etc. Portraits of authors and book trade figures.

Text: Serious, humorous, analytical, descriptive articles connected with the book trade, plus author interviews.
Overall freelance potential: Only for those freelances who have good access to the book trade.
Fees: Variable; depends on material.

BRITISH BAKER

William Reed Publishing, Broadfield Park, Crawley, West Sussex RH11 9RT.
Tel: 01293 846595. Fax: 01293 846538. E-mail: sylvia.macdonald@william-reed.co.uk
Editor: Sylvia Macdonald.
Fortnightly business-to-business news magazine covering the entire baking industry.
Illustrations: Interesting photographs relating to working bakeries, especially news items such as shop openings, promotions, charity events, etc. Also good stock shots of bakery products.
Text: Short news stories (300 words) or features (500–1,000 words) on any baking industry topic.
Overall freelance potential: Fair, for those who can supply relevant material.
Fees: £125 per 1,000 words for text; photographs by negotiation.

CABINET MAKER

Manning Publishing Ltd, The Irwin Centre, Scotland Road, Dry Drayton, Cambridge CB23 8AR.
Tel: 01954 212906. Fax: 01954 212105. E-mail: info@cabinet-maker.co.uk
Features **Editor:** James Dickson. News **Editor:** Katie Matthews.
Weekly publication for all those in the furniture and furnishing trade and industry.
Illustrations: Freelances commissioned to cover news assignments in the trade. Some scope for pictures to illustrate features.
Text: Features about companies making furniture for sale to retailers and interior designers.
Overall freelance potential: Around 10 per cent contributed, including news coverage.
Editor's tips: Approach the editor for a brief before submitting.
Fees: By agreement.

CATERER & HOTELKEEPER

Reed Business Information Ltd, Quadrant House, The Quadrant, Sutton, Surrey SM2 5AS.
Tel: 020 8652 4210. Fax: 020 8652 8973. E-mail: mark.lewis@rbi.co.uk
Editor: Mark Lewis. **Art Editor:** Chris Russell. Picture Librarian: Sue Hockins.
Weekly magazine for the hotel and catering trade.
Illustrations: News pictures relevant to hotel and catering establishments – openings, extensions, refurbishments, people, etc. Special interest in regional material. Commissions possible to cover establishments, equipment and food.
Text: Specialist articles of interest to the trade, by commission only.
Overall freelance potential: Mainly limited to those with connections within the trade.
Editor's tips: Also welcomes tip-offs concerning the industry, for which a fee of £15–£25 is paid.
Fees: On a rising scale according to size of reproduction or length of text.

CHEMIST AND DRUGGIST

CMP Information Ltd, Riverbank House, Angel Lane, Tonbridge TN9 1SE.
Tel: 01732 377487. Fax: 01732 367065. E-mail: chemdrug@cmpinformation.com
Editor: Gary Paragpuri.
Weekly news publication for retail pharmacists; the pharmaceutical, toiletries and cosmetics industries; pharmaceutical wholesalers, etc.
Illustrations: B&W and colour. Digital files preferred. News pictures concerning individual retailers and retailing related events, plus industry events relating to pharmaceutical companies.
Text: Local news stories relating to community pharmacy.
Overall freelance potential: Limited.
Fees: On a rising scale, according to contribution.

CONTAINERISATION INTERNATIONAL
Informa UK Ltd, 69-77 Paul Street, London EC2A 4LQ.
Tel: 020 7017 4820. Fax: 020 7017 4976. E-mail: john.fossey@informa.com
Editor: John Fossey. **Art Editor:** Ralph Murray.
Monthly business-oriented magazine on issues facing the international container transport industry.
Illustrations: Unusual pictures of container shipping activities, especially in exotic locations overseas, or interesting/amusing uses for containers.
Text: Well-researched and exclusive articles, preferably on some aspect of the container transport business not covered by staff writers. Around 2,000 words.
Overall freelance potential: Limited.
Fees: By agreement.

CONVENIENCE STORE
William Reed Ltd, Broadfield Park, Crawley, West Sussex RH11 9RT.
Tel: 01293 613400. Fax: 01293 610330. E-mail: david.rees@william-reed.co.uk
Editor: David Rees.
Fortnightly magazine for independent neighbourhood retailers and convenience stores, and their wholesale suppliers.
Illustrations: Photographs usually to illustrate specific features; little scope for pictures on their own.
Text: Illustrated features or stories concerning late-night, local, food-based stores. Should ideally feature a retailer who is doing something a bit different, or who has been highly successful in some way.
Overall freelance potential: Modest.
Fees: By negotiation.

DRAPERS
EMAP Ltd, Greater London House, Hampstead Road, London NW1 7EJ.
Tel: 020 7728 5000. E-mail: jessica.price-brown@emap.com
Editor: Jessica Price-Brown. **Art Editor:** Alison Fisher.
Weekly news publication for clothing and textile retailers.
Illustrations: News pictures of interest to the clothing and fashion trade. Some scope for portraits and fashion shoots by commission.
Text: Features, fashion and news items of relevance to retailers in the fashion and textile fields.
Overall freelance potential: Limited for news; fair for commissioned work.
Editor's tips: Do not send unsolicited material – call the art editor first.
Fees: Good; on a rising scale according to size of illustration or length of feature.

EUROFRUIT MAGAZINE
Market Intelligence Ltd, 4th Floor, Market Towers, One Nine Elms Lane, London SW8 5NQ.
Tel: 020 7501 3700. Fax: 020 7498 6472. E-mail: michael@fruitnet.com
Editor: Mike Knowles.
Monthly magazine of the European fresh fruit and vegetable trade. Aimed at producers, exporters, importers, merchants and buyers.
Illustrations: Subjects such as harvesting fruit, loading on to ships or lorries, quality checks on fruit, packing etc. Photographs accepted mostly for the magazine's own picture library.
Text: Topical features on fruit and vegetables, e.g. Chilean apples in Europe, French Iceberg lettuce, Egypt's expanding export range, Norway as an alternative market, etc. 1,250–2,000 words.
Overall freelance potential: Quite good. Some regular contributors, but scope for the freelance writer who can also supply pictures.
Editor's tips: It is best to work in close contact with the editorial department to get names of people who would be of interest to the publication.
Fees: Negotiable.

FISHING NEWS/FISHING NEWS INTERNATIONAL

IntraFish Media, 6th Floor, Eldon House, 2 Eldon Street, London EC2M 7LS.
Tel: 020 7650 1030. Fax: 020 7650 1050. E-mail: cormac.burke@intrafish.com
Editor: Cormac Burke.
Fishing News is a weekly newspaper for the commercial fishing industry in Britain and Ireland.
Fishing News International is the leading monthly newspaper for the global commercial fishing
industry.
Illustrations: Captioned news pictures covering any subject relating to the UK/Irish and
international commercial fishing industries.
Text: Illustrated news stories always considered.
Overall freelance potential: Very good; a lot of photographs are used.
Fees: Standard £25 per picture.

THE FLORIST & WHOLESALE BUYER

Wordhouse Publishing Group Ltd, 68 First Avenue, Mortlake, London SW14 8SR.
Tel: 020 8939 6470. Fax: 020 8878 9983. E-mail: info@thewordhouse.co.uk
Editor: Austin Clark.
Publication for retail florists, published 10 times a year.
Illustrations: News pictures about the trade and other interesting pictures of floristry in the retail
context, i.e. special displays, promotions, etc.
Text: Features on anything relating to floristry and retailing, shop profiles, practical aspects,
advertising and promotion, etc.
Overall freelance potential: Limited.
Fees: Text, £150 per 1,000 words published; pictures by agreement.

FOOD TRADER FOR BUTCHERS

National Federation of Meat & Food Traders, 1 Belgrove, Tunbridge Wells, Kent TN1 1YW.
Tel: 01892 541412. Fax: 01892 535462. E-mail: info@nfmft.co.uk
Editor: Jayne Cottrell.
Official magazine of the National Federation of Meat & Food Traders. Published 10 times a year.
Illustrations: Topical pictures related to news and issues in the meat and related food industry.
Text: Topical features on the food industry, primarily the meat trade. Up to 2,000 words.
Overall freelance potential: Fair for those in close contact with the trade.
Editor's tips: Only exclusive material will be considered.
Fees: By negotiation.

FORECOURT TRADER

William Reed Publishing Ltd, Broadfield Park, Crawley, West Sussex RH11 9RT.
Tel: 01293 610219. Fax: 01293 610330. E-mail: merril.boulton@william-reed.co.uk
Editor: Merril Bolton.
Monthly magazine for petrol station operators.
Illustrations: News pictures relating to petrol stations and the petrol sales business generally.
Text: News and features relating to all areas of petrol retailing.
Overall freelance potential: Fair.
Fees: Text, £120 per 1,000 words; pictures according to use.

FORESTRY JOURNAL

PO Box 7570, Dumfries DG2 8YD.
Tel/fax: 01387 702272. E-mail: editor@forestryjournal.co.uk
Editor: Mark Andrews.
Monthly magazine covering all aspects of forestry and timber production – arboriculture, estate
management, harvesting, haulage, and recreational use of forests and woodland.
Illustrations: Plenty of photographs used, but usually only as accompaniment to features on topics
as above/below.

Text: Always seeking freelances to produce well-illustrated local stories on forestry topics, and for profiles of individual contractors etc. Write or e-mail the editor with suggestions and/or details of areas covered.
Overall freelance potential: Good for complete illustrated features.
Fees: £150 per published page.

INDEPENDENT RETAIL NEWS
Metropolis Business Publishing, 6th Floor Davis House, 2 Robert Street, Croydon, CR0 1QQ.
Tel: 020 8253 8704. Fax: 01322 616375. E-mail: david.shrimpton@metropolis.co.uk
Editor: David Shrimpton.
Fortnightly publication for independent, convenience, licensed and CTN retailers. Assists them in being more profitable and aware of new products and campaigns.
Illustrations: Captioned news pictures and picture stories of interest to independent grocery and convenience store traders. Stock images to illustrate people buying goods in independent/corner stores, retail crime, under-age sales, bootlegging, national lottery sales, etc.
Text: Articles and stories relevant to small retailers.
Overall freelance potential: Fair.
Editor's tips: A sample copy of the magazine is available to potential contributors. Always phone first with ideas.
Fees: Photographs according to how sourced, but up to £150 for features and £50-£100 for news stories. For commissioned features £170 per 1,000 words and negotiable for news stories.

MEAT TRADES JOURNAL
William Reed Ltd, Broadfield Park, Crawley, West Sussex RH11 9RT.
Tel: 01293 846567. Fax: 01293 610330. E-mail: ed.bedington@william-reed.co.uk
Editor: Ed Bedington.
Fortnightly journal for the whole meat and poultry trade.
Illustrations: Pictures relating to any current meat trade issue, including legislation, food scares, court cases, etc.
Text: Stories on current issues as above. Illustrated features on current food issues, research, technology, and profiles of individual businesses.
Overall freelance potential: Good for those in a position to cover this industry.
Editor's tips: It is much preferred if material offered is exclusive.
Fees: Negotiable, according to use.

PET PRODUCT MARKETING
Bauer Active Ltd, Media House, Lynchwood, Peterborough PE2 6EA.
Tel: 01733 468000. E-mail: sandra.pearce@bauermedia.co.uk
Editor in Chief: Matt Clarke.
Monthly publication for the pet trade, supplying information about new products, pet market news and business advice.
Illustrations: Will consider high-quality portfolios of common pets, companion animals and exotic pet species, including portrait or action shots.
Text: Will consider features written by those with experience in the pet trade.
Fees: Negotiable.

WORLD FISHING
Mercator Media Limited, The Old Mill, Lower Quay, Fareham, Hampshire PO16 0RA.
Tel: 01329 825335. Fax: 01329 825330. E-mail: cwills@worldfishing.net
Editor: Carly Wills.
Monthly journal for the commercial fishing industry. Covers fisheries and related industries from an

international perspective.

Illustrations: Mainly to accompany specific articles, but some scope for scene-setting shots of commercial fishing activity in specific locations worldwide.

Text: Illustrated articles on any commercial fishing topic. Should always contain some international interest. Maximum 1,500 words.

Overall freelance potential: Good for those with connections in the industry.

Fees: By negotiation.

Transport

COACH AND BUS WEEK

Rouncy Media Ltd, 3 The Office Village, Cygnet Park, Peterborough PE7 8GX.

Tel: 01733 293240. Fax: 0845 2802927. E-mail: andrew.sutcliffe@rouncymedia.co.uk

Editorial Director: Andrew Sutcliffe. News Reporter: Gareth Evans. Editor, 'Out & About': Bernard Horton. Editor, 'Minibus': Martin Cole.

Weekly news magazine covering coach and bus operations. Aimed at licensed coach, bus and tour operators. Includes monthly supplements 'Out & About', containing tourism information for drivers and tour organisers, and 'Minibus' for minibus operators.

Illustrations: Pictures as illustrations to features mentioned below; coach and bus related news items. Places of interest to coach parties.

Text: Features on coach and bus operators, hotels, ferry operations, resorts and venues, anything that would be of interest to a coach party or an operator. Articles on subjects that an operator might find useful in their day-to-day business. Up to 1,000 words.

Overall freelance potential: Always interested in seeing work from freelances.

Fees: By negotiation.

COMMERCIAL MOTOR

Reed Business Information Ltd, Quadrant House, The Quadrant, Sutton, Surrey SM2 5AS.

Tel: 020 8652 3500. Fax: 020 8652 8969. E-mail: justin.stanton@rbi.co.uk

Editor: Justin Stanton.

Weekly publication devoted to the road haulage industry. Aimed at vehicle enthusiasts as well as industry readers.

Illustrations: Mostly commissioned; arrange to show portfolio to the art editor first. Possible interest in professional stock photographs of commercial vehicles and aspects of road haulage – send lists of subjects available.

Text: Technical articles on road haulage topics, from expert contributors only.

Overall freelance potential: Only for experienced contributors.

Fees: Day rate around £250–£300 plus expenses. Other material by negotiation.

OLD GLORY

Mortons Media Group Ltd, PO Box 43, Horncastle, Lincs LN9 6JR.

Tel: 01507 529306. Fax: 01507 529301. E-mail: ctyson@mortons.co.uk

Editor: Colin Tyson.

Monthly devoted to industrial/commercial transport and machinery heritage and vintage restoration including traction engines, tractors, etc.

Illustrations: Pictures of all forms of traction engines, tractors, buses, commercial vehicles, fairground machinery and maritime subjects such as old steamboats. News pictures of individual machines, restoration projects, etc. Detailed captions necessary including where and when picture taken. Covers: colourful pictures of traction engines in attractive settings.

Text: Illustrated articles on subjects as above.

Overall freelance potential: A lot of scope for good colour material.

Fees: Pictures £20–£75 dependent on size used.

ROADWAY
Roadway House, 35 Monument Hill, Weybridge, Surrey KT13 8RN.
Tel: 01932 838922. E-mail: roadway@rha.uk.net
Editor: Caroline Bullock.
Monthly news magazine for the road haulage industry. Official magazine of the Road Haulage Association.
Illustrations: Pictures of trucks on motorways, at depots etc. Should be newsworthy or of unusual interest.
Text: Articles on any aspect of the road haulage industry. Length by prior agreement with the editor.
Overall freelance potential: Limited.
Fees: By arrangement.

TOWPATH TALK
Mortons Media Group Ltd, Media Centre, Morton Way, Horncastle, Lincs LN9 6JR.
Tel: 01507 523456. E-mail: jrichardson@mortons.co.uk
Editor: Janet Richardson.
Specialist monthly newspaper covering all aspects of Britain's waterways.
Illustrations: News pictures and picture stories relevant to all forms of waterways and towpath use, including boating, cycling, horse riding, angling or walking.
Text: Will consider news stories and features on anything concerning the UK's waterways, such as the environment, canal restoration and heritage. Also specialist articles on technical matters such as engine maintenance and boat care.
Overall freelance potential: Good.
Fees: According to use.

TRACTOR
Mortons Media Group Ltd, Media Centre, Morton Way, Horncastle, Lincs LN9 6JR.
Tel: 01507 529304. Fax: 01507 529495. E-mail: thoyland@mortons.co.uk
Editor: Tony Hoyland.
Monthly magazine celebrating the farm tractor and its development.
Illustrations: Mainly colour; archive B&W. Images of interesting classic or vintage tractors, restoration projects, tractor rallies and events. Detailed captions about individual machines and their history always essential. Also archive pictures depicting farm life and machinery from WW1 to the 1960s.
Text: Well-illustrated articles on relevant subjects always considered.
Overall freelance potential: Very good.
Fees: By negotiation.

TRACTOR & MACHINERY
Kelsey Publishing Group, Cudham Tithe Barn, Berry's Hill, Cudham, Kent TN16 3AG.
Tel: 01959 541444. Fax: 01959 541400. E-mail: martin.oldaker@kelsey.co.uk
Editor: Martin Oldaker.
Monthly magazine for tractor enthusiasts, covering classic, vintage and contemporary machines from all parts of the world.
Illustrations: Pictures of tractors in the news, classic and vintage gatherings, unusual and interesting tractors, and related machinery. Captions must include details of type, model and year of tractor and name of driver. Contact editor before preparing a submission.
Text: Those who can add words to their images are welcomed.
Overall freelance potential: Good.
Fees: By arrangement.

TRUCK & DRIVER
Reed Business Information, Quadrant House, The Quadrant, Sutton, Surrey SM2 5AS.
Tel: 020 8652 3500. Fax: 020 8652 8988. E-mail: will.shiers@rbi.co.uk
Editor: Will Shiers.
Monthly magazine for truck drivers.
Illustrations: Interesting individual trucks, unusual situations involving drivers and their vehicles, news items and some studio work.
Text: Commissioned features on anything of interest to truck drivers. Looks for freelances with ideas.
Overall freelance potential: Very good.
Fees: By negotiation.

Travel

AUSTRALIA & NEW ZEALAND
Evolve Digital Publishing Ltd, Unit 3, The Old Estate Yard, North Stoke Lane, Upton Cheyney, Bristol BS30 6ND.
Tel: 0117 932 3586. E-mail: leanne.voisey@edpltd.co.uk
Editor: Leanne Voisey.
Monthly magazine aimed at both holidaymakers and migrants.
Illustrations: Very limited scope for photography on its own as much is sourced from the travel and migration trade. Pictures only required as part of complete feature packages as below, or possibly for covers which usually feature action shots of people on beaches.
Text: Well-illustrated features of around 1,200 – 2,000 words. Real-life stories of those who have emigrated to Australia or NZ, plus coverage of specific locations, cities, activities, food and culture. Should have wide rather than niche appeal. Submit ideas only in the first instance, along with examples of previous work.
Overall freelance potential: Good for experienced travel freelances who can provide the complete package.
Editor's tips: Looking for material that strikes a good balance between inspiration and information.
Fees: Up to £200 for cover images. Features £180 per 1,000 words inclusive of pictures.

BUSINESS TRAVELLER
Panacea Publishing International Ltd, 2nd Floor, Cardinal House, Albemarle Street, London W1S 4TE.
Tel: 020 7647 6330. Fax: 020 7647 6331. E-mail: editorial@businesstraveller.com
Editor: Tom Otley. **Art Editor:** Annie Harris.
Monthly consumer publication aimed at the frequently travelling international and domestic business executive.
Illustrations: Pictures to illustrate destination features on a wide variety of cities around the world – request features list of upcoming destinations.
Text: Illustrated features on business travel, but only by prior consultation with the editor.
Overall freelance potential: Around 65 per cent of the magazine is contributed by freelances.
Editor's tips: Submit low-res digital or dupes in the first instance.
Fees: Pictures from £50 up to £180 for a full page; covers £250. Text, £200 per 1,000 words.

CONDE NAST TRAVELLER
The Condé Nast Publications Ltd, Vogue House, Hanover Square, London W1S 1JU.
Tel: 020 7499 9080. Fax: 020 7493 3758. E-mail: cntraveller@condenast.co.uk

Editor: Sarah Miller. **Director of Photography:** Caroline Metcalfe.
Heavily-illustrated glossy monthly for the discerning, independent traveller.
Illustrations: Colour and occasional B&W. Top quality photo-feature material covering all aspects of travel, from luxury hotels and food, restaurant interiors to adventure travel, ecological issues, and reportage, etc. Very stylish and striking B&W photography also sought. Always interested in hearing from experienced photographers who are planning specific trips.
Text: Mostly commissioned from top name writers.
Overall freelance potential: Very good for material of the highest quality.
Editor's tips: The magazine seeks to use material with an original approach. Particularly interested in hearing from photographers who can produce excellent work but who are not necessarily travel specialists.
Fees: Variable depending on what is offered, but top rates paid for suitable material.

FOOD AND TRAVEL
Green Pea Publishing, Suite 51, The Business Centre, Ingate Place, Queenstown Road, London SW8 3NS.
Tel: 020 7501 0511. E-mail: edits@foodandtravel.com
Editor: TBA. **Creative Director:** Angela Dukes.
Up-market monthly for affluent people interested in food, wine and travel.
Illustrations: High quality food and travel photography, invariably produced on commission. Specialist photographers are advised to contact the creative director with details of experience and ideas. No scope for travel stock material since most is commissioned.
Text: Ideas for articles always considered, but invariably produced on commission by specialist writers.
Overall freelance potential: Good for specialists; better for travel than for food.
Fees: By negotiation.

FRANCE
Archant House, Oriel Road, Cheltenham, Gloucestershire GL50 1BB.
Tel: 01242 216050. Fax: 01242 216094. E-mail: editorial@francemag.com
Editor: Carolyn Boyd. **Art Editor:** Adam Vines.
Monthly magazine for Francophiles, with the emphasis on the real France.
Illustrations: Picture stories, and top quality individual pictures to illustrate articles, on French regions, annual events, cuisine, travel, arts and history. Covers: pictures that capture the essence of France. Photographs also required for annual calendar – selected early in each new year.
Text: Lively and colourful illustrated features on the life, culture and history of France. Normally around 1,200 words, but up to 2,000 words considered. Factual accuracy essential.
Overall freelance potential: Good for top quality material but much supplied by regular writers.
Editor's tips: E-mail with outlines/summary before submitting material. Features list fills 6-12 months in advance.
Fees: Photographs from £25 up to £100 for cover or DPS. £100 per 1,000 words.

FRENCH MAGAZINE
Horizon New Media,12 George Street, Bath BA1 2EH.
Tel: 01225 329381. E-mail: justin@horizonnewmedia.com
Editor: Justin Postlethwaite.
Monthly magazine for regular travellers to France and those with, or seeking, property there.
Illustrations: Digital files preferred. Typical French images for general illustration purposes –

Are you working from the latest edition of The Freelance Photographer's Market Handbook? It's published on 1 October each year. Markets are constantly changing, so it pays to have the latest edition

---

historic sites, vineyards, food/restaurants, activities, and homes and interiors etc. Submit lists of subjects available in the first instance. Commissions may be available to photographers with medium format or high-end digital equipment.
Text: Well-illustrated articles always welcomed, especially on gastronomy, buying property and regional features. Around 1,500 words plus 8-10 illustrations.
Overall freelance potential: Excellent.
Fees: Single pictures according to use; features from £150 per 1,000 words; packages negotiable.

GEOGRAPHICAL
Circle Publishing, One Victoria Villas, Richmond, Surrey TW9 2GW.
Tel: 020 8332 2713. Fax: 020 8332 9307. E-mail: magazine@geographical.co.uk
Editor: Geordie Torr. **Art Director:** Liz Fensome.
Monthly magazine of the Royal Geographical Society. Covers a wide spread of topics including travel, culture, environment, wildlife, conservation, history and exploration.
Illustrations: Mainly looking for photo-stories on geographical topics – human, political, ecological, economic and physical. Relevant news pictures always considered.
Text: Well-illustrated articles on any geographical subject, written in an informative but accessible way. Feature proposals should be sent to proposals@geographical.co.uk in the form of a 150-200 word synopsis.
Overall freelance potential: Excellent for the right type of material.
Fees: Negotiable, but in the region of £100 per published page. Single pictures according to use.

ITALIA!
Anthem Publishing Limited, Suite 6, Picadilly House, London Road, Bath BA1 3PL.
Tel: 01225 489984. Fax: 01225 489980. E-mail: debra.hughes@anthem-publishing.com
Editor: Amanda Robinson. **Art Editor:** Debra Hughes.
Highly-pictorial monthly covering regional travel and property in Italy. Also has sister-title Taste Italia focusing on Italian food and drink.
Illustrations: Happy to hear from photographers, particularly those based in or regularly visiting Italy, and those with large collections of existing images. Pictures used mainly scenic/landscape and people/local colour images.
Text: little scope as the magazine generates most topics in-house and commissions from known writers.
Overall freelance potential: Fair.
Fees: By negotiation.

LIVING FRANCE
Archant Life, Archant House, Oriel Road, Cheltenham GL50 1BB.
Tel: 01242 216050. Fax: 01242 216074. E-mail: editorial@livingfrance.com
Editor: Eleanor O'Kane.
Monthly magazine for those thinking of buying property in or moving to France, or hoping to work there.
Illustrations: Images reflecting working and living in France – property, French lifestyle, working life in France, retirement in France, children's education. Submit subject lists to deputy editor in the first instance. Covers: Images showing an aspirational and obviously French house, with space for coverlines.
Text: Suggestions for articles always considered. Main scope for destination pieces, interviews/profiles with expats in France, practical articles on buying property, living and working in France. E-mail synopsis in the first instance.
Overall freelance potential: Fair.
Fees: Individual pictures according to use; illustrated articles £300 for 1,000–1,500 words.

A PLACE IN THE SUN
APITS Ltd, 2nd Floor, Rear West Office, 16 Winchester Walk, London, SE1 9AQ

Tel: 020 3207 2920. E-mail: simong@apits.com
Editor: Richard Way. **Art Editor:** Simon Grover.
Glossy monthly for prospective buyers of overseas property. Official magazine of the C4 TV series of the same name.
Illustrations: Mostly by commission, though some stock images are used. Will consider sets of images based around people moving or living abroad, or suggestions for subjects, which could lead to a full-scale commission. Other general commissions also possible – submit details of experience and a few samples in the first instance.
Text: Illustrated feature stories as above.
Overall freelance potential: Good for the more experienced worker.
Fees: By negotiation.

REAL TRAVEL

Create Publishing, Castlemead, Lower Castle Street, Bristol, BS1 3AG.
Tel: 0117 917 5099. E-mail: hannah@realtravelmag.com
Editor: Hfu Reisenhofer. **Art Editor:** Dave Partridge.
Magazine for "active travellers" rather than holidaymakers.
Illustrations: Pictures of real people experiencing the world on career breaks or gap years or just for adventure, charity work, sporting activity, etc. Also stock pictures of less "touristy" destinations; submit details of coverage available in the first instance.
Text: Will always consider illustrated features focusing on "exciting yet attainable" destinations. From the more experienced contributor, expert advice and travel tips, on practical topics such as health, staying safe, etc.
Overall freelance potential: Good for the right sort of material as described.
Editor's tips: Contributions must have been clearly produced by active travellers from their own personal experience.
Fees: By negotiation.

SPAIN

The Media Company Publications Ltd, 21 Royal Circus, Edinburgh EH3 6TL.
Tel: 0131 226 7766. Fax: 0131 226 4567. E-mail: sue.hitchen@googlemail.com
Editor: Sue Hitchen.
Monthly magazine for lovers of Spain, especially those owning or aiming to buy property in the country or with an interest in the culture and history of Spain.
Illustrations: Commissions may be available to photographers resident in or visiting Spain. Stock images mostly sourced from agencies though photographers with in-depth collections may find it worthwhile to submit lists of subjects available.
Text: Ideas for illustrated features welcomed, on topics such as property, food and drink, travel and leisure activities. Submit outline first.
Overall freelance potential: Fair.
Fees: Negotiable and dependent on what is on offer.

THE SUNDAY TIMES TRAVEL MAGAZINE

Times Newspapers Ltd, 1 Pennington Street, London E98 1ST.
Tel: 020 7782 5000. E-mail: firstname.surname@sundaytimes.co.uk
Editor: Ed Grenby. **Picture Editor:** Polly Teller.
Monthly glossy aimed at up-market travellers. Published on behalf of The Sunday Times.
Illustrations: Will always consider high-quality travel material on spec, including especially striking single images for use in double-page spreads. Lists of stock material always of interest. Only limited scope for commissions.
Text: Will always consider suggestions for original illustrated travel features.
Overall freelance potential: Good for top-quality work.
Fees: Negotiable and according to use.

TRAVELLER
& Publishing for WEXAS International Ltd, 45-49 Brompton Road, London SW3 1DE.
Tel: 020 7581 6156. E-mail: traveller@and-publishing.co.uk
Editor: Amy Sohanpaul.
Quarterly publication containing narrative features on unusual and adventurous travel, usually in the developing countries of the world. Aimed at the independent traveller who prefers to travel off the beaten track.
Illustrations: High quality documentary travel pictures, usually from developing countries, rarely Europe or North America. Usually required as an integral part of illustrated articles as below, but there is also a six-page photo-essay (action/reportage). No tourist brochure-type shots.
Text: Well-illustrated travel articles from contributors with in-depth knowledge of the area/subject covered. Around 900 words, plus about 10 pictures. Unusual subject matter preferred, including coverage of world hot spots.
Overall freelance potential: Good, but limited by the magazine's frequency.
Editor's tips: Excellent photographic work is essential.
Fees: Photographs, From £50, full-page £80, £150 for cover. Text, £200 per 1,000 words.

WANDERLUST
Wanderlust Publications Ltd, PO Box 1832, Windsor, Berks SL4 1EB.
Tel: 01753 620426. Fax: 01753 620474. E-mail: info@wanderlust.co.uk
Editor: Dan Linstead. **Art Director:** Graham Berridge.
Magazine for the "independent-minded" traveller, published eight times a year.
Illustrations: Colour transparency or digital files (should be available at 60MB, no upsizing). Majority required for use in conjunction with features. Send a summary stock list in the first instance with a small selection of sample work. Covers: Always looking for bold, bright and uncluttered images that shout "travel", preferably with strong colours such as blue/yellow or red/orange.
Text: Well-illustrated features on independent and special interest travel at any level and in any part of the world. Contributors must have in-depth knowledge of their subject area and be prepared to cover both good and bad aspects. Short pieces up to 750 words; longer articles from 1,800–2,500 words.
Overall freelance potential: Excellent for complete packages of words and pictures.
Editor's tips: Don't send unsolicited originals; photocopies or prints will do as samples. Detailed "Notes for Contributors" and "Guidelines for Photographers" can be viewed on website: www.wanderlust.co.uk.
Fees: Photographs by negotiation and according to use; text £200 per 1,000 words.

Women's Interest

BELLA
H. Bauer Publishing Ltd, Academic House, 24-28 Oval Road, London NW1 7DT.
Tel: 020 7241 8000. Fax: 020 7241 8056. E-mail: lizzie.rowe@bauerconsumer.co.uk
Editor: Julia Davis. **Picture Editor:** Lizzie Rowe.
Weekly magazine for women, covering human interest stories, fashion, cookery and celebrities.
Illustrations: Pictures of celebrities and royalty, off-beat pictures and curiosities considered on spec. Fashion and food, mostly commissioned.
Text: Some scope for exclusive human interest features and celebrity interviews. Always check with the editor first.
Fees: By negotiation.

BEST

National Magazine Company, 72 Broadwick Street, London W1F 9EP.
Tel: 020 7439 5000. Fax: 020 7437 6886. E-mail: alison.thurston@natmags.co.uk
Editor: Jackie Hatton. **Picture Editor:** Alison Thurston.
Weekly magazine for women, covering affordable fashion, health matters, cookery, home
improvements, features etc.
Illustrations: Scope for off-beat, general human interest and curiosity shots, and informal celebrity
material. Commissioned coverage of fashion, food, features, etc.
Text: Articles with a practical slant, aimed at working women.
Overall freelance potential: Quite good.
Fees: Commissioned photography by negotiation; other material according to use.

CLOSER

Bauer Consumer Media, Endeavour House, 189 Shaftesbury Avenue, London WC2H 8JG.
Tel: 020 7859 8685. Fax: 020 7859 8685. E-mail: emma.peel@bauerconsumer.co.uk
Editor: Lisa Burrow. **Picture Editor:** Emma Peel.
Weekly women's magazine with the emphasis on celebrities and true-life stories.
Illustrations: Mainly by commission. Opportunities for experienced photographers to shoot a range
of celebrity material, from paparazzi street photography to studio work. Exclusive paparazzi
material also considered on spec, but much is sourced from agencies. Photographers in all parts of
the UK also needed to shoot portraits to illustrate true-life stories – submit details of experience and
area of the country covered.
Text: True-life stories about ordinary people always wanted – submit brief details in the first
instance.
Overall freelance potential: Good for those with some experience in these areas.
Fees: Photography by negotiation or according to job. True-life stories, up to £500.

COMPANY

National Magazine Company Ltd, 72 Broadwick Street, London W1F 9EP.
Tel: 020 7439 5000. Fax: 020 7312 3051. E-mail: abi.dillon@natmags.co.uk
Editor: Victoria White. **Picture Editor:** Abi Dillon.
Monthly magazine aimed at up-market young women in their twenties.
Illustrations: Photographs to illustrate features on fashion, beauty, relationships, careers, travel
and personalities, invariably by commission.
Text: Articles on the above topics, of varying lengths. Also, more topical and "newsy" features.
Overall freelance potential: Fair scope for experienced contributors.
Fees: By negotiation.

COSMOPOLITAN

National Magazine Company Ltd, 72 Broadwick Street, London W1V 2BP.
Tel: 020 7439 5000. Fax: 020 7439 5016. E-mail: joan.tinney@natmags.co.uk
Editor: Louise Court. **Creative Director:** Stuart Selner. **Picture Editor:** Joan Tinney.
Monthly magazine for women in the 18–34 age group.
Illustrations: Photographs to illustrate features on fashion, style and beauty, by commission only.
Some top quality stock situation pictures may be used to illustrate more general features on
emotional, sexual or social issues.
Text: Articles of interest to sophisticated young women. Always query the editor first
Overall freelance potential: Only for the experienced contributor to the women's press.
Fees: By negotiation.

ELLE

Hachette Filipacchi (UK) Ltd, 64 North Row, London W1K 7LL.
Tel: 020 7150 7348. Fax: 020 7150 7670. E-mail: hannah.ridleyl@hf-uk.com
Editor: Lorraine Candy. **Picture Editor:** Hannah Ridley.

Up-market monthly magazine with the emphasis on fashion.
Illustrations: Top quality images of fashion and style subjects, portraiture and still life, always by commission.
Text: Some scope for top quality feature articles, usually by commission and from established contributors.
Overall freelance potential: Good for contributors experienced at the top level of magazine journalism.
Fees: By negotiation.

ESSENTIALS

IPC Media Ltd, Blue Fin Building, 110 Southwark Street, London SE1 0SU.
Tel: 020 3148 5000. E-mail: tracey_pocock@ipcmedia.com
Editor: Julie Barton-Breck. **Creative Director:** Stuart Thomas. **Picture Editor:** Tracey Pocock.
Monthly mass-market magazine for women with the emphasis on practical matters.
Illustrations: Images of health, interior decoration, travel, food, etc. Some commissioned work available.
Text: Practical articles, health, features of interest to women. Synopsis essential in first instance.
Overall freelance potential: Good for experienced contributors to quality women's magazines.
Fees: By negotiation.

GLAMOUR

The Condé Naste Publications Ltd, 6-8 Old Bond Street, London W1S 4PH.
Tel: 020 7499 9080. Fax: 020 7491 2551. lucy.slade@condenast.co.uk
Editor: Jo Elvin. Features **Editor:** Corrie Jackson. Picture Director: Lucy Slade.
Mid-market general interest monthly for the 18-32 age group.
Illustrations: Mostly by commission to shoot features, portraiture, still life and interiors; make an appointment to show portfolio. Possible but limited scope for stock, including celebrity material.
Text: Always interested in celebrity interviews, investigative articles and features on relationships, careers, fashion, health and fitness. Send short synopsis in the first instance.
Overall freelance potential: Good for the experienced worker.
Fees: By negotiation.

GOOD HOUSEKEEPING

National Magazine Company Ltd, National Magazine House, 72 Broadwick Street, London W1V 2BP.
Tel: 020 7439 5000. Fax: 020 7439 5591. E-mail: contact@goodhousekeeping.co.uk
Editorial Director: Lindsay Nicholson. **Picture Editor:** Laura Meckiff.
General interest magazine for up-market women. Concentrates on home and family life.
Illustrations: Interiors, gardening, food, fashion, travel and reportage. Usually by commission to illustrate specific articles.
Text: Articles of interest to up-market women – interesting homes (with photos), gardening, personality profiles, emotional features, humorous articles, etc.
Overall freelance potential: Good scope for the highest quality material.
Fees: By negotiation.

GRAZIA

Bauer Media, Endeavour House, 189 Shaftesbury Avenue, London WC2H 8JG.
Tel: 020 7437 9011. Fax: 020 7520 6599. E-mail: deborah.brown@graziamagazine.co.uk
Editor: Jane Bruton. **Picture Director:** Deborah Brown.
Britain's first women's glossy to be published on a weekly basis, offering a mixture of celebrity coverage, real life stories, reportage, fashion and beauty.
Illustrations: Pictures of leading personalities at premieres, parties and generally out and about, plus paparazzi street shots. Pictures also required for news section containing hard news with the focus on women's issues and interests alongside celebrity stories. News pictures can be submitted on

spec to graziapics1@graziamagazine.co.uk. Opportunities for experienced workers in portraiture, beauty, still life and interiors; contact the picture director in the first instance with details of prior experience and coverage offered.

Text: Little freelance scope.

Overall freelance potential: Wide range of opportunities for experienced photographers.

Editor's tips: Celebrity coverage must be strictly A list, not C or D list. A short lead time means the magazine goes to press on Friday for sale the following Tuesday.

Fees: By negotiation.

HARPER'S BAZAAR

National Magazine Company Ltd, 72 Broadwick Street, London W1F 9EP.

Tel: 020 7439 5000. Fax: 020 7439 5506.

Editor: Lucy Yeomans. **Picture Director:** Chloe Limpkin. **Picture Editor:** Liz Pearn.

Monthly glossy magazine featuring fashion, design, travel, interiors, beauty and health.

Illustrations: Colour and high-quality B&W. Top quality photography to illustrate subjects as above, only by commission.

Text: General interest features of very high quality. 1,500–3,000 words. Only by commission.

Overall freelance potential: Good for those who can produce the right material.

Fees: Good; on a rising scale according to length of feature.

HELLO!

Hello Ltd, Wellington House, 69/71 Upper Ground, London SE1 9PQ.

Tel: 020 7667 8700. Fax: 020 7667 8711. E-mail: pictures@hellomagazine.com

Editor: Kay Goddard. **Picture Editor:** Freddie Sloan.

Weekly magazine for women covering people and current events.

Illustrations: Pictures and picture stories on personalities and celebrities of all kinds. People in the news and current news events. Off-beat pictures. Dramatic picture stories of bravery, courage or rescue.

Text: Interviews and/or reports to accompany photos.

Overall freelance potential: Excellent for quality material.

Editor's tips: The magazine has short lead times which it likes to exploit to the full – can include late stories in colour up to the Friday of the week before publication.

Fees: By negotiation.

THE LADY

The Lady, 39–40 Bedford Street, Strand, London WC2E 9ER.

Tel: 020 7379 4717. Fax: 020 7836 4620. E-mail: editors@lady.co.uk

Editor: Rachel Johnson. **Picture Editor:** Tamsan Barratt.

Weekly general interest magazine for women.

Illustrations: Photographs only required to accompany particular articles. Covers: Lifestyle images of women aged 35–50 years, travel or occasional famous faces.

Text: Illustrated articles on British and foreign travel, the countryside, human interest, wildlife, pets, cookery, gardening, fashion, beauty, British history and commemorative subjects. 700–850 words.

Overall freelance potential: Excellent for complete illustrated articles.

Fees: Pictures from £18, text £80 per 1,000 words.

LOOK

IPC Media Ltd, Blue Fin Building, 110 Southwark Street, London SE1 0SU.

Tel: 020 3148 5000. E-mail: jo_walker@ipcmedia.com

Editor: Ali Hall. **Picture Editor:** Desney Ryan.

Young women's weekly offering a mix of affordable fashion, celebrity style and gossip, and true life stories.

Illustrations: Mostly by commission. Those seeking fashion or portrait work should make an

appointment to show their portfolio. Those experienced in "real-life" work should make initial contact by e-mail. Celebrity images or other material that may be relevant to the target readership will be be considered on spec.
Text: Little scope.
Overall freelance potential: Good opportunities for experienced workers in this field.
Fees: By negotiation.

LOVE IT!
Hubert Burda Media UK, Swan House, 37-39 High Holborn, London WC1V 6AA.
Tel: 0845 481 0661. E-mail: arlene.brown@burdamagazines.co.uk
Editor: Jo Checkley. **Picture Editor:** Arlene Brown. **Deputy Picture Editor:** Verina Durand.
Real life weekly aimed at younger women.
Illustrations: Freelances around the country needed to shoot reportage, portraits and some studio work. Sample portfolios or CDs should be sent by post or e-mail to the picture desk.
Text: Original and exclusive real life stories always required.
Overall freelance potential: Excellent for the experienced worker.
Fees: Dependent on the nature of the job, but full day rate is £350, more typically £250 For shorter shoots.

MARIE CLAIRE
European Magazines Ltd, Blue Fin Building, 110 Southwark Street, London SE1 0SU.
Tel: 020 3148 5000. E-mail: sian_parry@ipcmedia.com
Editor: Trish Halpin. **Picture Editor:** Sian Parry.
Fashion and general interest monthly for sophisticated women in the 25–35 age group.
Illustrations: Top quality fashion, beauty, portraits, reportage, interiors, still life, etc, usually by commission.
Text: In-depth articles, features and profiles aimed at an intelligent readership. Up to 4,000 words.
Overall freelance potential: Very good for experienced contributors in this field.
Fees: By negotiation.

MORE
Bauer Media, Endeavour House, 189 Shaftesbury Avenue, London WC2H 8JG.
Tel: 020 7208 3397. Fax: 020 7208 3595. E-mail: tijen.denizmen@moremagazine.co.uk
Editor: Chantelle Horton. Picture Director: Tijen Denizmen.
Weekly magazine for young women in the 18–24 age group.
Illustrations: Up-to-date news pictures featuring celebrities, formal and informal. Fashion, beauty, health and pictures to illustrate specific articles, always by commission.
Text: Articles and features, often with a practical slant, of general interest to young women. Submit ideas only in the first instance.
Overall freelance potential: Quite good for quality material.
Editor's tips: No unsolicited features – commissions only.
Fees: By negotiation.

NOW
IPC Media Ltd, Blue Fin Building, 110 Southwark Street, London SE1 0SU.
Tel: 020 3148 5000. E-mail: nowpictures@ipcmedia.com
Editor: TBA. **Picture Editor:** Francesca D'Avanzo.
Weekly entertainment for women with the focus on celebrities and "true-life" stories.
Illustrations: Digital files preferred. Topical coverage of current film and TV stars, both formal and informal shots. Some commissions available to illustrate fashion, true-life stories and general features.
Text: Ideas for stories and interviews always considered.
Overall freelance potential: Limited.
Fees: Variable according to the material or assignment; top rates paid for good exclusives.

OK!
Northern & Shell plc, Northern & Shell Building, Number 10 Lower Thames Street, London EC3R 6EN.
Tel: 0871 434 1010. Fax: 0871 520 7766. E-mail: sophie.mutter@express.co.uk
Editor: Lisa Byrne. Picture Director: Tarkan Algin. **Picture Editor:** Sophie Mutter. **Picture Researcher:** Anna Williams.
Weekly, picture-led magazine devoted to celebrity features and news pictures.
Illustrations: Shots of celebrities of all kinds considered on spec, especially exclusives or unpublished archive material. Commissions available to experienced photographers.
Text: Exclusive stories/interviews with celebrities always of interest.
Overall freelance potential: Excellent for the right type of material.
Fees: Negotiable; depends on nature of the material or assignment.

PICK ME UP
IPC Media Ltd, Blue Fin Building, 110 Southwark Street, London SE1 0SU.
Tel: 020 3148 6441. Fax: 020 3148 8112. E-mail: natalie_jones@ipcmedia.com
Editor: June Smith-Sheppard. **Picture Editor:** Natalie Jones.
True life weekly presenting stories more graphically and in more detail than its rivals. Includes a limited amount of health material, but no celebrities.
Illustrations: Happy to hear from capable photographers around the country who are able to shoot stories as they arise. Initial contact should be made in writing, giving details of area covered and of any previous experience in the field.
Text: Suggestions for stories always welcomed, not only UK-based but also from overseas.
Overall freelance potential: Good for experienced contributors in this field.
Editor's tips: More is asked of contributors than is usually the case with real life material. Photographers will be expected to cover more angles, such as going to where an event took place or covering other aspects of a story.
Fees: Variable depending on what the photographer is required to do and how much travel is involved.

PRIMA
National Magazine Company, 72 Broadwick Street, London W1F 9EP.
Tel: 020 7439 5000. Fax: 020 7312 4100. E-mail: jo.lockwood@natmags.co.uk
Editor: Maire Fahey. **Art Director:** Jacqueline Hampsey. **Picture Editor:** Jo Lockwood. **Picture Researcher:** Bianca Topham.
General interest women's monthly with a strong emphasis on practical subjects. Major topics covered include cookery, gardening, crafts, health, fashion and homecare.
Illustrations: Top quality work in the fields of food, fashion, still-life, interiors and portraiture, usually by commission. Some scope for good stock shots of family and domestic situations, food, pets, etc that could be used for general illustration purposes, but query needs before before submitting.
Text: Short, illustrated practical features with a "how-to-do-it" approach.
Overall freelance potential: The magazine relies heavily on freelances.
Fees: Commissioned photography in the region of £400 per day. Other fees according to use.

PSYCHOLOGIES
Hachette Filipacchi (UK) Ltd, 64 North Row, London W1K 7LL.
Tel: 020 7150 7000. Fax: 020 7150 7001. E-mail: liz.simon@hf-uk.com
Editor: Louise Chunn. **Features Editor:** Rebecca Alexander. **Photo Editor:** Liz Simon.
Up-market women's monthly with the focus on "positive living", including topics such as work,

---

Are you working from the latest edition of The Freelance Photographer's Market Handbook? It's published on 1 October each year. Markets are constantly changing, so it pays to have the latest edition

health, family and social issues, travel.
Illustrations: Digital files preferred. Interested in both high-quality stock and in commissioning for specific features. Most images used are lifestyle-based, but relaxed and natural. Also opportunities for top-quality portraiture and beauty images. Initial approach should be by e-mail or telephone.
Text: Possible scope for high-quality lifestyle features.
Overall freelance potential: Good for experienced photographers.
Editor's tips: Examine the magazine closely to get a feel for its style.
Fees: By negotiation.

REAL PEOPLE
ACP-NatMag, 33 Broadwick Street, London W1F 0DQ.
Tel: 020 7439 5000. Fax: 020 7339 4650. E-mail: sue.miles@natmags.co.uk
Editor: Samm Taylor. **Picture Editor:** Sue Miles.
Real life weekly for women.
Illustrations: Requires experienced freelances in all parts of the country who may be available to undertake reportage and portrait shoots to illustrate stories. Initial contact by e-mail is preferred, giving brief details of any previous experience.
Text: Real life stories always required.
Overall freelance potential: Excellent for the experienced worker.
Fees: Around £150–£200 per assignment, depending on the nature of the shoot and rights licensed. Up to £500 for real life stories.

RED
Hachette Filipacchi (UK) Ltd, 64 North Row, London W1K 7LL.
Tel: 020 7150 7000. Fax: 020 7150 7001. E-mail: beverley.croucher@hf-uk.com
Editor: Sam Baker. **Art Director:** Jonathan Whitelocke. **Picture Editor:** Beverley Croucher.
Sophisticated monthly aimed at women in their 30s.
Illustrations: High quality commissioned photography covering portraiture, fashion, interior design, food and celebrities. Telephone to make an appointment to drop off portfolio in the first instance. Little scope for stock material.
Text: Ideas always welcome from experienced writers.
Overall freelance potential: Good for the experienced worker.
Fees: By negotiation.

REVEAL
The National Magazine Company Ltd, 33 Broadwick Street, London W1F 0DQ.
Tel: 020 7339 4524. E-mail: dara.levan-harris@natmags.co.uk
Editor: Jane Ennis. **Picture Editor:** Dara Levan-Harris.
A "five magazines in one" weekly package, with a mix of celebrities, real-life stories, fashion, lifestyle and TV listings.
Pictures: Good scope for celebrity shots, especially paparazzi-style pictures. Happy to hear from freelances if they think they have something, but ideally should be an exclusive. Send an e-mail first rather than sending images. Many opportunities for commissions to shoot celebrity, real-life or lifestyle features.
Text: Good, illustrated real-life stories always being sought; e-mail features.reveal@natmags.co.uk with suggestions.
Overall freelance potential: Excellent for the right type of material.
Fees: Photography by negotiation; £500 upwards for real-life stories.

As a member of the Bureau of Freelance Photographers, you'll be kept up-to-date with markets through the BFP Market Newsletter, published monthly. For details of membership, turn to page 9

SHE

National Magazine Company, National Magazine House, 72 Broadwick Street, London W1V 2BP.
Tel: 020 7439 5000. Fax: 020 7439 5350. E-mail: editor@shemagazine.co.uk
Editor: Claire Irvin. **Art Director:** Chris Lupton. **Picture Editor:** Chloe Trayler-Smith.
General interest monthly for the 30-something woman.
Illustrations: Most material by commission for specific articles; anything else only considered by appointment.
Text: Top quality features of interest to intelligent women; suggestions welcomed but always query the editor first.
Overall freelance potential: Little unsolicited material used, but quite good for commissions.
Editor's tips: Please study the content and style before contacting magazine.
Fees: By arrangement.

THAT'S LIFE!

H.Bauer Publishing Ltd, 24-28 Oval Road, London NW1 7DT.
Tel: 020 7241 8000. Fax: 020 7241 8008. E-mail: jim.taylor@bauer.co.uk
Editor: Sophie Hearsey. **Picture Editor:** Matt Wevill.
Popular women's weekly concentrating on true-life stories and confessions.
Illustrations: Mostly commissioned shots of people to accompany stories; photographers who can produce good informal portrait work should write to the picture editor enclosing a couple of samples. Also limited opportunities in fashion, food and still life. Quirky and amusing "readers' pictures" always considered on spec – should be accompanied by a brief story or anecdote.
Text: Personal true-life stories always of interest – shocking, scandalous, embarrassing, tear-jerking, etc. Around 300 words. Contact the editor with suggestions first.
Overall freelance potential: Good.
Fees: Story shoots around £150; readers' pictures £25; other photography by negotiation. £200 for true stories.

WI LIFE

NFWI, 104 New Kings Road, Fulham, London SW6 4LY.
Tel: 020 7731 5777. Fax: 020 7736 4061. E-mail: h&ced@nfwi.org.uk
Editor: Neal Maidment.
Published eight times a year for Women's Institute members, includes WI news and features.
Illustrations: Pictures of WI events, members, craft and cookery projects.
Text: Mostly written in-house.
Overall freelance potential: Modest scope for picture sales.
Editor's tips: Always consult the editor before submitting.
Fees: By agreement.

WOMAN

IPC Media Ltd, Blue Fin Building, 110 Southwark Street, London SE1 0SU.
Tel: 020 3148 5000. E-mail: michelle_filmer@ipcmedia.com
Editor: Karen Livermore. **Picture Editor:** Michelle Filmer.
Weekly magazine devoted to all women's interests.
Illustrations: Most pictures commissioned to illustrate specific features. Some scope for human interest shots which are dramatic, off-beat or unusual.
Text: Interviews with leading personalities, human interest stories. Other features mostly staff-produced. Submit a synopsis in the first instance.
Overall freelance potential: Only for experienced contributors in the field.
Fees: Good; on a rising scale according to size of reproduction or length of articles.

WOMAN & HOME
IPC Media Ltd, Blue Fin Building, 110 Southwark Street, London SE1 0SU.
Tel: 020 3148 5000. Fax: 020 3148 8120. E-mail: sharon_mears@ipcmedia.com
Editor: Sue James. **Picture Editor:** Sharon Mears.
Monthly magazine for all women concerned with family and home.
Illustrations: All photography commissioned from experienced freelances, to illustrate subjects including cookery, fashion, beauty, interior design, DIY, gardening, travel, topical issues and personality articles.
Text: Articles on personalities, either well-known or who lead interesting lives. 1,500 words.
Overall freelance potential: Very good for the experienced worker. Including regular contributors, about 50 per cent of the magazine is produced by freelances.
Fees: By negotiation.

WOMAN'S OWN
IPC Media Ltd, Blue Fin Building, 110 Southwark Street, London SE1 0SU.
Tel: 020 3148 5000. Fax: 020 3148 8112. E-mail: fran_jepps@ipcmedia.com
Editor: Vicky Mayer. **Picture Editor:** Fran Jepps.
Weekly publishing articles and practical features of interest to women.
Illustrations: Mostly commissioned to illustrate features on fashion, interior design, crafts, etc.
Text: Mostly staff-produced. Send a brief outline of any proposed feature in the first instance to the features editor.
Overall freelance potential: Fair for commissioned work, but much is produced by regulars.
Fees: Good; on a rising scale according to size of reproduction or length of article.

WOMAN'S WEEKLY
IPC Media Ltd, Blue Fin Building, 110 Southwark Street, London SE1 0SU.
Tel: 020 3148 6628. E-mail: sue_de_jong@ipcmedia.com
Editor: Diane Kenwood. **Art Editor:** Fiona Watson. **Picture Editor:** Sue De Jong.
General interest family-oriented magazine for women in the 35+ age group.
Illustrations: Mostly by commission to illustrate features on fashion, beauty, cookery, decoration, etc.
Text: Practical features on general women's topics, plus human interest stories and celebrity pieces.
Overall freelance potential: Fairly good for the experienced contributor.
Fees: By negotiation.

NEWSPAPERS

In this section we list the national daily and Sunday newspapers, and their associated magazine supplements. While the supplements may publish a wide range of general interest subject matter, the parent papers are obviously only likely to be interested in hard news pictures and stories of genuine interest to a nationwide readership.

News pictures

Despite the heavy presence of staff and agency photographers at major events, it is still perfectly possible for an independent freelance to get the shot that makes the front page. And when it comes to the unexpected, the freelance is often the only one on the spot to capture the drama.

If you think you have obtained a "hot" news picture or story, the best plan is to telephone the papers most likely to be interested as soon as possible and let them know what you have to offer.

Note that newspapers prefer to work from digital files and will not want to handle transparencies. They will, however, accept colour print or negative if that is all that is available.

In the listings that follow, as well as the main switchboard number you will find direct line telephone numbers which take you directly through to the picture desk of the paper concerned.

There should be little cause to use fax numbers for newspapers these days, but if you do it is advisable to always check the correct number for the department you want. Newspaper offices have numerous fax machines; the numbers listed here are necessarily general editorial numbers and if used without checking might delay your message getting to the department you need.

Other material

There is some scope for other material apart from hard news in most of the papers. Some use the occasional oddity or human interest item as a "filler", while in the tabloids there is always a good market for celebrity pictures.

Finally, of course, there is a market for top quality glamour material of the "Page 3" variety in several of the tabloids.

The supplements operate much like any other general interest magazine. Most of their content is commissioned from well-established photographers and writers, though some will accept exceptional photojournalistic features or exclusives on spec.

Fees

Fees paid by newspapers can vary tremendously according to what is offered and how it is used. However, it can be taken for granted that rates paid by the national papers listed here are good.

Generally, picture fees are calculated on standard rates based on the size of the reproduction, with the minumum fee you might expect from a national newspaper being around £65.

However, for material that is exclusive or exceptional the sky is almost literally the limit. If you think you have something very special and are prepared to offer it as an exclusive, make sure you negotiate a fee, and perhaps get several offers, before committing the material to anyone.

National Daily Newspapers

DAILY EXPRESS
Express Newspapers, 10 Lower Thames Street, London EC3R 6EN.
Tel: 020 8612 7000. Picture desk: 020 8612 7171.
E-mail: expresspix@express.co.uk
Editor: Peter Hill. **Picture Editor:** Neil McCarthy.

DAILY MAIL
The Daily Mail Ltd, Northcliffe House, 2 Derry Street, London W8 5TT.
Tel: 020 7938 6000. Picture desk: 020 7938 6373. Fax: 020 7937 5560.
E-mail: pictures@dailymail.co.uk
Editor: Paul Dacre. **Picture Editor:** Paul Silva.

DAILY MIRROR
Mirror Group Newspapers Ltd, Canary Wharf Tower, 1 Canada Square, London E14 5AP.
Tel: 020 7293 3000. Picture desk: 020 7293 3851. Fax: 020 7293 3983.
E-mail: picturedesk@mirror.co.uk
Editor: Richard Wallace. **Picture Editor:** Ian Down.

DAILY RECORD
The Scottish Daily Record and Sunday Mail Ltd, One Central Quay, Glasgow G3 8DA.
Tel: 0141 309 3000. Picture desk: 0141 309 3245. ISDN: 0141 309 4879.
E-mail: a.baird@dailyrecord.co.uk
Editor: Bruce Waddell. **Picture Editor:** Alasdair Baird.

DAILY SPORT
Sport Newspapers Ltd, 19 Great Ancoats Street, Manchester M60 4BT.
Tel: 0161 236 4466. Picture desk: 0161 238 8169. Fax: 0161 236 4535.
E-mail: pictures@sportnewspapers.co.uk
Editor: Pam McVitie. **Picture Editor:** Paul Currie.

DAILY STAR
Express Newspapers, 10 Lower Thames Street, London EC3R 6EN.
Tel: 020 8612 7000. Picture desk: 020 8612 7382.
E-mail: rob.greener@dailystar.co.uk
Editor: Dawn Neesom. **Picture Editor:** Rob Greener.

THE DAILY TELEGRAPH
Telegraph Media Group, Victoria Plaza, 111 Buckingham Palace Road, London SW1W 0SR.
Tel: 020 7931 2000. Picture desk: 020 7931 2660.
E-mail: photo@telegraph.co.uk
Editor: Tony Gallagher. **Picture Editor:** Kim Scott-Clark.
TELEGRAPH MAGAZINE
Editor: Michele Lavery. **Picture Editor:** Cheryl Newman.

As a member of the Bureau of Freelance Photographers, you'll be kept up-to-date with markets through the BFP Market Newsletter, published monthly. For details of membership, turn to page 9

FINANCIAL TIMES
The Financial Times Ltd, Number One Southwark Bridge, London SE1 9HL.
Tel: 020 7873 3000. Picture desk: 020 7873 3151.
E-mail: jamie.han@ft.com
Editor: Lionel Barber. **Picture Editor:** Jamie Han.

THE GUARDIAN
Kings Place, 90 York Way, London N1 9GU.
Tel: 020 3353 2000. Picture desk: 020 3353 4070.
E-mail: pictures@guardian.co.uk
Editor: Alan Rusbridger. **Picture Editor:** Roger Tooth.
WEEKEND GUARDIAN
Editor: Merope Mills. **Picture Editor:** Kate Edwards.

THE HERALD
200 Renfield Street, Glasgow G2 3QB.
Tel: 0141 302 7000. Picture desk: 0141 302 6668. Fax: 0141 333 1147. ISDN: 0141 302 2101.
E-mail: pictures@theherald.co.uk
Editor: Jonathan Russell. **Picture Editor:** Brodie Duncan.

THE INDEPENDENT
Independent News & Media Plc, Northcliffe House, 2 Derry Street, London W8 5TT.
Tel: 020 7005 2000. Picture desk: 020 7005 2830. Fax: 020 7005 2086.
E-mail: picturedesk@independent.co.uk
Editor: Simon Kelner. **Picture Editor:** Lynn Cullen.
THE INDEPENDENT MAGAZINE
Picture Editor: Nick Hall.

THE SCOTSMAN
The Scotsman Publications Ltd, Barclay House, 108 Holyrood Road, Edinburgh EH8 8AS.
Tel: 0131 620 8620. Picture desk: 0131 620 8560.
E-mail: tspics@scotsman.com
Editor: John McLellan. **Picture Editor:** Andy O'Brien.

THE SUN
News International Newspapers Ltd, 1 Virginia Street, London E98 1SN.
Tel: 020 7782 4000. Picture desk: 020 7782 4199. Fax: 020 7782 4335.
E-mail: pictures@thesun.co.uk; john.edwards@thesun.co.uk
Editor: Dominic Mohan. **Picture Editor:** John Edwards.

THE TIMES
News International Newspapers Ltd, 1 Pennington Street, London E98 1TT.
Tel: 020 7782 5000. Picture desk: 020 7782 5877. Fax: 020 7782 5449.
E-mail: pictures@thetimes.co.uk
Editor James Harding. **Picture Editor:** Paul Sanders.
THE TIMES MAGAZINE
Editor: Louise France. **Picture Editor:** Graham Wood.

National Sunday Newspapers

THE INDEPENDENT ON SUNDAY
Independent News & Media Plc, Northcliffe House, 2 Derry Street, London W8 5TT.
Tel: 020 7005 2000. Picture desk: 020 7005 2837/2828. Fax: 020 7005 2086.
E-mail: picturedesk@independent.co.uk
Editor: John Mullin. **Picture Editor:** Sophie Batterbury.
THE SUNDAY REVIEW
Editor: Lisa Markwell. **Picture Editor:** Hannah Brenchley.

THE MAIL ON SUNDAY
Northcliffe House, 2 Derry Street, Kensington, London W8 5TS.
Tel: 020 7938 6000. Picture desk: 020 7938 7017. Fax: 020 7938 6609.
E-mail: pix@mailonsunday.co.uk
Editor: Peter Wright. **Picture Editor:** Liz Cocks.
YOU MAGAZINE
Editor: Sue Peart. **Picture Editor:** Eve George.
NIGHT & DAY
Editor: Gerard Greaves. **Picture Editor:** Sam Reilly.

NEWS OF THE WORLD
News International Newspapers Ltd, Virginia Street, London E1 9XR.
Tel: 020 7782 4000. Picture desk: 020 7782 4421. Fax: 020 7782 4463.
ISDN: 020 7680 1010/7702 9140. E-mail: nowpicture@newsint.co.uk
Editor: Colin Myler. **Picture Editor:** Paul Ashton.
FABULOUS
Editor: Sally Eyden. **Picture Director:** Kim Mayers.

THE OBSERVER
Kings Place, 90 York Way, London N1 9GU.
Tel: 020 3353 2000. Picture desk: 020 3353 4304. E-mail: picture.desk@observer.co.uk
Editor: John Mulholland. **Picture Editor:** Greg Whitmore.
THE OBSERVER MAGAZINE
Editor: Tim Lewis. **Picture Editors:** Kit Burnet and Matthew Glynn.
OBSERVER FOOD MONTHLY
Editor: Allan Jenkins. **Picture Editor:** Kit Burnet and Matthew Glynn.

THE PEOPLE
Mirror Group plc, 1 Canada Square, Canary Wharf, London E14 5AP.
Tel: 020 7293 3000. Picture desk: 020 7293 3901. Fax: 020 7293 3810.
ISDN: 020 7572 5801 (Easy Transfer); 020 7513 2427 (Foresight).
E-mail: pictures@people.co.uk
Editor: Lloyd Embley. **Picture Editor:** Mark Moylan.
TAKE IT EASY
Editor: Hannah Tavner. **Picture Editor:** TBC.

SCOTLAND ON SUNDAY
The Scotsman Publications Ltd, Barclay House, 108 Holyrood Road, Edinburgh EH8 8AS.
Tel: 0131 620 8438. Fax: 0131 620 8491. ISDN: 0131 556 5379/1230.
E-mail: sospics@scotsman.com
Editor: Ian Stewart. **Picture Editor:** Alan Macdonald.

SUNDAY EXPRESS
Express Newspapers, 10 Lower Thames Street, London EC3R 6EN.
Tel: 020 8612 7000. Picture desk: 020 8612 7172 / 7176.
E-mail: sundayexpresspix@express.co.uk
Editor: Martin Townsend. **Picture Editor:** Terry Evans.
SUNDAY EXPRESS MAGAZINE
Editor: Louise Robinson. **Picture Editor:** Jane Woods.

SUNDAY HERALD
200 Renfield Street, Glasgow G2 3QB.
Tel: 0141 302 7000. Picture desk: 0141 302 7876. Fax: 0141 302 7815. ISDN: 0141 302 2103.
E-mail: sunday.pictures@sundayherald.com
Editor: Richard Walker. **Picture Editor:** Elaine Livingstone.
SUNDAY HERALD MAGAZINE
Editor: Susan Flockhart. **Picture Editor:** Leanne Thompson.

THE SUNDAY MAIL
The Scottish Daily Record and Sunday Mail Ltd, 1 Central Quay, Glasgow G3 8DA.
Tel: 0141 309 7000. Picture desk: 0141 309 3434. Fax: 0141 309 3587.
ISDN: 0141 309 4884/4886. E-mail: a.hosie@sundaymail.co.uk
Editor: Bruce Waddell. **Picture Editor:** Andy Hosie.

SUNDAY MIRROR
Mirror Group plc, 1 Canada Square, Canary Wharf, London E14 5AP.
Tel: 020 7293 3000. Picture desk: 020 7293 3335/6. Fax: 020 7510 6991.
E-mail: pictures@sundaymirror.co.uk
Editor: Tina Weaver. **Picture Editor:** Ivor Game.
CELEBS ON SUNDAY
Editor: Mel Brodie. **Picture Editor:** Jo Aspill.

THE SUNDAY POST
D. C. Thomson & Co Ltd, Courier Place, Dundee DD1 9QJ.
Tel: 01382 223131. Fax: 01382 201064. ISDN: 01382 575935.
E-mail: mail@sundaypost.com
Editor: Domald Martin. **News Editor:** Tom McKay. **Picture Editor:** Alan Morrison.
POST PLUS MAGAZINE
Editor: Jan Gooderham.

SUNDAY SPORT
Sport Newspapers Ltd, 19 Great Ancoats Street, Manchester M60 4BT.
Tel: 0161 236 4466. Picture desk: 0161 238 8169. Fax: 0161 236 4535.
E-mail: paul.currie@sportnewspapers.co.uk
Editor: Nick Appleyard. **Picture Editor:** Paul Currie.

THE SUNDAY TELEGRAPH
Telegraph Media Group, Victoria Plaza, 111 Buckingham Palace Road, London SW1W 0SR.
Tel: 020 7931 2000. Picture desk: 020 7931 3542.
E-mail: stpics@telegraph.co.uk
Editor: Ian McGregor. **Picture Editor:** Mike Spillard.
STELLA
Editor: Anna Murphy.

THE SUNDAY TIMES
Times Newspapers Ltd, 1 Pennington Street, London E98 1ST.
Tel: 020 7782 5000. Picture desk: 020 7782 5666. Fax: 020 7782 5563.
E-mail: pictures@sunday-times.co.uk
Editor: John Witherow. **Picture Editor:** Ray Wells.
THE SUNDAY TIMES MAGAZINE
Editor: Sarah Baxter. **Picture Editor:** Monica Allende.

BOOKS

Books represent a substantial and ever-growing market for the photographer. In an increasingly visual age the market for heavily illustrated books continues to expand, with hundreds of new titles being published every year.

In this section we list major book publishers, and specifically those companies that make considerable use of photographic material.

As well as regular publishers, also included here are book packagers. These are companies that offer a complete editorial production service and specialise in producing books that can be sold as finished packages to publishers internationally. The majority of their products are of the heavily illustrated type, and thus these companies can often present a greater potential market for photographic material than do the mainstream publishers.

Making an approach

In this field the difficulty for the individual freelance is that there is no easy way of knowing who wants what and when.

Obviously book publishers only require pictures of specific subjects when they are currently working on a project requiring such material. Much of the time they will rely heavily on known sources such as picture libraries, but this does not mean that there is not good scope for the individual photographer who has a good collection of material on particular subjects, or who may be able to produce suitable work to order.

The solution for the photographer, therefore, is to place details of what he or she has to offer in front of all those companies that might conceivably require material of that type.

The initial approach is simply to send an introductory letter outlining the sort of material that you can supply. A detailed list of subjects can be attached where appropriate.

There is little point however, in sending any photographs at this stage, unless it be one or two samples to indicate a particular style. And one should not expect an immediate response requesting that work be submitted; most likely the publisher will simply keep your details on file for future reference.

Preceding the listings of book publishers is a subject index that should assist in identifying the most promising markets for those areas in which you have good coverage.

In the listings that follow, the major areas of activity for each publisher are detailed under "Subjects". Of course, the larger companies publish on the widest range of subjects and therefore their coverage may be stated as "general", but in most entries you will find a list of specific subject areas. These are by no means a complete list of all the subjects handled by each publisher, but indicate those areas where the company is most active and therefore most likely to be in need of photographic material.

In some entries a "Contact" name is given. However, in a lot of cases it is not possible to give a specific name as larger book publishers usually have large numbers of editorial personnel with constantly shifting responsibilities for individual projects. In addition, many companies frequently use the services of freelance picture researchers. A general approach should therefore simply be addressed to the editorial director.

Rights and fees

Whereas the rights sold in the magazine world are invariably for UK use only, book publishers – and especially packagers – make a good deal of their profit from selling their products to other publishers in overseas markets.

It is therefore quite likely that when work is chosen for use in a particular book the publisher may at some stage request, in addition to British publishing rights, rights for other areas such as "Commonwealth", "North American", "French language", etc. These differing rights will, of course, affect the fees that the photographer receives – the more areas the book sells into, the higher the fees.

Other major factors affecting fees are the size of reproduction on the page and the quantity of the print-run.

Thus there is no easy way to generalise about the sort of fees paid in this field. On the whole, however, fees in book publishing are quite good and comparable with good magazine rates. For packages destined for the international co-edition market they can be substantially higher.

A word about names and imprints

The use by large publishers of a multiplicity of names for different divisions can be quite confusing.

Many famous publishing names, though still in existence, now belong to huge publishing conglomerates. A few are still run as separate companies, but most have effectively become "imprints".

These imprints are used by large publishers for specific sections of their list. In the past many imprints were run as completely separate operations, but in an age of consolidation most have now been incorporated into their parent company.

Only especially relevant imprints are given full listings here, that is those that are run as separate operations and use photography to any extent. Most imprints are simply listed under their parent company.

Subject Index

Gardening

Anness Publishing
Antique Collectors' Club Ltd
Breslich & Foss
Kyle Cathie Ltd
The Crowood Press
Focus Publishing
W. Foulsham & Co Ltd
Guild of Master Craftsman Publications Ltd
Hodder Headline Ltd
Frances Lincoln Ltd
New Holland Publishers
Octopus Publishing Group Ltd
Orion Publishing Group Ltd
Pan Macmillan
Quarto Group
Reader's Digest Association Ltd
Ryland, Peters & Small
Souvenir Press Ltd

Health/Medical

Anova Books
Breslich & Foss
Cambridge University Press
Carroll & Brown Publishers
Kyle Cathie Ltd
Constable & Robinson
Ebury Publishing
Focus Publishing
W. Foulsham & Co Ltd
Grub Street
Piatkus Books
Quarto Group
Simon & Schuster
Souvenir Press Ltd
Transworld Publishers

Interior Design

Ebury Publishing
Frances Lincoln Ltd
New Holland Publishers
Octopus Publishing Group Ltd
Orion Publishing Group Ltd
Ryland, Peters & Small
Thames & Hudson

Military

Ian Allan Publishing
Amber Books Ltd
Anova Books

Cassell Military
Constable & Robinson
The Crowood Press
Robert Hale Ltd
The History Press Ltd
Osprey Publishing
Transworld Publishers
Weidenfeld & Nicolson Ltd

Motoring

Ian Allan Publishing
The Crowood Press
Haynes Publishing

Music

Cambridge University Press
Ebury Publishing
Faber & Faber Ltd
Guinness Publishing Ltd
Robert Hale Ltd
Hodder Headline Ltd
Omnibus Press/Book Sales Ltd
Pan Macmillan
Plexus Publishing Ltd
Thames & Hudson
Virgin Books Ltd

Natural History

Appletree Press
A & C Black (Publishers) Ltd
Cambridge University Press
The Crowood Press
Robert Hale Ltd
Christopher Helm Publishers Ltd
Kingfisher Publications
New Holland Publishers
Orion Publishing Group Ltd
T & A D Poyser
Reader's Digest Association Ltd
Souvenir Press Ltd
Usborne Publishing

Photography

David & Charles Publishing Ltd
Derby Books Publishing Ltd
Phaidon Press Ltd
Photographer's Institute Press
RotoVision
Thames & Hudson Ltd

Politics/Current Affairs

Bloomsbury Publishing Ltd
Chatto & Windus
Constable & Robinson
Faber & Faber Ltd
Hutchinson
Pan Macmillan
Yale University Press

Railways

Ian Allan Publishing
The History Press Ltd
Railways – Milepost 92½

Science

Amber Books Ltd
Cambridge University Press
Lutterworth Press
Orion Publishing Group Ltd
Transworld Publishers

Sport

A & C Black (Publishers) Ltd
The Crowood Press
Derby Books Publishing Ltd
Ebury Publishing
Focus Publishing

W. Foulsham & Co Ltd
Guinness Publishing Ltd
Robert Hale Ltd
The History Press Ltd
Hodder Headline Ltd
Octopus Publishing Group Ltd
Orion Publishing Group Ltd
Transworld Publishers
Virgin Books Ltd

Travel

AA Publishing
Amber Books Ltd
Appletree Press
Bloomsbury Publishing Ltd
Cambridge University Press
Chatto & Windus
Constable & Robinson
The Crowood Press
Ebury Publishing
W. Foulsham & Co Ltd
Robert Hale Ltd
Hutchinson
New Holland Publishers
Octopus Publishing Group Ltd
Orion Publishing Group Ltd
Pan Macmillan
Quarto Group
Sheldrake Press
Thames & Hudson Ltd

Book Publishers

AA PUBLISHING
Automobile Association, Fanum House, Basingstoke, Hampshire RG21 2EA.
Tel: 01256 491588. Fax: 01256 492440. E-mail: travelimages@theaa.com
Contact: Ian Little, Head of Picture Library.
Subjects: Travel images for guide books, maps and atlases. Commissions only.

IAN ALLAN PUBLISHING
Riverdene Business Park, Molesey Road, Hersham, Surrey KT12 4RG.
Tel: 01932 266600. Fax: 01932 266601.
Web: www.ianallanpublishing.com
Subjects: Aviation, military, motoring, railways, road transport.

AMBER BOOKS LTD
Bradley's Close, 74-77 White Lion Street, London N1 9PF.
Tel: 020 7520 7600. Fax: 020 7520 7606. E-mail: terry@amberbooks.co.uk
Web: www.amberbooks.co.uk
Contact: Terry Forshaw, Picture Manager.
Subjects: General; aviation, fitness and survival, military, naval, popular science, transport.

ANNESS PUBLISHING LTD
Hermes House 88-89 Blackfriars Road, London SE1 8HA.
Tel: 020 7401 2077. Fax: 020 7633 9499. E-mail: info@anness.com
Web: www.lorenzbooks.com
Contact: Picture Library Manager.
Imprints: Aquamarine, Hermes House, Lorenz Books, Southwater.
Subjects: Crafts, cookery, gardening, health, reference.

ANOVA BOOKS
10 Southcombe Street, London W14 0RA.
Tel: 020 7605 1400. Fax: 020 7605 1401.
Web: www.anovabooks.com
Imprints: Batsford, Collins & Brown, Conway Maritime Press, Pavilion, Robson.
Subjects: General illustrated; architecture, arts & crafts, biography, cookery, fashion, health, military, transport.

ANTIQUE COLLECTORS CLUB LTD
Sandy Lane, Old Martlesham, Woodbridge, Suffolk IP12 4SD.
Tel: 01394 389950. Fax: 01394 389999.
Web: www.antique-acc.com
Contact: Diana Steel, Managing Director (by letter only).
Subjects: Antiques, architecture, art, gardening. (Digital not accepted).

Are you working from the latest edition of The Freelance Photographer's Market Handbook? It's published on 1 October each year. Markets are constantly changing, so it pays to have the latest edition

APPLETREE PRESS LTD
The Old Potato Station, 14 Howard Street South, Belfast BT7 1AP.
Tel: 028 90 243074. Fax: 028 90 246756. E-mail: editorial@appletree.ie
Web: www.appletree.ie
Subjects: Irish and Scottish interest; arts & crafts, cookery, nature, UK travel.

A & C BLACK (PUBLISHERS) LTD
38 Soho Square, London W1D 3HB.
Tel: 020 7758 0200. Fax: 020 7758 0222. E-mail: enquiries@acblack.co.uk
Web: www.acblack.com
Imprints: Adlard Coles Nautical, Christopher Helm, Methuen Drama, T&AD Poyser.
Subjects: Arts and crafts, children's educational, nautical, natural history, reference, sport, theatre.

BLOOMSBURY PUBLISHING PLC
36 Soho Square, London W1D 3QY.
Tel: 020 7494 2111. Fax: 020 7434 0151. E-mail: csm@bloomsbury.com
Web: www.bloomsbury.com
Subjects: General; biography, children's, current affairs, reference, travel.

BRESLICH & FOSS LTD
2a Union Court, 20-22 Union Road, London, SW4 6JP
Tel: 020 7819 3990. Fax: 020 7819 3998. E-mail: sales@breslichfoss.com
Web: www.breslichfoss.co.uk
Contact: Janet Ravenscroft.
Subjects: Arts, children's, crafts, gardening, health, lifestyle.

CAMBRIDGE UNIVERSITY PRESS
The Edinburgh Building, Shaftesbury Road, Cambridge CB2 8RU.
Tel: 01223 312393. Fax: 01223 315052. E-mail: information@cambridge.org
Web: www.cambridge.org
Subjects: Archaeology, architecture, art, astronomy, biology, drama, geography, history, medicine, music, natural history, religion, science, sociology, travel.

CARROLL & BROWN PUBLISHERS LTD
20 Lonsdale Road, London NW6 6RD.
Tel: 020 7372 0900. Fax: 020 7372 0460. E-mail: mail@carrollandbrown.co.uk
Web: www.carrollandbrown.co.uk
Contact: Chrissie Lloyd, Art Director.
Subjects: General illustrated reference, health, parenting.

KYLE CATHIE LTD
122 Arlington Road, London NW1 7HP.
Tel: 020 7692 7215. Fax: 020 7692 7260. E-mail: vicki.murrell@kyle-cathie.com
Web: www.kylecathie.com
Contact: Vicki Murrell, Editorial Assistant.
Subjects: Beauty, food and drink, gardening, health, reference.

CHATTO & WINDUS LTD
Random House, 20 Vauxhall Bridge Road, London SW1V 2SA.
Tel: 020 7840 8540. Fax: 020 7233 6117. E-mail: chattoeditorial@randomhouse.co.uk
Web: www.randomhouse.co.uk
Subjects: General; biography and memoirs, current affairs, history, travel.

THE CROWOOD PRESS LTD
The Stable Block, Crowood Lane, Ramsbury, Marlborough, Wiltshire SN8 2HR.
Tel: 01672 520320. Fax: 01672 520280. E-mail: enquiries@crowood.com
Web: www.crowoodpress.co.uk
Subjects: Angling, aviation, climbing, country interests, crafts, DIY, equestrian, gardening, motoring, military, natural history, sport, travel.

DAVID & CHARLES PUBLISHING LTD
Brunel House, Newton Abbot, Devon TQ12 4PU.
Tel: 01626 323200. Fax: 01626 323317.
Web: www.davidandcharles.co.uk
Contact: Prudence Rogers.
Subjects: Crafts, nostalgia, photography, railways.

DERBY BOOKS PUBLISHING CO LTD
3 The Parker Centre, Mansfield Road, Derby DE21 4SZ.
Tel: 01332 384235. Fax: 01332 292755. E-mail: steve.caron@dbpublishing.co.uk
Web: www.dbpublishing.co.uk
Contact: Steve Caron, Managing Director; Alex Morton, Publishing Manager.
Subjects: Archive photography, British heritage and local history, sport (especially football).

EBURY PUBLISHING
Random House, 20 Vauxhall Bridge Road, London SW1V 2SA.
Tel: 020 7840 8400. Fax: 020 7840 8406. E-mail: eburyeditorial@randomhouse.co.uk
Web: www.eburypublishing.co.uk
Imprints: BBC Books, Ebury Press, Rider, Time Out Guides,Vermilion.
Contact: Vicky Orchard, Editorial Assistant.
Subjects: Biography, cookery, crafts, current affairs, decorating and interiors, health and beauty, history, mind, bidy spirit, music, parenting, sport, travel guides.

FABER & FABER LTD
Bloomsbury House, 74-77 Great Russell Street, London WC1B 3DA.
Tel: 020 7927 3800. Fax: 020 7927 3801. E-mail: gadesign@faber.co.uk
Web: www.faber.co.uk
Contact: Design Department.
Subjects: Biography, film, music, politics, theatre, wine.

FOCUS PUBLISHING (SEVENOAKS) LTD
11A St Botolph's Road, Sevenoaks, Kent TN13 2EB.
Tel: 01732 742456. Fax: 01732 743381. E-mail: info@focus-publishing.co.uk
Web: www.focus-publishing.co.uk
Contact: Guy Crofton, Managing Director.
Subjects: General illustrated; crafts, DIY, food and drink, gardening, health, photography, sport, transport.

W. FOULSHAM & CO
The Oriel, Thames Valley Court, 183-187 Bath Road, Slough, Berkshire SL1 4AA.
Tel: 01753 526769. Fax: 01753 535003. E-mail: marketing@foulsham.com
Web: www.foulsham.com
Contact: Barry Belasco, Managing Director.
Subjects: Crafts, collecting, cookery, DIY, gardening, health, hobbies, sport, travel.

GRUB STREET PUBLISHING
4 Rainham Close, London SW11 6SS.
Tel: 020 7924 3966. Fax: 020 7738 1009. E-mail: post@grubstreet.co.uk
Web: www.grubstreet.co.uk
Subjects: Aviation history, cookery.

GUILD OF MASTER CRAFTSMAN PUBLICATIONS LTD
86 High Street, Lewes, East Sussex BN7 1XN.
Tel: 01273 477374. Fax: 01273 402849.
Web: www.thegmcgroup.com/www.pipress.co.uk
Imprints: Photographers' Institute Press
Contact: Anthony Bailey, Chief Photographer.
Subjects: Crafts; gardening, needlework, photography, woodworking.

GUINNESS WORLD RECORDS LTD
3rd Floor, 184 Drummond Street, London NW1 3HP.
Tel: 020 7891 4567. Fax: 020 7891 4501.
Web: www.guinnessworldrecords.com
Contact: Design Department.
Subjects: Guinness World Records book, TV and merchandising, sport and popular music.

HALDANE MASON
PO Box 34196, London NW10 3YB.
Tel: 020 8459 2131. Fax: 020 8728 1216. E-mail: info@haldanemason.com
Web: www.haldanemason.com
Contact: Ron Samuel, Art Director.
Subjects: Children's illustrated non-fiction.

ROBERT HALE LTD
Clerkenwell House, 45-47 Clerkenwell Green, London EC1R 0HT.
Tel: 020 7251 2661. Fax: 020 7490 4958.
Web: www.halebooks.com
Contact: Nikki Edwards, Non Fiction Editor
Subjects: General; architecture, cookery, crafts, equestrian, gemmology, horology, mind, body and spirit, military, music, natural history, sport, topography, travel.

HARPERCOLLINS PUBLISHERS
77-85 Fulham Palace Road, London W6 8JB.
Tel: 020 8741 7070. Fax: 020 8307 4440. E-mail: enquiries@harpercollins.co.uk
Web: www.harpercollins.co.uk
Imprints: Collins, Fourth Estate, HarperElement, HarperPress, HarperSport, HarperThorsons.
Subjects: General.

HARVILL SECKER
Random House, 20 Vauxhall Bridge Road, London SW1V 2SA.
Tel: 020 7840 8540. Fax: 020 7233 6117. E-mail: harvillseckereditorial@randomhouse.co.uk
Web: www.randomhouse.co.uk
Contact: Lily Richards.
Subjects: General non-fiction.

HAYNES PUBLISHING
Sparkford, Yeovil, Somerset BA22 7JJ.
Tel: 01963 440635. Fax: 01963 440023.
Web: www.haynes.co.uk
Imprints: G.T.Foulis, Patrick Stephens.
Contact: Christine Smith, Adminstration Manager.
Subjects: Transport, DIY.

CHRISTOPHER HELM PUBLISHERS/T&AD POYSER
(Imprints of A&C Black Publishers)
36 Soho Square, London W1D 3QY.
Tel: 020 7758 0200. Fax: 020 7758 0222. E-mail: nredman@acblack.com
Web: www.acblack.com
Contact: Nigel Redman, Commissioning Editor.
Subjects: Ornithology and natural history.

THE HISTORY PRESS LTD
The History Press Ltd, The Mill, Brimscombe Port, Stroud, Gloucestershire GL5 2QG.
Tel: 01453 883300. Fax: 01453 883233. E-mail: submissions@thehistorypress.co.uk
Web: www.thehistorypress.co.uk
Contact: Katie Beard, Head of Design & Origination.
Imprints: Pathfinder, Phillimore, Pitkin, Spellmount, Stadia, Sutton, Tempus.
Subjects: Archaeology, arts, biography, crime, general history, local interest, military, royalty, social history, sport, transport & industrial, walking guides.

HODDER EDUCATION GROUP
338 Euston Road, London NW1 3BH.
Tel: 020 7873 6000. Fax: 020 7873 6325.
Web: www.hodderheadline.co.uk
Contact: Helen Townson, Design Manager.
Subjects: Education including geography, health, history, science, travel.

HODDER HEADLINE LTD
338 Euston Road, London NW1 3BH.
Tel: 020 7873 6000. Fax: 020 7873 6024.
Web: www.hodderheadline.co.uk
Contact: Picture Manager, c/o division.
Imprints: Hachette Children's Books, Headline, Hodder Education, Hodder & Stoughton.
Subjects: General; academic, biography, children's, food and wine, history, music, sport.

HUTCHINSON
Random House, 20 Vauxhall Bridge Road, London SW1V 2SA.
Tel: 020 7840 8564. Fax: 020 7233 6127. E-mail: hutchinsoneditorial@randomhouse.co.uk
Web: www.randomhouse.co.uk
Contact: Sue Freestone.
Subjects: Biography, current affairs, history, travel.

LAURENCE KING PUBLISHING LTD
361–373 City Road, London EC1V 1LR.
Tel: 020 7841 6900. Fax: 020 7841 6969. Web: www.laurenceking.com
Contact: Julia Ruxton, Picture Manager.
Subjects: Arts and architecture, design, fashion. (Digital not accepted).

KINGFISHER PUBLICATIONS
The Macmillan Building, 20 New Wharf Raoad, London N1 9RR.
Tel: 020 7014 4166. E-mail: c.weston-baker@macmillan.co.uk
Web: www.kingfisherpub.com
Contact: Cee Weston-Baker.
Subjects: Children's non-fiction, natural history, reference.

FRANCES LINCOLN LTD
4 Torriano Mews, Torriano Avenue, London NW5 2RZ.
Tel: 020 7284 4009. Fax: 020 7485 0490. E-mail: fl@frances-lincoln.com
Web: www.franceslincoln.com
Contact: Sue Gladstone, Picture Department.
Subjects: General; architecture, art, gardening, travel.

LITTLE, BROWN BOOK GROUP
100 Victoria Embankment, London EC4Y 0DY.
United KingdomTel: 020 7911 8000. Fax: 020 7911 8100. E-mail: info@littlebrown.co.uk
Web: www.littlebrown.co.uk
Imprints: Little, Brown; Abacus; Piatkus; Sphere.
Subjects: General.

THE LUTTERWORTH PRESS
P O Box 60, Cambridge CB1 2NT.
Tel: 01223 350865. Fax: 01223 366951. E-mail: publishing@lutterworth.com
Web: www.lutterworth.com
Contact: Adrian Brink.
Subjects: Antiques, art and architecture, biography, crafts, natural history, reference, religion, science.

NEW HOLLAND PUBLISHERS (UK) LTD
Garfield House, 86-88 Edgware Road, London W2 2EA.
Tel: 020 7724 7773. Fax: 020 7258 1293. E-mail: enquires@nhpub.co.uk
Web: www.newhollandpublishers.com
Subjects: Biography, crafts, cookery, gardening, history, interior design, natural history, sports and outdoor pursuits, travel.

OCTOPUS PUBLISHING GROUP LTD
2-4 Heron Quays, London E14 4JP.
Tel: 020 7531 8400. Fax: 020 7531 8650. E-mail: info@octopus-publishing.co.uk
Web: www.octopus-publishing.co.uk
Imprints: Cassell Illustrated, Conran Octopus, Gaia Books, Godsfield Press, Hamlyn, Mitchell Beazley.
Subjects: Illustrated general reference and non-fiction.

OMNIBUS PRESS/MUSIC SALES LTD
14-15 Berners Street, London W1T 3LJ.
Tel: 020 7612 7400. Fax: 020 7612 7545.
Contact: Chris Charlesworth, Editor; Jacqui Black, Picture Researcher.
Subjects: Rock, pop and classical music.

ORION PUBLISHING GROUP LTD
Orion House, 5 Upper St Martin's Lane, London WC2H 9EA.
Tel: 020 7240 3444. Fax: 020 7240 4822.
Web: www.orionbooks.co.uk
Contact: Design Department.
Imprints: Orion; Gollancz; Weidenfeld & Nicolson; Cassell Military; Halban Publishers; Allen & Unwin.
Subjects: General; biography, cookery, design, gardening, history, interiors, natural history, popular science, sport, travel.

OSPREY PUBLISHING LTD
Midland House, West Way, Botley, Oxford OX2 0HP.
Tel: 01865 727022. Fax: 01865 727017. E-mail: editorial@ospreypublishing.com
Web: www.ospreypublishing.com
Contact: Kate Moore, Publisher.
Subjects: Illustrated military history and aviation.

OXFORD UNIVERSITY PRESS
Great Clarendon Street, Oxford OX2 6DP.
Tel: 01865 556767. Fax: 01865 556646.
Web: www.oup.co.uk
Imprints: Clarendon Press, Oxford Paperbacks.
Subjects: General; academic, educational, reference.

PAN MACMILLAN
20 New Wharf Road, London N1 9RR.
Tel: 020 7014 6000. Fax: 020 7014 6001. E-mail: nonfiction@macmillan.co.uk
Web: www.panmacmillan.com
Imprints: Boxtree, Macmillan, Pan, Picador, Sidgwick & Jackson.
Subjects: General; biography, crafts, current affairs, gardening, music, popular history, practical, travel.

PENGUIN GROUP (UK)
80 Strand, London WC2R 0RL.
Tel: 020 7010 3000. Fax: 020 7010 3294. E-mail: lesley.hodgson@uk.penguingroup.com
Web: www.penguin.co.uk
Imprints: Allen Lane, Hamish Hamilton, Michael Joseph, Penguin, Viking.
Contacts: Lesley Hodgson, Samantha Johnson (Picture Editors).
Subjects: General.

PHAIDON PRESS LTD
Regent's Wharf, All Saints Street, London N1 9PA.
Tel: 020 7843 1000. Fax: 020 7843 1010. E-mail: enquiries@phaidon.com
Web: www.phaidon.com
Subjects: Architecture, decorative and fine arts, design, photography.

PHOTOGRAPHERS' INSTITUTE PRESS
(Imprint of GMC Publications)
166 High Street, Lewes, East Sussex BN7 1XN.
Tel: 01273 477374. Fax: 01273 402849. E-mail: jonathonb@thegmcgroup.com
Web: www.pipress.co.uk
Contact: Jonathan Bailey, Associate Publisher.
Subjects: Photography.

PIATKUS BOOKS LTD
Little, Brown Book Group, 100 Victoria Embankment, London EC4Y 0DY.
Tel: 020 7911 8000. Fax: 020 7911 8100. E-mail: info@littlebrown.co.uk
Web: www.piatkus.co.uk
Contact: Managing Editor.
Subjects: Biography, health, leisure, lifestyle, mind body & spirit, popular culture, women's interests.

PLAYNE BOOKS LTD
Park Court Barn, Trefin, Haverfordwest, Pembrokeshire SA62 5AU.
Tel: 01348 837073. Fax: 01348 837063. E-mail: info@playne.books.co.uk
Web: www.playnebooks.co.uk
Contact: Gill Davies, Editorial Director.
Subjects: General illustrated books for adults and children.

PLEXUS PUBLISHING LTD
25 Mallinson Road, London SW11 1BW.
Tel: 020 7924 4662. Fax: 020 7924 5096. E-mail: info@plexusuk.demon.co.uk
Web: www.plexusbooks.com
Contact: Sandra Wake, Editorial Director.
Subjects: Biography, fashion, film, music, popular culture.

THE QUARTO GROUP
26 City Road, London EC1V 2TT.
Tel: 020 7700 9000. Fax: 020 7253 4437. E-mail: info@quarto.com
Web: www.quarto.com
Contact: Caroline Guest, Art Director.
Subjects: General; arts and crafts, cookery, gardening, health, home interest, new age, reference, travel.

RAILWAYS – MILEPOST 92½
Newton Harcourt, Leicestershire LE8 9FH.
Tel: 0116 259 2068. E-mail: studio@railphotolibrary.com
Contacts: Colin Garratt, Director; Colin Nash, Picture Library Manager.
Subjects: Railways worldwide – past and present.

RANDOM HOUSE UK LTD
Random House, 20 Vauxhall Bridge Road, London SW1V 2SA.
Tel: 020 7840 8400. Fax: 020 7233 8791.
Web: www.randomhouse.co.uk
Contact: Suzanne Dean, Creative Director.
Imprints: Bodley Head, Jonathan Cape, Century, Chatto & Windus, Harvill Secker, William Heinemann, Hutchinson, Pimlico, Yellow Jersey.
Subjects: Various; see individual imprints.

READER'S DIGEST ASSOCIATION
11 Westferry Circus, Canary Wharf, London E14 1HE.
Tel: 020 7715 8000. Fax: 020 7715 8181.
Web: www.readersdigest.co.uk
Subjects: General illustrated; cookery, crafts, DIY, encyclopaedias, folklore, gardening, guide books, history, natural history.

ROTOVISION
Sheridan House, 112-116 Western Road, Hove BN3 1DD.
Tel: 01273 727268. Fax: 01273 727269. E-mail: isheetam@rotovision.com
Web: www.rotovision.com
Contact: Isheeta Mustafi, Commissioning Editor.
Subjects: Design, photography.

ROUTLEDGE
2 Park Square, Milton Park, Abingdon, Oxon OX14 4RN.
Tel: 020 7017 6000. Fax: 020 7017 6699.
Web: www.routledge.com
Contact: Design Department.
Subjects: Built environment, education, humanities, nursing and health, social sciences.

RYLAND PETERS & SMALL LTD
20-21 Jockey's Fields, London WC1R 4BW.
Tel: 020 7025 2200. Fax: 020 7025 2201. E-mail: leslie.harrington@rps.co.uk
Web: www.rylandpeters.com
Contact: Leslie Harrington, Art Director.
Subjects: Body and soul, food and drink, gift, home and garden.

SHELDRAKE PRESS LTD
188 Cavendish Road, London SW12 0DA.
Tel: 020 8675 1767. Fax: 020 8675 7736. E-mail: jsr@sheldrakepress.demon.co.uk
Web: www.sheldrakepress.co.uk
Contact: Simon Rigge, Publisher.
Subjects: Cookery, history, travel.

SHIRE PUBLICATIONS
Midland House, West Way, Botley, Oxford OX2 0HP.
Tel: 01865 727022. Fax: 01865 727017. E-mail: editorial@shirebooks.co.uk
Web: www.shirebooks.co.uk
Contact: Nick Wright, Publisher.
Subjects: Art & antiques, archaeology,history and motoring.

SIMON & SCHUSTER
1st Floor, 222 Gray's Inn Road, London, WC1X 8HB.
Tel: 020 7316 1900. Fax: 020 7316 0332. E-mail: Editorial.enquiries@simonandschuster.co.uk
Web: www.simonandschuster.co.uk
Imprints: Simon & Schuster, Pocket Books.
Subjects: Biography, cookery, health, history, self-help, childrens books and lifestyle.

SOUVENIR PRESS LTD
43 Great Russell Street, London WC1B 3PD.
Tel: 020 7580 9307. Fax: 020 7580 5064. E-mail: souvenirpress@ukonline.co.uk
Subjects: General; archaelogy, art, animals, childcare, cookery, gardening, health, hobbies, plants, practical, sociology.

As a member of the Bureau of Freelance Photographers, you'll be kept up-to-date with markets through the BFP Market Newsletter, published monthly. For details of membership, turn to page 9

THAMES & HUDSON LTD
181a High Holborn, London WC1V 7QX.
Tel: 020 7845 5000. Fax: 020 7845 5050. E-mail: s.ruston@thameshudson.co.uk
Web: www.thamesandhudson.com
Contact: Sam Ruston, Head of Picture Research.
Subjects: Art, architecture, archaeology, anthropology, cinema, fashion, interior design, music, photography, practical guides, religion and mythology, theatre, travel.

TOUCAN BOOKS LTD
3rd Floor, 89 Charterhouse Street, London EC1M 6HR.
Tel: 020 7250 3388. Fax: 020 7250 3123. E-mail: info@toucanbooks.co.uk
Web: www.toucanbooks.co.uk
Contact: Christine Vincent, Picture Manager
Subjects: General illustrated.

TRANSWORLD PUBLISHERS
61-63 Uxbridge Road, London W5 5SA.
Tel: 020 8579 2652. Fax: 020 8579 5479. E-mail: info@transworld-publishers.co.uk
Web: www.transworld-publishers.co.uk
Imprints: Bantam, Doubleday, Expert.
Subjects: General non-fiction; biography, food & drink, health, military, music, popular science, social history, sport, travel.

USBORNE PUBLISHING
83-85 Saffron Hill, London EC1N 8RT.
Tel: 020 7430 2800. Fax: 020 7242 0974. E-mail: mail@usborne.co.uk
Web: www.usborne.com
Contacts: Steve Wright; Mary Cartwright.
Subjects: General children's; crafts, natural history, practical, reference.

VIRGIN BOOKS LTD
Random House, 20 Vauxhall Bridge Road, London SW1V 2SA.
Tel: 020 7840 8352. E-mail: lstevens@virgin-books.co.uk
Web: www.virgin-books.co.uk
Contacts: Lucy Stevens (design department), Louisa Joyner, Editorial Director.
Subjects: Biography, current affairs, health, lifestyle, music, sport.

WEIDENFELD & NICOLSON LTD
Orion House, 5 Upper St Martin's Lane, London WC2H 9EA.
Tel: 020 7240 3444. Fax: 020 7240 4822.
Web: www.orionbooks.co.uk
Imprints: Cassell Military, Weidenfeld.
Subjects: Biography, history, military.

YALE UNIVERSITY PRESS
47 Bedford Square, London WC1B 3DP.
Tel: 020 7079 4900. Fax: 020 7079 4901. E-mail: x.x@yaleup.co.uk
Web: www.yalebooks.co.uk
Contact: Picture Manager.
Subjects: Architecture, art, history, politics, sociology.

CARDS, CALENDARS, POSTERS & PRINTS

This section lists publishers of postcards, greetings cards, calendars, posters and prints, along with their requirements. There is some overlap here, with many of the companies listed producing a range of products that fall into more than one of these categories,

With the exception of traditional viewcard producers, who have always offered rather meagre rates for freelance material, fees in this area are generally good. However, only those who can produce precisely what is required as far as subject matter, quality and format are concerned, are likely to succeed.

Market requirements

While digital is generally accepted here, a number of companies continue to express a preference for transparencies – particularly large format such as 6x7cm or 6x9cm.

But whether it's digital or film, the need for material of the highest quality cannot be too strongly emphasised. The market is highly specialised with very specific requirements. If you aim to break into this field, you must be very sure of your photographic technique. You must be able to produce professional quality material that is pin sharp and perfectly exposed with excellent colour saturation.

You must also know and be able to supply *exactly* what the market requires. The listings will help you, but you should also carry out your own field study by examining the photographic products on general sale.

After a period in the doldrums the photographic greetings card has been making something of a comeback in recent years. Neverthless, the big mass-market card publishers still employ mostly art or graphics. Those that do use photography tend to be smaller, specialised companies, many of them publishing a full range of photographic products. These companies also use a lot of work from top photographers or picture libraries, which means that there is greater competition than ever to supply material for these products.

The calendar market is equally demanding, though fortunately there are still large numbers of calendars using photographs being produced every year. Many calendar producers obtain the material they need from picture agencies, but this is not to say that individual photographers cannot successfully break into this field. Once again, though, you must be sure of your photographic technique and be able to produce really top quality work.

Make a point of studying the cards, calendars or posters that you see on general sale or hanging up in places you visit. Don't rely solely on what *you* think would make a good card or calendar picture; familiarise yourself with the type of pictures actually being used by these publishers.

Finally, it is worth noting that whilst many firms will consider submissions at any time, some in the calendar or greetings card market only select material at certain times of the year or when they are renewing their range. So when contemplating an approach to one of these firms, always check first to see if they are accepting submissions at the time.

Rights and fees

Where provided by the company concerned, fee guidelines are quoted. Some companies prefer to negotiate fees individually, depending upon the type of material you offer. If you are new to this field, the best plan is to make your submission (preferably after making an initial enquiry, outlining the material you have available) and let the company concerned make you an offer. Generally speaking, you should not accept less than about £75 for Greetings Card or Calendar Rights.

Remember, you are not selling your copyright for this fee; you are free to submit the same photograph to any *non-competitive* market (for example, a magazine) at a later date. But you should not attempt to sell the picture to another greetings card publisher once you have sold Greetings Card Rights to a competing firm.

CHRIS ANDREWS PUBLICATIONS LTD
15 Curtis Yard, North Hinksey Lane, Oxford OX2 0LX.
Tel: 01865 723404. Fax: 01865 725294. E-mail: chris.andrews1@btclick.com
Web: www.cap-ox.co.uk
Contact: Chris Andrews (Proprietor).
Products: Calendars, postcards, guidebooks, diaries, address books.
Requirements: Atmospheric colour images of recognisable places (towns, villages) throughout central England, specifically the Cotswolds, Oxfordshire, Cherwell Valley, Thames and Chilterns. Expanding range now covers London, the Thames, Isle of Wight, Windsor/Eton, Portsmouth/Gosport, Bristol, Winchester, Gloucester and York. Winterscapes especially welcome. Photographs not required for immediate use may be accepted into the Oxford Picture Library which is run in parallel.
Formats: Digital files on CD/DVD.
Fees: By negotiation.

THOMAS BENACCI
Unit 12, Bessemer Park, 250 Milkwood Road, London SE24 0HG.
Tel: 020 7924 0635. Fax: 020 7924 0636. E-mail: thomasbenacciltd@btconnect.com
Web: www.thomasbenacci.co.uk
Contact: Massimo Carminati (Manager).
Products: Postcards.
Requirements: Always interested in new views of London for sale to the tourist market – landmarks, scenes and buildings that are easily recognisable or interesting to tourists. Images should be bright and lively.
Formats: All considered.
Fees: £50 for postcard rights.

GB EYE LTD
1 Russell Street, Kelham Island, Sheffield S3 8RW.
Tel: 0114 292 0088. E-mail: mike@gbeye.com
Web: www.gbeye.com
Contact: Mike Cunsolo (Creative Executive).
Products: Posters, prints, postcard packs, 3D lenticulars, badges, stickers, etc.
Requirements: Pin-up type images of youth-culture celebrities – contemporary pop stars, young film and TV actors/actresses, popular young sports stars. Colour or B&W, but must have immediate appeal to the youth market. Also open to new ideas for possible generic subjects – landscapes, animals, humour, etc.
Formats: 35mm transparencies considered but medium format preferred. Digital accepted, 32x45cm at 300dpi.
Fees: Negotiable.

HALLMARK CARDS PLC
Bingley Road, Heaton, Bradford BD9 6SD.
Tel: 01274 252000. Fax: 01274 252675.
Web: www.hallmark.co.uk
Contact: (Studio Manager).
Products: Greetings cards, postcards, giftwrap.
Requirements: Will consider any images suitable for these products.
Formats: All considered.
Fees: Dependent on work and use.

IMAGES & EDITIONS LTD/OTTER HOUSE LTD
Water Lane, Haven Banks, Exeter EX2 8BY.
Tel: 01392 427 333. E-mail: m.jennings@ottherhouse.co.uk

Web: www.images-editions.co.uk/www.otterhouse.co.uk
Contact: Michelle Jennings (Art Studio Manager).
Products: Greetings cards, calendars and stationery.
Requirements: Will consider British landscapes and wildlife, domestic pets (especially cats, dogs, horses), florals, transport, travel.
Formats: Digital files preferred, transparencies considered.
Fees: By negotiation for purchase or on royalty basis.

INDIGO ART LTD

Indigo House, Brunswick Place, Liverpool L20 8DT.
Tel: 0151 933 9779. Fax: 0151 922 1524. E-mail: info@indigoart.co.uk
Web: www.indigoart.co.uk
Contact: Dave Bertram (Proprietor).
Products: Large-scale display prints for use in interior design projects.
Requirements: Striking colour or B&W images with a modern/contemporary look. Wide variety of styles considered: abstracts, close-ups, experimentation with light, angles or digital manipulation. Work in series preferred. See the Indigo Collection on website for current range of styles. Submission guidelines are available for download.
Formats: Digital (20–50MB), transparencies, prints or high-res scans (50MB).
Fees: On a royalties basis, 10% of wholesale print price.

INFOCADO

Gooch's Court, Stamford, Lincs PE9 2RE.
Tel: 01780 481498Fax: 01780 766031. E-mail: submissions@infocado.co.uk
Web: www.infocado.co.uk
Contact: Brian Oliver (General Manager).
Products: Calendars.
Requirements: Anything depicting "the true character of Britain". British countryside; architecture and heritage; flowers and gardens; animals both domestic and wild, natural and humorous; transport.
Formats: Digital submissions only (50MB TIFF). See website for full submission guidelines.
Fees: Subject to negotiation.

JUDGES POSTCARDS LTD

176 Bexhill Road, St Leonard's on Sea, East Sussex TN38 8BN.
Tel: 01424 710377. Fax: 01424 438538. E-mail: michelle.renno@judges.co.uk
Web: www.judges.co.uk
Contact: Michelle Renno (Product Co-ordinator).
Products: Postcards, calendars, greetings cards.
Requirements: Images of England and Wales, local and regional, appealing to the tourist industry. Must be bright, sunny and vibrant. Landscapes, flowers, animals and any other imagery may be considered.
Formats: Film and digital. Small JPEG files may be sent for viewing purposes. Final digital submission must be to A3 at 300dpi, TIFFs in CMYK (convert RGB before submitting). Prefer unretouched original files.
Fees: Dependent on quality and quantity.

KARDORAMA LTD

PO Box 85, Potters Bar, Herts EN6 5AD.
Tel: 01707 271710.
Web: www.kardorama.co.uk
Contact: Brian Elwood (Managing Director).
Products: Postcards.
Requirements: Always seeking new views of London – major tourist sights or subjects that tourists

would consider typical such as red buses, phone boxes, policemen, taxis, etc. Should be good record shots but with "a hint of romance" and plenty of detail in the main subject. Also, humorous images, any subject or location providing the image needs no explanation, but must be sharp and well exposed under good lighting conditions.
Formats: Digital files preferred (with print copy); 35mm and medium format transparencies also considered.
Fees: Variable, depending on quality of work, subject matter and quantities

PHOTODIMENSION
600 Liverpool Road, Ainsdale, Southport PR8 3BQ.
Tel: 07840 918131. E-mail: ian@photodimension.co.uk
Web: www.photodimension.co.uk
Contact: Ian Homewood (Proprietor).
Products: Limited edition fine art and canvas prints, sold via website.
Requirements: Top quality images suitable for large format decoration and wall display in hotels, bars, businesses or homes. Any subject considered but mainly landscapes, florals, abstracts, architecture, portraiture, wildlife/captive animals, sports/action, documentary and photographic art. Must be eligible for limited edition sales.
Formats: Digital files, JPEGs sized to A3 at 300dpi.
Fees: 75 per cent of net sale profit (after printing, shipping and transaction costs) to the photographer.

PINEAPPLE PARK LTD
Unit 9, Henlow Trading Estate, Henlow, Bedfordshire, SG16 6DS.
Tel: 01462 814817. Fax: 01462 819443. E-mail: sarah@pineapplepark.co.uk
Web: www.pineapplepark.co.uk
Contact: Sarah M Parker (Director).
Products: Greetings cards.
Requirements: Seek high quality colour images of: 1) Florals – contemporary and traditional needed for female-orientated range of greetings cards. Country kitchen type arrangements including china, country dressers etc also needed. 2) Male subjects, eg collection of wine bottles, sporting items, cars etc for male-orientated greetings cards. 3) Gardens and gardening.
Formats: Digital files or colour transparencies. Check website for submission details.
Fees: By negotiation, for worldwide greetings card rights.

PORTFOLIO COLLECTION LTD
105 Golborne Road, London W10 5NL.
Tel: 020 8960 1826/3051. Fax: 020 8960 6570. E-mail: jayne@portfoliocards.com
Contact: Jayne Diggory (Director).
Products: Greetings cards and posters.
Requirements: Specialists in creative black and white photography. Strong, contemporary, expressive images – landscapes, cityscapes, people, etc. Also nostalgic images from the '60s and '70s – pop stars, swinging London, flower power, etc.
Formats: Prints from 10x8in up.
Fees: Usually on royalty basis at 12 per cent of distribution price. Flat fees may be negotiated.

Are you working from the latest edition of The Freelance Photographer s Market Handbook? It s published on 1 October each year. Markets are constantly changing, so it pays to have the latest edition

---

NIGEL QUINEY PUBLICATIONS

Cloudesley House, Shire Hill, Saffron Walden, Essex CB11 3FB.
Tel: 01799 520200. Fax: 01799 520100. E-mail: abutterworth@nigelquiney.com
Web: www.nigelquiney.com
Contact: Alison Butterworth (Creative Director).
Products: Greetings cards.
Requirements: Top quality colour images of animals (domestic and wild) in humorous or interesting situations, and florals – bright, modern, contemporary. Will also consider images suitable for anniversary, new baby, etc.
Formats: Digital files.
Fees: Dependent on product/design, for world rights for five years.

RIVERSIDE CARDS

Jubilee Way, Grange Moor, Wakefield WF4 4TD.
Tel: 01924 840500. Fax: 01924 840600. E-mail: design@riversidecards.com
Web: www.riversidecards.com
Contact: Design Studio.
Products: Greetings cards.
Requirements: B&W and colour images of cute domestic animals (kittens, puppies, etc), landscapes, seascapes, countryside scenes, artistic/natural florals, dramatic/atmospheric sunsets and sunrise.
Formats: Any considered including digital files (low-res JPEG for initial submission; high res TIFF required once order confirmed).
Fees: By negotiation.

ROSE OF COLCHESTER LTD

Clough Road, Severalls Industrial Park, Colchester CO4 9QT.
Tel: 01206 844500. Fax: 01206 845872. E-mail: simon@rosecalendars.co.uk
Web: www.rosecalendars.co.uk/www.reeve-calendars.com
Contact: Simon Williams (Publishing Manager).
Products: Calendars for business promotion.
Requirements: British and worldwide landscapes and wildlife. Also glamour, classic cars and supercars, adventure sport. Submit January for annual selection process, but material accepted throughout the year.
Formats: Full resolution files from high-end digital cameras or professional scans from medium and large format transparencies. All files must have accurate metadata embedded detailing subject matter, with exact location for scenic submissions.
Fees: Negotiable depending on subject matter.

SANTORO GRAPHICS

Rotunda Point, 11 Hartfield Crescent, Wimbledon, London SW19 3RL.
Tel: 020 8781 1100. Fax: 020 8781 1101. E-mail: submissions@santorographics.com
Web: santorographics.com
Contact: J. Freeman
Products: Postcards and greetings cards.
Requirements: Striking and attractive images appealing to the typical young poster and card buyer: nostalgic, retro, contemporary, romantic, humorous and cute images of people, animals and situations. B&W a speciality, but colour images in contemporary styles are also sought.
Formats: Any considered.
Fees: By negotiation for worldwide rights.

AGENCIES

Picture libraries and agencies are in the business of selling pictures. They are not in the business of teaching photography or advising photographers how to produce saleable work – although they can sometimes prove remarkably helpful in the latter respect to those who show promise. Their purpose is strictly a business one: to meet the demand for stock pictures from such markets as magazine and book publishers, advertising agencies, travel operators, greetings card and calendar publishers, and many more.

Many photographers look upon an agency as a last resort; they have been unable to sell their photographs themselves, so they think they might as well try unloading them on an agency. This is the wrong attitude. No agency will succeed in placing pictures which are quite simply unmarketable. In any event, the photographer who has had at least some success in selling pictures is in a far better position to approach an agency.

Agency requirements

If you hope to interest an agency in your work, you must be able to produce pictures which the agency feels are likely to sell to one of their markets. Although the acceptance of your work by an agency is no guarantee that it will sell, an efficient agency certainly will not clutter up its files with pictures which do not stand a reasonably good chance of finding a market.

Agents handle pictures of every subject under the sun. Some specialise in particular subjects – sport, natural history, etc – while others act as general agencies, covering the whole spectrum of subject matter. Any photograph that could be published in one form or another is a suitable picture for an agency.

Even if you eventually decide that you want to place all your potentially saleable material with an agency, you cannot expect to leave every aspect of the business to them. You must continue to study the market, watching for trends; you must continue to study published pictures.

For example, if your speciality is travel material, you should use every opportunity to study the type of pictures published in current travel brochures and other markets using such material. Only by doing this – by being aware of the market – can you hope to continue to provide your agency with marketable pictures.

Nowadays agencies do most of their business online and maintain extensive websites displaying the images they hold. Though some still accept film images, most only want digitally-captured images or high-resolution scans.

Although agency websites are primarily aimed at potential picture buyers, they are equally valuable to the photographer considering an approach since they give a good indication of the type of subject and style of work the agency handles.

Commission and licensing

Agencies generally work on a commission basis, 50 per cent being the most usual rate – if they receive £100 for reproduction rights in a picture, the photographer gets £50 of this. Some agencies have more variable rates, depending on who handles keywording, scanning, etc should these be required.

The percentage taken may seem high, but it should be remembered that a picture agency, like any other business, has substantial overheads to account for.

There can also be high costs involved in making prospective buyers aware of the pictures that are available. Some larger agencies produce lavish colour catalogues featuring selections of their best pictures, while smaller agencies regularly send out flyers. All are involved in constantly maintaining and updating their websites.

Agencies do not normally sell pictures outright. As would the individual photographer, they merely sell reproduction rights, the image being licensed to the buyer for a specific purpose. Images may be licensed by size of reproduction, by territory in which they are published, by the medium in which they are reproduced, by time and/or quantity of reproductions, and can be exclusive or non-exclusive. Selling in this way is known as "rights-managed" licensing.

Other forms of selling undertaken by certain agencies are "royalty-free" and "microstock". Under these methods images are sold for a flat fee and pre-licensed for a specified range of uses. Fees are generally low, but this disadvantage may be offset by multiple sales of the same image.

A long-term investment

When dealing with a photographer for the first time, most agencies require a minimum initial submission – which can consist of anything from a few to 500 or more pictures. Most also stipulate that you must keep your material with them for a minimum period of anything from one to five years.

When an agency takes on the work of a new photographer, they are involved in a lot of work – categorising, filing, keywording, cross-indexing and more.

The next step will be to make it known to picture buyers that these new pictures are available, perhaps including reproductions of them in any new catalogues or publicity material and getting an initial selection onto the website.

Having been involved in all this work and expense, it is not unreasonable for them to want to be given a fair chance to market the pictures. If the photographer were able to demand the withdrawal of the images after only a few months, the agency will have been involved in a lot of work and expense for nothing.

Dealing with an agency must therefore be considered a long-term investment. Having initially placed, say, a few hundred pictures with an agency, it could be at least several months before any are selected by a picture buyer, and even longer before any monies are seen by the photographer.

Normally, the photographer will also be expected to regularly submit new material to the library. Indeed, only when you have several hundred pictures lodged with the library can you hope for regular sales – and a reasonable return on your investment.

Making an approach

When considering placing work with an agency, the best plan is to make an initial short-list of those that seem most appropriate to your work.

Then contact the agency or agencies of your choice outlining the material you have available. It may also be worth mentioning details of any sales you have made yourself. If an agency is interested they will probably ask that you first post or e-mail some samples to them. Later they may suggest an appointment when you can bring a wider selection material to show them in person.

But remember that there is little point in approaching an agency until you have a sizeable collection of potentially saleable material. Most will not feel it worth their while dealing with a photographer who has only a dozen or so marketable pictures to offer – it just wouldn't be worth all the work and expense involved. And the chance of the photographer seeing a worthwhile return on just a dozen pictures placed with an agency are remote indeed; you'd be lucky to see more than one cheque in ten years!

In the listings that follow you'll find information on established agencies seeking work from new contributors: the subjects they handle, the markets they supply, the formats they stock, their terms of business (including any minimum submission quantity and minimum retention period), and their standard commission charged on sales.

Prefacing the listings you'll find an Agency Subject Index. This is a guide to agencies which have a special interest in those subjects, though many other agencies may also cover the same subjects within their general stock.

Remember: simply placing material with an agency doesn't guarantee sales. And no agency can sell material for which there is no market. On the other hand, if you are able to produce good quality, marketable work, and can team up with the right agency, you could see a very worthwhile return from this association.

An asterisk against an agency name in the main listings indicates membership of the British Association of Picture Libraries & Agencies (BAPLA).

174

Subject Index

Aerial

Geo Aerial Photography
Skyscan Photolibrary

Agriculture

Ecoscene
NHPA/Photoshot
Oxford Scientific (OSF) Ltd
Panos Pictures
Papilio
Royal Geographical Society Picture Library

Architecture

Arcblue
Loop Images
View Pictures Ltd
Elizabeth Whiting & Associates

Botanical/Gardens

FLPA – Images of Nature
Garden Picture Library
Garden World Images
NHPA/Photoshot
Natural Science Photos
Oxford Scientific (OSF) Ltd
Papilio
PictureNature
Shorelark
Elizabeth Whiting & Associates
TTL Plus

Business/Industry

Eye Ubiquitous
Footprint Images
Leslie Garland Picture Library
Getty Images
Robert Harding World Imagery
Impact Photos
Link Picture Library
Newscast Ltd
Photolibrary.com
Panos Pictures
Picturebank Photo Library Ltd
SCR Photo Library
StockScotland.com

Food/Drink

Bubbles Photo Library
Eyecatchers
Food Features
Foodanddrinkphotos.com
Fresh Food Images
Stockfood Ltd
Travel Ink
Elizabeth Whiting & Associates

General (all subjects)

Adams Picture Library
Alamy
Art Directors/TRIP Photo Library
Corbis
Eye Ubiquitous
Getty Images
Robert Harding World Imagery
Imagestate
Photoshot
Pictures Colour Library
TheImagefile.com

Geography/Environment

Allan Cash Picture Library
Ecoscene
Eye Ubiquitous
FLPA – Images of Nature
Impact Photos
Link Picture Library
NHPA/Photoshot
Natural Science Photos
Oxford Scientific (OSF) Ltd
Panos Pictures
Papilio
Picturebank Photo Library Ltd
Royal Geographical Society Picture Library
SCR Photo Library

Glamour

Camera Press Ltd
Picturebank Photo Library Ltd

Historical

Bridgeman Art Library
Royal Geographical Society Picture Library

Landscapes

Arcangel Images
Collections
Cornish Picture Library
Epicscotland
Fotomaze
Loop Images
NHPA/Photoshot
Oxford Scientific (OSF) Ltd
PictureNature
Shorelark
StockScotland
TTL Plus

Music

Arena PAL
Camera Press Ltd
Capital Pictures
Famous
Getty Images
Jazz Index Photo Library
Lebrecht Photo Library
Retna Pictures Ltd

News/Current Affairs

Camera Press Ltd
Express Syndication
Getty Images News & Sport
London Media Press
Press Association Images
Rex Features Ltd
World Picture News
Zenith Image Library

People/Lifestyle

Allan Cash Picture Library
Bizarre Archive
Latitude Stock
PYMCA
Picturebank Photo Library Ltd
Photolibrary.com
Photofusion Picture Library
Retna Pictures Ltd
Shorelark
Socialstock

Personalities/Celebrities

Big Pictures
Camera Press Ltd

Capital Pictures
Eyevine
Express Syndication
Famous
Getty Images News & Sport
Lebrecht Photo Library
London Media Press
Newscast Ltd
Nunn Syndication
Press Association Images
Retna Pictures Ltd
Rex Features Ltd
Writer Pictures

Science/Technology

Camera Press Ltd
Oxford Scientific (OSF) Ltd
Picturebank Photo Library Ltd
Science Photo Library

Social Documentary

Allan Cash Picture Library
Arkreligion
Bubbles Photo Library
Collections
E & E Image Library
Eye Ubiquitous
Impact Photos
Link Picture Library
PYMCA
Panos Pictures
Photofusion Picture Library
Socialstock
Zenith Image Library

Sport

Action Images Ltd
Getty Images News & Sport
Kos Picture Source Ltd
Photolibrary.com
Press Association Images
Skishoot
Skyscan Photolibrary

Transport

Alvey & Towers
Cody Images
Railphotolibrary.com
Skyscan Photolibrary
Slick Stock Images

Travel/Tourist

Andalucia Plus Image Library
Andes Press Agency
Allan Cash Picture Library
Eye Ubiquitous
Eyecatchers
Footprint Images
Fresh Food Images
Kos Picture Source Ltd
Latitude Stock
Photolibrary.com
Picturebank Photo Library Ltd
Pictures Colour Library
Skishoot
Spectrum Colour Library
The Travel Library
World Pictures/Photoshot

Underwater

FLPA – Images of Nature
Kos Picture Source Ltd
Natural Science Photos
Oxford Scientific (OSF) Ltd
Papilio
PictureNature

Wildlife

FLPA – Images of Nature
NHPA/Photoshot
Natural Science Photos
Oxford Scientific (OSF) Ltd
Papilio
PictureNature
TTL Plus

ACTION IMAGES*
1st Floor, Aldgate House, 33 Aldgate High Street, London EC3N 1DL.
Tel: 0845 155 6352 E-mail: info@actionimages.com
Web: www.actionimages.com
Contact: Gavin Clay (Head of Photography and Assignments).
Specialist subjects/requirements: High quality sports pictures, especially of any unusual or spectacular incident.
Markets supplied: Newspapers, magazines, books, etc.
Formats accepted: Digital only; minimum 18MB files.
Usual terms of business: No minimum initial submission, but phone first to discuss possible submissions.
Commission: Negotiable.
Additional information: Operates as the specialist sports arm of the Reuters news agency.

ADAMS PICTURE LIBRARY (APL)*
The Studio, Hillside Cottage, Hessenford, Cornwall PL11 3HH.
Tel: 01503 240475. Fax: 01503 240890. E-mail: tam@adamspicturelibrary.com
Web: www.adamspicturelibrary.com
Contact: Dave Jarvis, Tamsyn Jarvis (Partners).
Specialist subjects/requirements: All subjects, with special interest in retro fashion.
Markets supplied: All markets including advertising, publishing, calendars and posters.
Formats accepted: Digital files preferred (50MB).
Usual terms of business: Minimum initial submission: 100 images. Minimum retention period: 5 years; 1 year's notice required for withdrawal.
Commission: 50 per cent (for exclusive images).

ALAMY*
127 Milton Park, Abingdon, Oxon OX14 4SA.
Tel: 01235 844640. Fax: 01235 844650. E-mail: memberservices@alamy.com
Web: www.alamy.com
Contact: Alan Capel (Head of Content); Alexandra Bortkiewicz (Director of Photography).
Specialist subjects/requirements: Quality images of all subjects – business, lifestyle, travel, vacations, sports, food, abstracts, concepts, still life, science, wildlife, people, celebrities, historical, reportage.
Markets supplied: Advertising, design, corporate and publishing worldwide.
Formats accepted: Digital files only, usually 48–70MB uncompressed RGB JPEG. See website for full technical requirements.
Usual terms of business: Requires initial test submission of four images; if accepted no minimum submission applies.
Commission: 60 per cent to photographer.
Additional information: Photographers must supply their own digital files and keywording. Alamy do not edit photographers' submissions but files are checked for technical accuracy before being allowed online. For initial approach first register on the website.

ALVEY & TOWERS*
The Springboard Centre, Mantle Lane, Coalville, Leicestershire LE67 3DW.
Tel/fax: 01530 450011. E-mail: office@alveyandtowers.com
Web: www.alveyandtowers.com
Contact: Emma Rowen (Library Manager).
Specialist subjects/requirements: All aspects of transport, air, sea and land, including associated industries and issues worldwide.

Markets supplied: Advertising, books, magazines, corporate brochures, calendars, audio visual.
Formats accepted: Digital only.
Usual terms of business: On application.
Commission: 40 per cent.
Additional information: It is essential that potential contributors make contact prior to making any submission in order to discuss precise requirements. Submission guidelines available via e-mail.

ANDES PRESS AGENCY
26 Padbury Court, London E2 7EH.
Tel: 020 7613 5417. Fax: 020 7739 3159. E-mail: photos@andespressagency.com
Web: www.andespressagency.com
Contact: Val Baker (Picture Editor).
Specialist subjects/requirements: Latin America, including the Caribbean; world religions.
Markets supplied: Books, newspapers, magazines.
Formats accepted: All considered.
Usual terms of business: Minimum initial submission: 100 transparencies. Minimum retention period: 3 years.
Commission: By negotiation.

ARCANGEL IMAGES LTD
Apartado 528, Calle Las Mimosas 85, Campo Mijas, Mijas Costa, 29649, Malaga, Spain.
Tel: 0871 218 1023. E-mail: submissions@arcangel-images.com
Web: www.arcangel-images.com
Contact: Michael Mascaro (Director).
Specialist subjects/requirements: creative and fine art imagery, from nudes to landscapes and with the emphasis on digital capture. Will consider all types of images and styles, from general high-quality stock to personal fine art work.
Markets supplied: Book publishing, music industry, design companies, etc.
Formats accepted: Digital files only (minimum 17MB, preferred 30-40MB).
Usual terms of business: Minimum initial submission: 20 accepted images. Minimum retention period: 3 years.
Commission: 50 per cent.
Additional information: British/Spanish company with head office in Spain. Prefer initial approach by e-mail with a few sample images (totalling no more than 500KB) or a link to a personal website.

ARCBLUE*
93 Gainsborough Road, Richmond, Surrey TW9 2ET.
Tel: 020 8940 2227. Fax: 020 8940 6570. E-mail: info@arcblue.com
Web: www.arcblue.com
Contact: Peter Durant (Library Manager).
Specialist subjects/requirements: Modern contemporary architecture and built environment. Also interiors and landscape.
Markets supplied: General publishing, advertising and design.
Formats accepted: Digital (60MB RGB TIFF).
Usual terms of business: Minimum initial submission: 30 images. Minimum retention period: 2 years.
Commission: 40 per cent.
Additional information: Prefer to see coherent sets of images that work together as well as individually. Send sample set of images in the first instance by e-mail, preferably 20–50 images in digital format.

ARENA PAL*
Thompson House, 42-44 Dolben Street, London SE1 0UQ.
Tel: 020 7403 8542. Fax: 020 7403 8561. E-mail: enquiries@arenapal.com
Web: www.arenapal.com
Contact: Mike Markiewicz (Submissions & Archive Manager).
Specialist subjects/requirements: Performing arts, the entertainment industry and relevant personalities – theatre, music, dance, opera, jazz, TV, film, circus, festivals and venues.
Markets supplied: All media including publishing, arts bodies, advertising, design companies.
Formats accepted: All formats, digital files preferred.
Usual terms of business: No minimum initial submission, but expect around 100 images.
Minimum retention period: 3 years.
Commission: 50 per cent.

ARKRELIGION.COM*
57 Burdon Lane, Cheam, Surrey SM2 7BY.
Tel: 020 8642 3593. Fax: 020 8395 7230. E-mail: images@artdirectors.co.uk
Web: www.arkreligion.com
Contact: Helene Rogers (Partner).
Specialist subjects/requirements: All religions worldwide, mainstream to alternate, ceremonies from birth to death, festivals and important events, people (priests, pilgrims, worshippers), artefacts, churches/temples, holy books, worship, meals and food, daily rituals.
Markets supplied: Advertising and editorial.
Formats accepted: All formats, but digital preferred (minimum 50MB 8-bit TIFF).
Usual terms of business: Minimum initial submission: 100 images. Minimum retention period: 3 years.
Commission: 50 per cent.
Additional information: Photographers' Guidelines can be viewed on the website.

ART DIRECTORS/TRIP PHOTO LIBRARY*
57 Burdon Lane, Cheam, Surrey SM2 7BY.
Tel: 020 8642 3593. Fax: 020 8395 7230. E-mail: images@artdirectors.co.uk
Web: www.artdirectors.co.uk
Contact: Bob Turner (Partner).
Specialist subjects/requirements: All subjects and all locations. Art Directors supplies images mainly for advertising; TRIP handles general travel material and in-depth, extensive coverage of all religions.
Markets supplied: Advertising and editorial.
Formats accepted: All formats; digital preferred (minimum 50MB 8-bit TIFF).
Usual terms of business: Minimum initial submission: 100 images. Minimum retention period: 3 years.
Commission: 50 per cent.
Additional information: Ask for Photographers' Guidelines or view them on website.

BIG PICTURES*
50-54 Clerkenwell Road, London EC1M 5PS.
Tel: 020 7250 3555. Fax: 020 7250 0033. E-mail: production@bigpictures.co.uk
Web: www.bigpictures.co.uk/www.mrpaparazzi.com
Contact: Tomasina Brittain (Picture Editor).
Specialist subjects/requirements: Current, well-known and preferably A-list celebrities, mainly informal paparazzi material.
Markets supplied: News media and magazines worldwide.

Formats accepted: Digital files preferred.
Usual terms of business: No minimum submission. Minimum retention period: Exclusive worldwide sales licence for 90 days.
Commission: 50 per cent, or outright purchase.
Additional information: Urgent images can be quickly uploaded via the agency's "Mr Paparazzi" website.

BIZARRE ARCHIVE
30 Cleveland Street, London W1T 4JD.
Tel: 020 7907 6485. E-mail: tom@bizarrearchive.com
Web: www.bizarrearchive.com
Contact: Tom Broadbent (Director).
Specialist subjects/requirements: Photo features on anything weird, quirky or bizarre – pin-up girls, alternative models, fetish and sex material, sideshows, bizarre people, odd animals, lowbrow artists, underground clubs, self-made freaks, alternative fashion, eccentric lifestyles and individuals, extreme tattoos and body modification, counterculture icons of music, performance and film.
Markets supplied: Magazines, newspapers and websites worldwide.
Formats accepted: Digital files preferred.
Usual terms of business: No minimum initial submission. Minimum retention period: None stated.
Commission: 50 per cent.
Additional information: Also stocks, syndicates and sells on material published in Bizarre magazine.

BRIDGEMAN ART LIBRARY*
17-19 Garway Road, London W2 4PH.
Tel: 020 7727 4065. Fax: 020 7792 8509. E-mail: info@bridgeman.co.uk
Web: www.bridgeman.co.uk
Contact: Adrian Gibbs (Collections Manager).
Specialist subjects/requirements: American, European and Oriental paintings and prints, antiques, antiquities, arms and armour, botanical subjects, ethnography, general historical subjects and personalities, maps and manuscripts, natural history, topography, transport, etc.
Markets supplied: Publishing, advertising, television, greetings cards, calendars, etc.
Formats accepted: Minimum 5x4in transparencies or 50MB digital files (RGB TIFF).
Usual terms of business: No minimum initial submission. Retention period negotiable.
Commission: 50 per cent.

BUBBLES PHOTO LIBRARY*
3 Rose Lane, Ipswich IP1 1XE.
Tel: 01473 288605. E-mail: info@bubblesphotolibrary.co.uk
Web: www.bubblesphotolibrary.co.uk
Contact: Sarah Robinson, Loisjoy Thurstun (Partners).
Specialist subjects/requirements: Babies, children, pregnancy, mothercare, child development, education (especially aspects of multiculturalism), teenagers, old age, family life, women's health and medical, still lives of food, vegetables, herbs, etc.
Markets supplied: Books, magazines, newspapers and advertising.
Formats accepted: All formats but digital files preferred (A3 at 300dpi)
Usual terms of business: Minimum initial submission: 100 images. Regular contributions expected. Minimum retention period: 3 years.
Commission: 50 per cent.
Additional information: Attractive women and children sell best. Always looking for multicultural and multiracial children/adults. Photographers must pay close attention to selecting models that are healthy-looking and ensure that backgrounds are uncluttered. Best clothes to wear are light coloured and neutral fashion.

CAMERA PRESS LTD*
21 Queen Elizabeth Street, London SE1 2PD.
Tel: 020 7378 1300. Fax: 020 7407 2635. E-mail: j.wald@camerapress.com
Web: www.camerapress.com
Contact: Jacqui Ann Wald (Editorial Director).
Specialist subjects/requirements: Photographs and illustrated features covering celebrity and personality portraiture, news, reportage, humour, music, food, fashion, beauty and interiors.
Formats accepted: Digital preferred (min 30MB) but scanning still undertaken.
Usual terms of business: By mutual agreement.
Commission: 50 per cent.

CAPITAL PICTURES*
85 Randolph Avenue, London W9 1DL.
Tel: 020 7286 2212. E-mail: sales@capitalpictures.com
Web: www.capitalpictures.com
Contact: Phil Loftus (Manager).
Specialist subjects/requirements: Celebrities and personalities from the worlds of showbusiness, film and TV, rock and pop, politics and royalty.
Markets supplied: UK and international magazines, newspapers, etc.
Formats accepted: Digital only.
Usual terms of business: Minimum initial submission: 100 images. Minimum retention period: 1 year.
Commission: 50 per cent.

THE ALLAN CASH PICTURE LIBRARY*
21 Ceylon Road, London W14 OPY.
Tel: 020 7371 2224. E-mail: david@allancashpicturelibrary.com
Web: www.allancashpicturelibrary.com
Contact: David Bromley (Manager).
Specialist subjects/requirements: Travel and documentary photography from around the world, including culture, industry, native peoples, nature, landmarks and historical images.
Markets supplied: Magazines, newspapers, advertising, travel trade.
Formats accepted: Digital files and film negatives.
Usual terms of business: Minimum initial submission: 100 images. Minimum retention period: 3 months.
Commission: 50 per cent.
Additional information: The library is based on the lifetime's work, covering over 75 countries, of the renowned 20th century travel photographer James Allan Cash FRPS, FIBP.

CLOWNFISHPHOTO
20 Millersdale Drive, West Bromwich, West Midlands B71 3PX.
E-mail: info@clownfishphoto.co.uk
Web: www.clownfishphoto.co.uk
Contact: Craig Stephens (Director).
Specialist subjects/requirements: Displays photographers' personal work for online sales of prints, posters and other items direct to the public. Also markets images to publishing contacts worldwide.
Markets supplied: General public and commercial/publishing industry.
Formats accepted: Digital only. Images for display to be no more than 15MB; if and when an image is sold the agency will contact the photographer and advise what size, format and resolution is required.

Usual terms of business: Minimum six month subscription. No image retention period.
Commission: Photographer receives 80 per cent on sales to commercial clients, 100 per cent on sales to the public.
Additional information: There is a monthly subscription fee of £3.00 for photographers. Subscribers have access to sales reports and hit count statistics for each of their uploaded images enabling monitoring and management of portfolio to maximise sales.

CODY IMAGES*
2 Reform Street, Beith KA15 2AE.
Tel: 0845 2235451. Fax: 0845 2235452. E-mail: ted@codymages.com
Web: www.codyimages.com
Contact: Ted Nevill (Director).
Specialist subjects/requirements: All aspects of aviation and defence – worldwide, historical and modern.
Markets supplied: Books, magazines, newspapers, multi-media, etc.
Formats accepted: All formats, digital files preferred.
Usual terms of business: Minimum initial submission: 200 images. Minimum retention period: 3 years.
Commission: 50 per cent.
Additional information: Ring first to discuss submission and agency requirements.

COLLECTIONS*
13 Woodberry Crescent, London N10 1PJ.
Tel: 020 8883 0083. Fax: 020 8883 9215. E-mail: sal.shuel@btinternet.com
Web: www.collectionspicturelibrary.com/www.collectionspicturelibrary.co.uk
Contact: Brian, Sal and Simon Shuel (Directors).
Specialist subjects: The British Isles and Ireland.
Markets supplied: All, particularly on the editorial side.
Formats accepted: All formats, digital preferred (min 26MB), will consider transparencies and B&W prints, but only in exceptional circumstances
Usual terms of business: By arrangement; "easy going and on the side of the contributor."
Commission: 50 per cent.
Additional information: The library aims to stock quality pictures of as many places, things, happenings on these islands as possible.

CORBIS*
111 Salusbury Road, London NW6 6RG.
Tel: 020 7644 7644. Fax: 020 7644 7645. E-mail: info@corbis.com
Web: www.corbis.com
Contact: Vanessa Kramer (Director of Artistic Relations).
Specialist subjects/requirements: General library handling most subjects, on both a licensed and royalty-free basis.
Markets supplied: Advertising, publishing, design, etc.
Formats accepted: Digital files only, minimum 10MB (current events) or 50MB (editorial/advertising).
Usual terms of business: Minimum initial submission variable. Minimum retention period: 3 years.
Commission: 20–50 per cent, depending on client and use.
Additional information: For detailed contributor submission information see http://studioplus.corbis.com

CORNISH PICTURE LIBRARY*
40b Fore Street, St Columb Major, Cornwall TR9 6RH.
Tel: 01637 880103. E-mail: paul@imageclick.co.uk

Web: www.imageclick.co.uk
Contact: Paul Watts (Proprietor).
Specialist subjects/requirements: Cornwall and the West Country (Devon, Dorset, Somerset, Wiltshire, Isles of Scilly, Channel Isles) – landscapes, historic sites, gardens, people, activities, attractions, wildlife.
Markets supplied: Magazines, books, tourism, etc.
Formats accepted: Digital files from 10MP cameras upwards, minimum 30MB TIFF; must be colour correct preferably with Adobe 1998 profile and with full picture details and keywords in metadata. Top quality medium format or larger transparencies accepted; no 35mm. B&W archive (pre-1960) images of Cornwall.
Usual terms of business: No minimum submission. Minimum retention period: 5 years.
Commission: 50 per cent.
Additional information: Contact by e-mail to request contributors' guidelines before sending submission. Browse website for more info and to view images already held; very similar images not required, only better shots or different views.

THE DEFENCE PICTURE LIBRARY LTD
14 Howeson Court, Mary Seacole Road, The Millfields Business Park, Plymouth PL1 3JY.
Tel: 01752 312061. Fax: 01752 312063. E-mail: dpl@defencepictures.com
Web: www.defencepictures.com
Contact: David Reynolds (Director).
Specialist subjects/requirements: Military images covering all aspects of the armed forces worldwide, in training and on operations. Pictures of UK and international forces across the globe are always of interest.
Markets supplied: Publishers, advertising agencies, national media.
Formats accepted: High-resolution TIFF files preferred, 35mm and medium format trasparencies accepted.
Usual terms of business: Minimum initial submission: 50 quality images. Minimum retention period: 5 years.
Commission: 50 per cent.
Additional information: The library is the UK's leading specialist source of military and defence images.

E & E IMAGE LIBRARY*
Beggars Roost, Woolpack Hill, Brabourne Lees, Nr Ashford, Kent TN25 6RR.
Tel: 01303 812608. E-mail: info@eeimages.co.uk
Web: www.eeimages.co.uk
Contact: Isobel Sindon (Proprietor).
Specialist subjects/requirements: World religions, festivals, manuscripts/illustrations, Biblelands, stained glass, architecture, places of interest, heritage, death (ceremonies, funerals, burials), eccentricities/oddities, transport, nature.
Markets supplied: General publishing, newspapers, TV, merchandising.
Formats accepted: Digital files preferred, with full caption and keywords.
Usual terms of business: Minimum initial submission: 50 images; less if specialist subject matter. Minimum retention period: 5 years.
Commission: 50 per cent.

ECOSCENE*
Empire Farm, Throop Road, Templecombe, Somerset BA8 0HR.
Tel: 01963 371700. E-mail: sally@ecoscene.com
Web: www.ecoscene.com
Contact: Sally Morgan (Proprietor).
Specialist subjects/requirements: Environmental issues worldwide including agriculture, conservation, energy, pollution, transport, sustainable development.

Markets supplied: Books, magazines, organisations, etc.
Formats accepted: Digital files at 50MB.
Usual terms of business: Minimum initial submission: 100 quality images. Minimum retention period: 4 years.
Commission: 55 per cent to photographer.
Additional information: Contributors' guidelines available on request – can also be found on the library's website along with details of specific current requirements.

EPICSCOTLAND
Unit 5, Hathaway Business Centre, 21-29 Hathaway Street, Glasgow G20 8TD.
Tel: 0141 945 0000. Email: info@epicscotland.com
Web: www.epicscotland.com
Contact: Emily Bevan-Pritchard (Picture Editor).
Specialist subjects/requirements: All aspects of Scotland and Scottish life.
Markets supplied: Newspapers, magazines, publishers, design agencies.
Formats accepted: All formats but digital preferred, above 20MB and of high quality.
Usual terms of business: No minimum terms.
Commission: 50 per cent.
Additional information: No submitting without prior contact. Digital files must be checked by e-mail before submission.

EXPRESS SYNDICATION
The Northern & Shell Building, 10 Lower Thames Street, London EC3R 6EN.
Tel: 0870 211 7884. Fax: 0870 211 7871. E-mail: mark.swift@express.co.uk
Web: www.expresspictures.com
Contact: Mark Swift (Syndication Manager).
Specialist subjects/requirements: Current news, features and personalities.
Markets supplied: Magazines and newspapers, UK and overseas.
Formats accepted: All formats.
Usual terms of business: Minimum retention period: 90 days.
Commission: 50 per cent.
Additional information: Represents the Daily and Sunday Express, Daily Star and OK! magazine as well as freelance photographers and other agencies.

EYE UBIQUITOUS & HUTCHISON*
65 Brighton Road, Shoreham, West Sussex BN43 6RE.
Tel: 01273 440113. Fax: 01273 440116. E-mail: library@eyeubiquitous.com
Web: www.eyeubiquitous.com
Contacts: Paul Seheult (Proprietor), Stephen Rafferty (Library Manager).
Specialist subjects/requirements: Material suitable for the travel/tourist industry (scenics, resorts, beaches, major sights), plus general stock and social documentary material (people, lifestyles, work, environment, etc). Also incorporates the Hutchison Picture Library offering in-depth documentary coverage of indigenous cultures worldwide.
Markets supplied: Publishing markets, travel industry, UK and European advertising agencies.
Formats accepted: Digital (50MB TIFF) or colour transparency.
Usual terms of business: Suggested minimum submission 200 images, but terms open to discussion.
Commission: 40 per cent.
Additional information: The collections are run as separate entities, though contributing photographers may have work with more than one.

EYECATCHERS
3 Cobden Road, Midhurst, West Sussex GU29 9JW.
Tel: 01730 812976. E-mail: info@eyecatchersphotopix.com

Web: www. eyecatchersphotopix.com
Contact: Antony Lynn-Hill (Director).
Specialist subjects/requirements: Food and drink, lifestyle images, wildlife, backgrounds, travel, London.
Markets supplied: Magazine and book publishers, web design, advertising.
Formats accepted: Digital.
Usual terms of business: Images are offered on a non-exclusive basis and may be withdrawn by giving 14 days notice in writing.
Commission: 80 per cent to photographer on monthly turnover of up to £1,000; 70 per cent on turnover of £1,000 – £3,000.
Additional information: All sales are on a royalty-free basis but the agency was specifically created to offer photographers a better deal than can be found with other RF-only agencies.

EYEVINE
3 Mills Studios,Three Mill Lane, London E3 3DU.
Tel: 020 8709 8709. E-mail: info@eyevine.com
Web: www.eyevine.com
Contact: Graham Cross (Director).
Specialist subjects/requirements: Portraiture, news and reportage.
Markets supplied: Worldwide editorial publishing (newspapers, magazines, books etc).
Formats accepted: Digital files preferred, minimum 30MB RGB JPEG. Colour/B&W print or transparency also accepted.
Usual terms of business: Minimum initial submission: 1 image. Minimum retention period: 3 years.
Commission rate: 50 per cent.
Additional information: Although a news, feature, personalities and assignments agency we are only looking to take on portraiture at this stage. See website for further information.

FLPA – IMAGES OF NATURE*
Pages Green House, Wetheringsett, Stowmarket, Suffolk IP14 5QA.
Tel: 01728 860789. Fax: 01728 860222. E-mail: pictures@flpa-images.co.uk
Web: www.flpa-images.co.uk
Contact: Jean Hosking, David Hosking (Directors).
Specialist subjects/requirements: Natural history and weather phenomena: birds, clouds, fish, fungi, insects, mammals, pollution, rainbows, reptiles, sea, snow, seasons, trees, underwater, hurricanes, earthquakes, lightning, volcanoes, dew, rain, fog, etc. Ecology and the environment. Horse, dog and cat breeds.
Markets supplied: Book publishers, advertising agencies, magazines.
Formats accepted: Digital files at 50MB (contact agency for guidelines).
Usual terms of business: Minimum initial submission: 20 images for evaluation. Minimum retention period: 4 years.
Commission: 50 per cent.
Additional information: Competition in the natural history field is fierce, so only really sharp, well-composed pictures are needed. Sales are slow to start with, and a really keen photographer must be prepared to invest money in building up stock to the 1,000 mark.

FAMOUS*
13 Harwood Road, London SW6 4QP.
Tel: 020 7731 9333. Fax: 020 7731 9330. E-mail: info@famous.uk.com
Web: www.famous.uk.com
Contact: Rob Howard (Managing Director).
Specialist subjects/requirements: Celebrity photographs, especially personalities in the TV, movie, music, fashion and Royal fields. Taken in any situation: red carpet, paparazzi, party, performance, studio and at home.

Markets supplied: General press and publishing.
Formats accepted: Digital only.
Usual terms of business: No minimum submission or retention period.
Commission: 50 per cent.
Additional information: Always looking for photographers who can supply relevant pictures fast.

FOOD FEATURES*
Beaconhurst, Chestnut Walk,Tangmere,West Sussex, PO20 2HH
Tel: 01243 532240. E-mail: frontdesk@foodpix.co.uk
Web: www.foodfeatures.net
Contact: Steve Moss, Alex Barker (Partners).
Specialist subjects/requirements: Food and drink, especially images involving people – dining, cooking, dinner parties, al fresco, chefs, etc.
Markets supplied: Publishing, advertising, etc.
Formats accepted: Digital files preferred, 30MB minimum, 50MB preferred. 35mm transparencies acceptable for location shots but larger formats preferred.
Usual terms of business: No minimum initial submission. Minimum retention period: 3 years.
Commission: By agreement.

FOODANDDRINKPHOTOS.COM*
Studio 4, Sun Studios, 30 Warple Way, London W3 0RX.
Tel: 020 8740 6610. Fax: 020 8762 9994. E-mail: info@foodanddrinkphotos.com
Web: www.foodanddrinkphotos.com
Contact: Charles Montgomery (Library Manager).
Specialist subjects/requirements: All food and drink related photography, all styles, both traditional and more conceptual.
Markets supplied: Editorial, advertising and design.
Formats accepted: Transparencies or digital files (35–80MB).
usual terms of business: Minimum initial submission: 20 images. Minimum retention period: 3 years.
Commission rate: 50 per cent.
Additional information: Transparencies scanned for free and digitised to high resolution.

FOOTPRINT IMAGES
PO Box 4610, Warwick CV34 9EY.
Tel: 0207 193 1192. E-mail: contributors@footprintimages.com
Web: www.footprintimages.com
Contact: Glyn Thomas, Mike Finn-Kelcey (Partners).
Specialist subjects/requirements: Travel, business, wildlife and conceptual/abstract photography.
Markets supplied: General publishing, advertising.
Formats accepted: Digital; minimum 2400 pixels on longest dimension.
Usual terms of business: Minimum initial submission: 10 sample images. No minimum retention period. Non-exclusive contract.
Commission: 65 per cent to photographer if images fully captioned and keyworded; otherwise 50 per cent.
Additional information: Prospective contributors can register on the website where there are full submission details or send initial samples via e-mail. Rights-managed sales only.

As a member of the Bureau of Freelance Photographers, you'll be kept up-to-date with markets through the BFP Market Newsletter, published monthly. For details of membership, turn to page 9

FOTOMAZE
12 Penlee Street, Penzance, Cornwall TR18 2DE.
Tel: 01736 350192. E-mail: admin@fotomaze.com
Web: www.fotomaze.com
Contact: Lee Searle (Managing Director).
Specialist subjects/requirements: All Cornwall-related subjects – landscapes, seascapes, lifestyle, music, etc. Also creative images suitable for wall display or decoration.
Markets supplied: Tourist/travel trade, publishing, advertising and design. Also sells display prints to business or public.
Formats accepted: Digital files, 300 dpi and over 5MB in size. All images to be uploaded online.
Usual terms of business: Minimum initial submission: 5 sample images. Minimum retention period: None stated.
Commission: 60 per cent to photographer.
Additional information: The agency is particularly interested in new talent. Contributors can choose to sell rights-managed or royalty-free. See website for further details.

FRESH FOOD IMAGES
2nd Floor, Waterside House, 9 Woodfield Road, London W9 2BA.
Tel: 020 7432 8200. Fax: 020 7432 8201. E-mail: creative@freshfoodimages.co.uk
Web: www.freshfoodimages.co.uk
Contact: Lee Wheatley (Creative Director).
Specialist subjects/requirements: Food and wine related images. High quality, original material on all aspects from farming, fishing, country trades, markets and vineyards to raw ingredients, finished dishes, chefs, restaurants and kitchens.
Markets supplied: Publishing, advertising, etc.
Formats accepted: Digital files required, shot on 10MP camera or high-end scans at 50MB.
Usual terms of business: Minimum initial submission: 50+ images for initial evaluation. Minimum retention period: 3 years.
Commission: 40 per cent to photographer.
Additional information: Formerly the Anthony Blake Photo Library, now part of the international Photolibrary Group. Only stocks images of the very highest standard. See www.freshfoodimages.co.uk/photographers.html for full submission details.

GARDEN PICTURE LIBRARY*
2nd Floor, Waterside House, 9 Woodfield Road, London W9 2BA.
Tel: 020 7432 8200. Fax: 020 7432 8201. E-mail: creative@gardenpicture.com
Web: www.gardenpicture.com
Contact: Lee Wheatley (Creative Director).
Specialist subjects/requirements: Gardens, plants (mainly cultivated), people and animals in the garden, practical gardening, food al fresco, outdoor living, flower shows, floral still life, and garden features.
Markets supplied: General publishing, greetings cards and calendars, advertising and design.
Formats accepted: Digital – see website for specifications.
Usual terms of business: Minimum initial submission: 100 images.
Commission: 40 per cent to photographer.
Additional information: Submission guidelines available on request or via website.

GARDEN WORLD IMAGES LTD*
Grange Studio, Woodham Road, Battlesbridge, Wickford, Essex SS11 7QU.
Tel: 01245 325725. Fax: 01245 429198. E-mail: info@gardenworldimages.com
Web: www.gardenworldimages.com
Contact: Tyrone McGlinchey (Director).
Specialist subjects/requirements: All aspects of horticulture, plants, vegetables, fruit, herbs, trees, gardens, pools, patios, etc. Also gardening action shots, people doing things, step-by-step,

making patios, etc. Creative abstract images.
Markets supplied: Publishing, calendars, seed catalogues, etc.
Formats accepted: Digital images preferred, minimum 50MB.
Usual terms of business: Minimum initial submission: 50 images. Minimum retention period: 2 years.
Commission: 50 per cent.
Additional information: Plant portraits must be identified with Latin name.

GEO AERIAL PHOTOGRAPHY*
4 Christian Fields, London SW16 3JZ.
Tel/fax: 020 8764 6292 or 0115 981 9418. E-mail: geo.aerial@geo-group.co.uk
Web: www.geo-group.co.uk
Contact: John Douglas (Director), Kelly White (Consultant).
Specialist subjects/requirements: Worldwide oblique aerial photographs.
Markets supplied: Books, magazines, advertising, etc.
Formats accepted: Digital files preferred, 35mm or larger format transparencies accepted.
Usual terms of business: Negotiable.
Commission: 50 per cent.
Additional information: Locations must be identified in detail. Do not send samples of work but contact by email first.

GETTY IMAGES*
101 Bayham Street, London NW1 0AG.
Tel: 020 7267 8988. Fax: 020 7267 6540. E-mail: editor@gettyartists.com
Web: http://creative.gettyimages.com
Contact: Editorial Submissions Team.
Specialist subjects/requirements: Conceptual and general stock photography on all subjects.
Markets supplied: Advertising, publishing, design agencies, etc.
Formats accepted: Digital.
Usual terms of business: On application, for rights-managed and royalty-free sales.
Commission: Variable.
Additional information: The Getty Images Creative division incorporates several major collections including Digital Vision, The Image Bank, Redferns, Stockbyte, Stone and Photodisc. For contributor information see www.gettyimages.com/contributors

GETTY IMAGES NEWS & SPORT*
116 Bayham Street, London NW1 0AG.
Tel: 0800 376 7981. E-mail: editorialsubmissions@gettyimages.com
Web: http://editorial.gettyimages.com
Contact: Hugh Pinney (Director of Photography).
Specialist subjects/requirements: Contemporary news, sport and entertainment images.
Markets supplied: Newspapers, magazines, television, etc.
Formats accepted: 35mm and digital (for news).
Usual terms of business: Minimum retention period: 3 years.
Commission: 50 per cent.

ROBERT HARDING WORLD IMAGERY*
Berkshire House, Queen Street, Maidenhead, Berkshire SL6 1NF.
Tel: 020 7478 4000. Fax: 020 7478 4161. E-mail: submissions@robertharding.com
Web: www.robertharding.com
Contact: Fraser Hall (Content Manager).
Specialist subjects/requirements: Travel.
Markets supplied: Publishers, advertising agencies, design groups, calendar publishers, etc.
Formats accepted: Digital only (48–52MB uncompressed TIFF).

Usual terms of business: Minimum initial submission: 150–300 images. Minimum retention period: 7 years; 12 months notice of withdrawal.
Commission: As per contract; usually 40% to photographer.
Additional information: For initial submission RAW files must also be included. Will only consider images from professional digital SLR cameras with a minimum data capability of 10 megapixels, shot as RAW files and converted to 16-bit TIFF. Will not accept images shot in TIFF or JPEG mode.

IMAGESTATE*

First Floor, Clerks Court, 18-20 Farringdon Lane, London EC1R 3AU.
Tel: 0207251 7100. E-mail: info@imagestate.com
Web: www.imagestate.com
Contact: Nathan Grainger (Content & Research Manager).
Specialist subjects/requirements: General contemporary stock – lifestyle, business, industry, landscapes, travel, leisure, etc
Markets supplied: Advertising and publishing, marketing, TV and film.
Formats accepted: Digital files preferred, at 50MB. Some transparency, negative and print depending on subject matter.
Usual terms of business: Minimum initial submission dependent on quality. Minimum retention period: 5 years.
Commission: Subject to contract.
Additional information: The agency sells both rights-managed and royalty-free stock. Model releases essential for people pictures.

IMPACT PHOTOS*

First Floor, Clerks Court, 18-20 Farringdon Lane, London EC1R 3AU.
Tel: 020 7251 7100. E-mail: library@impactphotos.com
Web: www.impactphotos.com
Contact: Nathan Grainger (Content & Research Manager).
Specialist subjects/requirements: Worldwide coverage of people in their environment – agriculture, industry, health, religion, transport, modernisation, education, social issues and travel.
Markets supplied: Newspapers, magazines, book, advertising, marketing, TV and film.
Formats accepted: Digital on CD preferred (50MB RGB TIFF uncompressed at 300dpi). Also 35mm transparencies in certain cases.
Usual terms of business: No minimum initial submission. Minimum retention period: 3 years.
Commission: Subject to contract.
Additional information: Digital contributors should also supply low-res images for quick edit.

JAZZ INDEX PHOTO LIBRARY*

26 Fosse Way, London W13 0BZ.
Tel: 020 8998 1232. E-mail: christianhim@jazzindex.co.uk
Web: www.jazzindex.co.uk
Contact: Christian Him (Principal).
Specialist subjects/requirements: Jazz, blues, world music and contemporary music. Good atmospheric shots of musicians (do not have to be well-known). Both contemporary and archive material of interest.
Markets supplied: Newspapers, book publishers, videos, television.
Formats accepted: All transparency formats; B&W prints or negs; digital at 300dpi.
Commission: 50 per cent.
Usual terms of business: No minimum submission.
Additional information: Always interested in jazz and rock photos from the '50s, '60s or '70s. Contributors must phone first to enquire if material is suitable.

KOS PICTURE SOURCE LTD*
PO Box 104, Midhurst, West Sussex GU29 1AS.
Tel: 020 7801 0044. Fax: 020 7801 0055. E-mail: images@kospictures.com
Web: kospictures.com
Contact: Chris Savage (Library Manager).
Specialist subjects/requirements: Water-related images from around the world. International yacht racing, all watersports, seascapes, underwater photography, and general travel.
Markets supplied: Advertising, design, publishing.
Formats accepted: Digital files (min 30MB).
Usual terms of business: No minimum initial submission. Minimum retention period: 2 years.
Commission: Variable.

LATITUDE STOCK*
The Old Coach House, 14 High Street, Goring-on-Thames, Berkshire RG8 9AR.
Tel: 01491 873011. Fax: 01491 875558. E-mail: info@latitudestock.com
Web: www.latitudestock.com
Contact: Felicity Bazell (Collections Manager), Stuart Cox.
Specialist subjects/requirements: All aspects of travel and tourism, from destinations to forms of transport, food, things to buy, famous sights, hotel shots to native lifestyles. All countries including the UK. Particularly interested in travel lifestyle images.
Markets supplied: Travel industry, magazines, books, newspapers, advertising etc.
Formats accepted: Digital only.
Usual terms of business: Minimum initial submission: 200 images. Minimum retention period: 3 years.
Commission: 40 per cent to photographer.
Additional information: Full submissions guidelines on website. If interested in submitting, please e-mail in the first instance.

LEBRECHT PHOTO LIBRARY*
3 Bolton Road, London NW8 0RJ.
Tel: 020 7625 5341. E-mail: pictures@lebrecht.co.uk
Web: www.lebrecht.co.uk; www.authorpictures.co.uk
Contact: Elbie Lebrecht (Proprietor).
Specialist subjects/requirements: Music & Arts Pictures – all aspects of music (classical, opera, jazz, rock) and the performing arts. Instruments, composers, musicians, singers, artists. Interiors and exteriors of concert halls and opera houses, statues and tombs of famous composers in the UK and abroad. Author Pictures – living and dead writers, novelists, politicians, scientists, philosophers, theologians. Playwrights and their plays; historic and modern performances.
Markets supplied: Specialist magazines, national press, book publishers.
Formats accepted: Digital submissions preferred (300dpi 50MB TIFF).
Usual terms of business: No minimum initial submission or retention period.
Commission: 50 per cent.
Additional information: The library has two connected divisions with their own websites – Music & Arts Pictures and Author Pictures.

LINK PICTURE LIBRARY*
41A The Downs, London SW20 8HG.
Tel: 020 8944 6933. E-mail: library@linkpicturelibrary.com
Web: www.linkpicturelibrary.com
Contact: Orde Eliason (Proprietor).
Specialist subjects/requirements: General documentary coverage of countries worldwide, but particularly Africa – communications, culture, education, environment, health, industry, people and politics. Special interest in South Africa, South East Asia, India and Israel.
Markets supplied: Newspapers, general publishing, educational publishing.

Formats accepted: Digital files preferred, at 300dpi for A4 output. 35mm transparencies also considered.
Usual terms of business: Minimum initial submission: 50 images. Minimum retention period: 3 years.
Commission: 50 per cent.
Additional information: Intial submission should be low-res images on CD.

LONDON MEDIA PRESS
11a Printing House Yard, London E2 7PR.
Tel: 020 7613 2548. Fax: 020 7729 9209. E-mail: pictures@london-media.co.uk
Web: www.london-media.co.uk
Contact: Rick Hewett, Andrew Buckwell (Directors).
Specialist subjects/requirements: News pictures, picture stories and features for worldwide syndication, especially celebrity/paparazzi material.
Markets supplied: National and international newspapers and magazines.
Formats accepted: Digital only.
Usual terms of business: No minimum initial submission. Minimum retention period: None stated.
Commission: 60 per cent to contributor.
Additional information: Freelance shift work frequently available.

LOOP IMAGES
The Studio, 61 Park Road, Woking, Surrey GU22 7BZ.
Tel/fax: 01483 830120. E-mail: paul@loopimages.com
Web: www.loopimages.com
Contact: Paul Mortlock (Library Manager).
Specialist subjects/requirments: Contemporary Britain photography (material shot in England, Scotland, Ireland and Wales) – landscape, cityscape, lifestyle, architecture, history, heritage, culture and the arts. Particular need for good town/city imagery.
Markets supplied: Magazine/book/newspaper publishers, design and ad agencies, travel and tourism industry in UK/US and Europe.
Formats accepted: Digital only – A4 300dpi TIFF (33MB) as library master.
Usual terms of business: Minimum initial submission: 50 images. Minimum retention period: Negotiable, but usually 2 years.
Commission rate: 50 per cent.
Additional information: Looking for quality material, not fillers.

MILLENNIUM IMAGES LTD*
17D Ellingfort Road, London, E8 3PA.
Tel: 020 8985 1144. Fax: 020 8525 6647. E-mail: mail@milim.com
Web: www.milim.com
Contact: Niall O'Leary (Art Director).
Specialist subjects/requirements: Creative contemporary photography with a strong individual style.
Markets supplied: Book publishers, advertising and design, general publishing.
Formats accepted: Digital files, 50-60MB TIFF.
Usual terms of business: Minimum initial submission: 20–40 images. Minimum retention period: 3 years.
Commission: 50 per cent.
Additional information: Particularly keen to see work from young innovative photographers. The agency not only sells reproductions rights but also arranges commissions and passes on image requests from picture buyers.

NHPA/PHOTOSHOT*
29-31 Saffron Hill, London EC1N 8SW.
Tel: 020 7421 6003. Fax: 020 7421 6006. E-mail: ldalton@photoshot.com
Web: www.nhpa.co.uk
Contact: Lee Dalton (Picture Editor).
Specialist subjects/requirements: Worldwide wildlife, domestic animals and pets, plants and gardens, landscapes, agriculture and environmental subjects. Endangered and appealing wildlife of particular interest.
Markets supplied: Books, magazines, advertising and design, cards and calendars, electronic publishing, exhibitions, etc (UK and overseas).
Formats accepted: Digital files preferred, transparencies accepted.
Usual terms of business: Minimum initial submission: 200 images.
Commission: 50 per cent.
Additional information: Pictures should be strong, active and well-composed. Full submissions guidelines available on website. NHPA forms the central wildlife and nature collection in the Photoshot group of companies.

NATURAL SCIENCE PHOTOS
PO Box 397, Welwyn Garden City, Herts AL7 9BA.
Tel: 01707 690561. Fax: 01707 690738. E-mail: natasha@naturalsciencephotos.com
Web: www.naturalsciencephotos.com
Contact: Natasha Jones (Partner).
Specialist subjects/requirements: Wildlife and nature, animals and plant life, plus geology, geography, landscape, weather and the environment.
Markets supplied: Books, magazines, newspapers, calendars, advertising, etc.
Formats accepted: Digital files preferred.
Usual terms of business: No minimum submission. Standard contract allows for 3 years retention and is non-exclusive.
Commission: 50 per cent.
Additional information: All material to be clearly captioned and well documented – English and scientific names, locality and photographer; also any useful additional information.

NEWSCAST LTD
First Floor, The Communications Building, 48 Leicester Square, London WC2H 7FG.
Tel: 020 3137 9137. Fax: 020 3137 1553. E-mail: photo@newscast.co.uk
Web: www.newscast.co.uk
Contact: Scott Draper (Head of Client Services).
Specialist subjects/requirements: Corporate, consumer and professional portrait photography.
Markets supplied: Magazines, newspapers, online publications and broadcasting media worldwide.
Formats accepted: Digital files preferred, minimum 18MB JPEG/TIFF.
Usual terms of business: No minimum requirements.
Commission: 50 per cent.
Additional information: This is an entirely Web-based syndication service. For image security the website is password-protected allowing the image owner to track daily downloads. All images are watermarked for protection.

NUNN SYNDICATION*
PO Box 56303, London SE1 2TD.
Tel: 020 7357 9000. Fax: 020 7231 3912. E-mail: production@nunn-syndication.com
Web: www.nunn-syndication.com
Contact: Robin Nunn (Managing Director).
Specialist subjects/requirements: All aspects of the British royal family, including state occasions, foreign tours, informal shots, etc. Also foreign royalty and general celebrities.
Markets supplied: General publishing.

Formats accepted: Digital files and 35mm transparencies.
Usual terms of business: No minimum terms specified.
Commission: 40 per cent.

ONIMAGE*

2 Independent Place, London E8 2HE.
Tel/fax: 020 7249 8384. E-mail: info@onimage.co.uk
Web: www.onimage.co.uk
Contact: Andre Pinkowski (Managing Director).
Specialist subjects/requirements: Contemporary and evocative imagery with a distinctive visual style and character.
Markets supplied: Advertising, design agencies, magazine publishing and book publishing.
Formats accepted: Digital files preferred, shot on at least a 12.5MP camera or scans of near drum scan quality at 50MB (for 35mm). Colour negative and transparency also accepted for in-house scanning.
Usual terms of business: Minimum initial submission: 40 images. Minimum retention period: 3 years.
Commission: 50 per cent.
Additional information: Potential contributors are advised to look at the website to gain an idea of the type and style of material required.

OXFORD SCIENTIFIC (OSF) LTD*

2nd Floor, Waterside House, 9 Woodfield Rd, London W9 2BA.
Tel: 020 7432 8200. Fax: 020 7432 8201. E-mail: creative@osf.co.uk
Web: www.osf.co.uk
Contact: Lee Wheatley (Creative Director).
Specialist subjects/requirements: High quality wildlife photography, plus the environment, botanical, science, travel, pollution and conservation, landscapes, agriculture, high-speed photography, special effects, underwater, creative plant shots, indigenous people, pets.
Markets supplied: Magazines, book publishers, advertising/design companies, merchandising etc.
Formats accepted: Digital (check website for accepted DSLR cameras).
Usual terms of business: Minimum initial submission 50 images. Minimum retention period: 5 years.
Commission: 40 per cent.
Additional information: See contributors' page website for full submission guidelines.

PYMCA*

2nd Floor, 71 St John's Street, London EC1M 4NJ.
Tel: 020 7251 8338. E-mail: james@pymca.com
Web: www.pymca.com
Contact: James Lange (Library Manager).
Specialist subjects/requirements: All images related to youth and subcultures, from the past (1940s/50s) to the present day, UK and abroad. Areas of particular interest: street fashions; lifestyle; social documentary; music/clubbing; recreational sport; related incidental imagery.
Markets supplied: General publishing, editorial, advertising, design, music industry etc.
Formats accepted: All formats, digital files preferred (min 28MB TIFF). Video footage.
Usual terms of business: Minimum initial submission: 20 pictures. Minimum retention period: 3 years.
Commission: 50 per cent.
Additional information: Particularly interested in model-released work for the Model Release collection, which is aimed primarily at commercial advertising and design markets. Also seeking video footage of youth subcultures, plus essays/text about different scenes and stories/experiences about being involved in these.

PANOS PICTURES*
1 Honduras Street, London EC1Y 0TH.
Tel: 020 7253 1424. Fax: 020 7253 2752. E-mail: pics@panos.co.uk
Web: www.panos.co.uk
Contact: Adrian Evans (Director).
Specialist subjects/requirements: Documentary coverage of the Third World and Eastern Europe, focusing on global social, economic and political issues and with special emphasis on enviroment and development.
Markets supplied: Newspapers and magazines, book publishers, development agencies.
Formats accepted: Digital only.
Usual terms of business: No minimum initial submission or retention period.
Commission: 50 per cent.
Additional information: 50 per cent of all profits from the library are covenanted to the Panos Institute, an international development studies group.

PAPILIO
155 Station Road, Herne Bay, Kent CT6 5QA.
Tel: 01227 360996. E-mail: library@papiliophotos.com
Web: www.papiliophotos.com
Contact: Justine Pickett or Robert Pickett (Directors).
Specialist subjects/requirements: All aspects of natural history worldwide, including plants, insects, birds, mammals and marine life.
Markets supplied: Books, magazines, advertising, etc.
Formats accepted: Digital preferred (shot as RAW in camera, minimum 18MB TIFF after conversion).
Usual terms of business: Minimum initial submission: 100 images. Minimum retention period: 5 years.
Commission: 50 per cent.
Additional information: Digital files preferred, but contact first before sending digital submissions to obtain full detailed requirements.

PHOTOFUSION PICTURE LIBRARY*
17a Electric Lane, Brixton, London SW9 8LA.
Tel: 020 7733 3500. Fax: 020 7738 5509. E-mail: library@photofusion.org
Web: www.photofusionpictures.org
Contact: Liz Somerville (Library Manager).
Specialist subjects/requirements: All aspects of contemporary life with an emphasis on environmental and social issues. Specialist areas include children, disability, education, environment, the elderly, families, health, housing & homelessness, plus people generally.
Markets supplied: UK book and magazine publishing, newspapers, charities, annual reports, etc.
Formats accepted: Digital files preferred (minimum 30MB TIFF), transparencies and prints accepted.
Usual terms of business: No minimum initial submission. Minimum retention period: 3 years.
Commission: 50 per cent.
Additional information: Particularly looking for photographers who have good access to cover education and health. Also coverage from Scotland and/or Northern Ireland.

PHOTOLIBRARY*
2nd Floor, Waterside House, 9 Woodfield Road, London W9 2BA.
Tel: 020 7432 8200. Fax: 020 7432 8201. E-mail: creative@photolibrary.com
Web: www.photolibrary.com
Contact: Lee Wheatley (UK Creative Director).
Specialist subjects/requirements: High-end, creative imagery primarily oriented to advertising and business-to-business markets. Mainly travel, lifestyle, business, nature and sport.

Markets supplied: Advertising, design agencies, business.
Formats accepted: Digital (30MB TIFF minimum).
Usual terms of business: Minimum initial submission: Up to 50 images for initial assessment. Minimum retention period: 5 years.
Commission: 50 per cent.
Additional information: The Photolibrary Group represents a wide range of individual stock agencies and offers worldwide distribution with offices in 10 countries. Releases always required for people, animals and property. See artists' page on website for full details.

PHOTOSHOT*

29-31 Saffron Hill, London EC1N 8SW.
Tel: 020 7421 6000. Fax: 020 7421 6006. E-mail: info@photoshot.com
Web: www.photoshot.com
Contact: Charles Taylor (Managing Director).
Specialist subjects/requirements: Wide variety of subject matter within various distinct collections including UPPA (news); Starstock and Stay Still (celebrity, entertainment); World Illustrated (culture, environment, heritage); Talking Sport (sport). Also several nature and travel collections including NHPA, PictureNature and World Pictures (see separate listings).
Markets supplied: Newspapers, magazines, book publishers, broadcasting, advertising, etc.
Formats accepted: All formats, digital preferred.
Usual terms of business: Variable.
Commission: Usually 50 per cent.
Additional information: See website for futher details on individual collections.

PICTURE HOOKED*

97 Field Avenue, Canterbury, Kent CT1 1TS.
Tel: 07769 696244. E-mail: info@picturehooked.co.uk
Web: www.picturehooked.co.uk
Contact: Kieran Orwin (Director).
Specialist subjects/requirements: Creative personal photography and artwork on any subject.
Markets supplied: Newspapers, magazines, book publishing. All images are also offered for sale as ready-to-hang canvas prints.
Formats accepted: Digital only, 300dpi RGB 8-bit uncompressed TIFFs.
Usual terms of business: No minimum initial submission. Minimum retention period: 3 years.
Commission: 50 per cent.
Additional information: Simple, standard stock images are not required; images must be able to stand on their own as pieces of "art".

PICTUREBANK PHOTO LIBRARY LTD*

Parman House, 30–36 Fife Road, Kingston-upon-Thames, Surrey KT1 1SY.
Tel: 020 8547 2344. Fax: 020 8974 5652. E-mail: info@picturebank.co.uk
Web: www.picturebank.co.uk
Contact: Martin Bagge (Managing Director).
Specialist subjects/requirements: Worldwide travel and tourism, UK cities and countryside, people (glamour, families, children, ethnic peoples), environment, animals (domestic and wild), business, industry and technology.
Markets supplied: Magazines, calendars, travel industry, advertising, etc.
Formats accepted: Digital files at 50MB+.
Usual terms of business: Minimum initial submission: 100 images. Minimum retention period: 5 years.
Commission: Variable – maximum 50 per cent.

PICTURENATURE*
Lyndhurst, Watson Street, Banchory AB32 5TR.
Tel: 0131 208 2006. E-mail: fenneke@picture-nature.com
Web: www.picture-nature.com
Contact: Fenneke Wolters-Sinke (Founder).
Specialist subjects/requirements: All images involving nature, including landscapes, seascapes, flowers, plants, wildlife, abstracts in nature. Also people interacting with the natural environment, such as outdoor pursuits, natural resources, cultural/traditional celebrations, architecture and outdoors lifestyles.
Markets supplied: General publishing, advertising, etc.
Formats accepted: Digital only.
Usual terms of business: Contact Fenneke Wolters-Sinke for more information.
Commission: By arrangement.
Additional information: The library is now part of the Photoshot group.

PICTURES COLOUR LIBRARY*
10 James Whatman Court, Turkey Mill, Ashford, Kent ME14 5SS.
Tel: 01622 609809. Fax: 01622 609806. E-mail: karen@picturescolourlibrary.co.uk
Web: www.picturescolourlibrary.co.uk
Contact: Karen McCunnall (Submissions Manager).
Specialist subjects/requirements: Travel and travel-related images; food and drink.
Markets supplied: Magazines, newspapers, travel companies, advertising and design, calendars and greetings cards.
Formats accepted: Digital only (minimum file size 50MB).
Usual terms of business: Minimum initial submission: 500 images. Minimum retention period: 3 years.
Commission: 50 per cent.

PRESS ASSOCIATION IMAGES*
Pavilion House, 16 Castle Boulevard, Nottingham NG7 1FL.
Tel: 0115 844 7447. Fax: 0115 844 7448. E-mail: images@pressassociation.com
Web: www.pressassociation.com/images
Contact: Neal Simpson (Photographic Director); Simon Galloway, Scott Wilson (Picture Desk Managers).
Specialist subjects/requirements: Worldwide news, sport and showbusiness, past and present.
Markets supplied: Newspapers, magazines, websites, advertising agencies, etc.
Formats accepted: Digital, film negative and transparency.
Usual terms of business: No minimum terms.
Commission: 50 per cent.
Additional information: Includes pictures from The Press Association, Empics Sport, Empics Entertainment and Associated Press.

RAILPHOTOLIBRARY.COM*
Newton Harcourt, Leicestershire LE8 9FH.
Tel: 0116 259 2068. Fax: 0116 259 3001. E-mail: studio@railphotolibrary.com
Web: www.railphotolibrary.com
Contact: Colin Nash (Library Manager).
Specialist subjects/requirements: Railways – all aspects, national and international, contemporary and archive.
Markets supplied: Advertising, publishing, design, corporate railways.
Formats accepted: Digital preferred (min 25MB JPEG/TIFF); colour transparencies accepted. Archive B&W.
Usual terms of business: Minimum initial submission: 25 pictures. No minimum retention period.
Commission: 50 per cent.

Additional information: All material must be of the highest quality. Transparencies must be mounted and captioned with brief, accurate details.

RETNA PICTURES*

29-31 Saffron Hill, London EC1N 8SW.
Tel: 0845 034 0645. Fax: 020 7421 6006. E-mail: info@retna.co.uk
Web: www.retna.co.uk
Contact: Steve Hodgson (Director).
Specialist subjects/requirements: Lifestyle images: men, women, couples, family life, health and beauty, leisure, babies, children, teenagers, business and food. Celebrity/music images: portraiture, studio and events photography.
Markets supplied: Newspapers, magazines, books, record companies, advertising.
Formats accepted: All formats but digital files preferred.
Usual terms of business: Minimum initial submission: 40–50 images. Minimum retention period: 3 years.
Commission: Negotiable, depending on material.
Additional information: Lifestyle images must be fully model-released.

REX FEATURES*

18 Vine Hill, London EC1R 5DZ.
Tel: 020 7278 7294. Fax: 020 7696 0974. E-mail: photogs@rexfeatures.com
Web: www.rexfeatures.com
Contact: Mike Selby, (Editorial Director), Gretchen Viehmann (Chief Editor).
Specialist subjects/requirements: Human interest and general features, current affairs, personalities, entertainment news, animals (singles and series), humour, travel.
Markets supplied: UK national newspapers and magazines, book publishers, audio visual, television and international press. Daily worldwide syndication.
Formats accepted: Digital preferred.
Usual terms of business: No minimum submission. Preferred minimum retention period: 2 years.
Commission: 50 per cent.

ROYAL GEOGRAPHICAL SOCIETY PICTURE LIBRARY*

1 Kensington Gore, London SW7 2AR.
Tel: 020 7591 3060. Fax: 020 7591 3001. E-mail: images@rgs.org
Web: www.rgs.org/images
Contact: Library Manager.
Specialist subjects/requirements: Exploration and geographical coverage, both historic and current. Travel photography from remote destinations: indigenous peoples and daily life, landscapes, environmental and geographical phenomena, agriculture, crafts, human impact on the environment.
Markets supplied: Commercial publishing and academic research.
Formats accepted: Digital files preferred; minimum 17MB digital capture, 50MB scans.
Usual terms of business: Minimum initial submission: 250 pictures. Minimum retention period: At least 2 years.
Commission: 50 per cent.

SCR PHOTO LIBRARY

Society for Co-operation in Russian and Soviet Studies, 320 Brixton Road, London SW9 6AB.
Tel: 020 7274 2282. Fax: 020 7274 3230. E-mail: ruslibrary@scrss.org.uk
Web: www.scrss.org.uk
Contact: John Cunningham (Librarian).
Specialist subjects/requirements: Pictures from Russia and all Republics of the former Soviet Union. General/everyday scenes, landscapes, architecture, towns and cities, politics, arts, industry, agriculture, science, etc.
Markets supplied: General.

Formats accepted: All formats.
Usual terms of business: No minimum submission. Minimum retention period: 2 years.
Commission: 50 per cent.

SCIENCE PHOTO LIBRARY (SPL)*
327-329 Harrow Road, London W9 3RB.
Tel: 020 7432 1100. Fax: 020 7286 8668. E-mail: info@sciencephoto.com
Web: www.sciencephoto.com
Contact: Rosemary Taylor (Director).
Specialist subjects/requirements: All types of science-related imagery including health and medicine people and lifestyle, flowers and nature, wildlife and environment, technology and industry, astronomy and space, history of science and medicine.
Markets supplied: Books, magazines, advertising, design, corporate, audio visual.
Formats accepted: Digital only, 50MB with no interpolation.
Usual terms of business: No minimum submission. Minimum retention period: 5 years.
Commission: 50 per cent.
Additional information: All photographs must be accompanied by full and accurate caption information.

SHORELARK
The Forum, 277 London Road, Burgess Hill, West Sussex RH15 9QU.
Tel: 01444 240244. E-mail: contributors@shorelark.co.uk
Web: www.shorelark.co.uk
Contact: Christopher Sutton (Director).
Specialist subjects/requirements: Images that celebrate life and the world around us, including landscapes, wildlife, heritage, missionary work, the developing world, major sports and people pictures.
Markets supplied: Editorial, commercial, print and display.
Formats accepted: Digital only, RGB files.
Usual terms of business: Minimum initial submission: 10 sample images on CD. No minimum retention period.
Commission: 50 per cent.
Additional information: Full contributor details available on website. Images are supplied at reduced rates to churches, charities and certain educational organisations.

SKISHOOT
Hall Place, Upper Woodcott, Whitchurch, Hants RG28 7PY.
Tel: 01635 255527. E-mail: pictures@skishoot.co.uk
Web: www.skishoot.co.uk
Contact: Felice Hardy (Partner), Claire Bicknell (Library Manager).
Specialist subjects/requirements: Skiing and snowboarding, ski resorts in Europe, Asia and North America.
Markets supplied: Travel industry, general publishing, and advertising.
Formats accepted: Digital files preferred.
Usual terms of business: Minimum initial submission: 50 images. No minimum retention period.
Commission: 50 per cent.

SKYSCAN PHOTOLIBRARY*
Oak House, Toddington, Cheltenham GL54 5BY.
Tel: 01242 621357. Fax: 01242 621343. E-mail: info@skyscan.co.uk
Web: www.skyscan.co.uk
Contact: Brenda Marks (Library Manager).
Specialist subjects/requirements: Anything aerial – air to ground; aircraft; general aviation; aerial sports (skydiving, ballooning, etc).

Markets supplied: Editorial, advertising, design, calendars.
Formats accepted: Prefer digital files of 28+MB (preferably 50+MB), uninterpolated.
Usual terms of business: Minimum initial submission: 20+ images. Minimum retention period: 2 years.
Commission: 50 per cent.
Additional information: Also operates a brokerage service which is sometimes more appropriate than agency terms. Photographs are retained by the photographer; picture requests are initiated and negotiated by Skyscan and fees split 50/50.

SLICK STOCK IMAGES
Unit 2, 681 Esplanade, Mornington, Victoria 3191, Australia.
Tel: +61 3 5975 1956. E-mail: info@slickstock.com
Web: www.slickstock.com
Contact: Kim Hearn (Partner).
Specialist subjects/requirements: Aviation, including aircraft (civil and military), air travel, passengers, airports, creative images for generic use.
Markets supplied: Worldwide publishing, advertising, design, etc.
Formats accepted: Digital only. 300dpi TIFF from digital origination, or 50MB scans from transparencies. Bulk submissions should be made on CD/DVD but FTP upload is available for urgent or newsworthy images.
Usual terms of business: Minimum initial submission: None specified but prefer to deal with photographers with substantial collections. No minimum retention period.
Commission: 50 per cent, or 55 per cent for exclusive images.
Additional information: Although based in Australia the library sources and sells images worldwide. Partner Kim Hearn was formerly in charge of the Flight Collection, once the UK's leading aviation stock library.

SOCIALSTOCK*
1.11 Paintworks, Bath Road, Bristol BS4 3EH.
Tel: 0117 971 9413. E-mail: nick.cooper@socialstock.co.uk
Web: www.socialstock.co.uk
Contact: Nick Fallowfield-Cooper (Picture Editor).
Specialist subjects/requirements: UK-specific social documentary imagery of all kinds including crime, community, education, healthcare, environment, housing, the elderly and transport. Seeks experienced photographers to provide social documentary images and undertake assignments.
Markets supplied: General publishing and other markets.
Formats accepted: Digital, minimum file size 6MB.
Usual terms of business: Minimum initial submission: None stated. Minimum retention period: 3 years.
Commission: 40 per cent to photographer on "pay-as-you-go" account. 60-80 per cent for assignment work.
Additional information: Photographers are available to clients to shoot on an assigment basis should they require a more bespoke service. A weekly shoot list is available to registered contributors.

SPECTRUM COLOUR LIBRARY
First Floor, Clerks Court, 18-20 Farringdon Lane, London EC1R 3AU.
Tel: 020 7251 7100. E-mail: nathan.grainger@heritage-images.com
Web: www.impactphotos.com
Contact: Nathan Grainger (Content & Research Manager).
Specialist subjects/requirements: Travel, people, culture, places, natural history.
Markets supplied: Advertising, magazines, newspapers, book publishing, travel brochures.
Formats accepted: Digital files preferred, at 50MB.
Usual terms of business: No minimum submission. Minimum retention period: 5 years.

Commission: By negotiation.
Additional information: The library is managed by Imagestate Media Partners Ltd.

STOCKFOOD LTD*
Ground Floor, 24 Conway Sreet, London W1T 6BG.
Tel: +49 89 747 202 22 (Munich); 020 7529 8640 (UK sales). E-mail: photographer@stockfood.com
Web: www.stockfood.com
Contact: Petra Thierry (Manager, Photographers & Art Department, Munich).
Specialist subjects/requirements: All types of food and drink imagery, including people eating
and drinking and other food-related lifestyle pictures, as well as interior design.
Markets supplied: Advertising, design, magazine and book publishing, etc.
Formats accepted: Digital (34MB+ from camera, 50MB from scan).
Usual terms of business: Minimum initial submission: 100 images. Minimum retention period:
5 years (exclusive representation required).
Commission: Commission to photographer 40 per cent for rights-managed, 30 per cent royalty-free.
Additional information: With its head office in Munich, Germany, the agency has representation
in 80 countries and is the largest source of food-related imagery in the world. All initial
photographer contact should be made via the website. UK address is sales office only.

STOCKSCOTLAND*
The Grange House, Lochside, Lairg, Sutherland IV27 4EG.
Tel: 01549 402295. E-mail: info@stockscotland.com
Web: www.stockscotland.com
Contact: Hugh Webster (Library Manager).
Specialist subjects/requirements: All aspects of Scotland and Scottish life – landscapes, castles,
Highland games, natural history, industry, whisky, people, lifestyles, etc.
Markets supplied: General publishing, advertising, travel industry.
Formats accepted: All formats. Prefer digital or high-res scans (30MB+).
Usual terms of business: No minimum initial submission. Minimum retention period: 3 years.
Commission: 50 per cent.
Additional information: Images should be edited rigorously before submission. Do not send lots of
very similar images. For more submission details see website.

THEIMAGEFILE.COM
3000 Hillswood Drive, Chertsey, Surrey KT16 0RZ.
Tel: 0845 118 0030. E-mail: membership@theimagefile.com
Web: www.theimagefile.com
Contact: James Duncan (Director).
Specialist subjects/requirements: All major commercial subjects.
Markets supplied: Advertising, design agencies, general publishing.
Formats accepted: Digital only.
Usual terms of business: No minimum initial submission or retention period.
Commission: 75 per cent to photographer, but because of the personalised facilities offered (see
below) there is a monthly subscription charge (discount to BFP members: 20%).
Additional information: Contributing photographers have their own account through which they
set their own prices for images sold. They are able to deal direct with purchasers if they wish and
also obtain commissions. Other facilities include direct uploading of images and real time payment
tracking.

THE TRAVEL LIBRARY
Unit 7, The Kiln Workshops, Pilcot Road, Crookham Village, Fleet, Hants GU51 5RY.
Tel: 01252 623770. Fax: 01252 812399. E-mail: info@travel-library.co.uk
Web: www.travel-library.co.uk
Contact: Chris Penn (Image Production Manager).

Specialist subjects/requirements: Top quality tourist travel material covering destinations worldwide.
Markets supplied: UK tour operators and travel industry, advertising, design and corporate.
Formats accepted: Digital RAW files saved and submitted as TIFF (minimum 24MB). Transparencies only accepted in exceptional circumstances.
Usual terms of business: Minimum initial submission: 100 images. Minimum retention period: 5 years.
Commission: Exclusive 50 per cent. Non-exclusive 40 per cent.

TRIGGER IMAGE*

Lavender Cottage, Brome Avenue, Eye, Suffolk IP23 7HW.
Tel: 01379 871358. E-mail: studio@triggerimage.co.uk
Web: wwww.triggerimage.co.uk
Contact: Tim Kahane (Director).
Specialist subjects/requirements: Personal, creative photography on any subject, especially images that are atmospheric, emotive or inspiring.
Markets supplied: Art buyers in publishing, design and advertising.
Formats accepted: Digital only, minimum 5100x3000 pixels.
Usual terms of business: Minimum initial submission: 10 sample images. Minimum retention period: 36 months.
Commission: Standard rate 50 per cent.
Additional information: Standard stock images are not accepted; study website first to see the type of work held. Creativity and expression is more important than experience.

TTL PLUS

Unit 7, The Kiln Workshops, Pilcot Road, Crookham Village, Fleet, Hants GU51 5RY.
Tel: 01252 623770. Fax: 01252 812399. E-mail: chris@ttl-plus.com
Web: www.ttl-plus.com
Contact: Chris Penn (Image Production Manager); Elizabeth Cawthorn (Picture Editor).
Specialist subjects/requirements: Professional quality images suitable for use on calendars, greetings cards and posters – cats, kittens, dogs, puppies, florals, nature, landscapes, panoramics, abstracts, railways, the seasons, colours, etc.
Markets supplied: Specialist paper product publishers, as above.
Formats accepted: Digital, minimum 24MB, 50–60MB preferred. Will view transparencies but any selected will require scanning after editing at the cost of the photographer.
Usual terms of business: No minimum initial submission. Minimum retention period: 5 years.
Commission: 50 per cent.
Additional information: Images must be of the highest standard and genuinely suitable for up-market products in relevant fields.

VIEW PICTURES LTD*

2 Whitacre Mews, 26-34 Stannary Street, London SE11 4AB.
Tel: 020 7840 5840. Fax: 020 7840 5841 . E-mail: dg@dennisgilbert.com/yvonne@viewpictures.co.uk
Web:.www.viewpictures.co.uk
Contact: Dennis Gilbert (Director), Yvonne Peeke-Vout (MD).
Specialist subjects/requirements: Top quality images of modern architecture and interior design, with the emphasis on recently-completed projects by leading architects. Classic modern buildings and historic structures also represented.
Markets supplied: Book and magazine publishers, advertising agencies, graphic designers.
Formats accepted: Digital preferred, 48MB TIFF files. Also medium/large format colour transparency.
Usual terms of business: Minimum initial submission: None stated. Minimum retention period: Negotiable.
Commission: 40 per cent to photographer.

Additional information: Seeks only top quality work from experienced architectural photographers. Commissions may also be available.

ELIZABETH WHITING & ASSOCIATES*
70 Mornington Street, London NW1 7QE.
Tel: 020 7388 2828. Fax: 020 7388 7587. E-mail: ewa@elizabethwhiting.com
Web: www.ewastock.com
Contact: Liz Whiting (Director).
Specialist subjects/requirements: Home interest topics – architecture, interiors, design, DIY, crafts, gardens, food. Some travel and scenic material.
Markets supplied: Book and magazine publishers, advertising, design companies.
Formats accepted: Digital files preferred (minimum 50 MB); colour transparencies accepted.
Usual terms of business: No minimum initial submission, but a contract is only entered into if both parties envisage a long-term commitment. Minimum retention period: 1 year.
Commission: 50 per cent.

WORLD PICTURE NETWORK
62 White Street, 3rd Floor, New York 10013, USA.
Tel: +1 212 871 1215. Fax: +1 212 925 4569. E-mail: info@worldpicturenews.com
Web: www.worldpicturenews.com
Contact: Senior Editor.
Specialist subjects/requirements: International news and photojournalism for on-line supply.
Markets supplied: National and international magazines, newspapers, broadcasting organisations.
Formats accepted: Digital.
Usual terms of business: No minimum terms.
Commission: 50 per cent.
Additional information: Originally established in London, HQ is now in New York. Business is conducted entirely on-line and photographers must first register on the website. Contributors must be familiar with scanning procedures, able to process images quickly and have the facility to up-load on-line. For further information see website.

WORLD PICTURES/PHOTOSHOT*
29-31 Saffron Hill, London EC1N 8SW.
Tel: 020 7421 6004. Fax: 020 7421 6006. E-mail: mail@worldpictures.co.uk
Web: www.worldpictures.co.uk
Contact: David Brenes (Library Manager).
Specialist subjects/requirements: Travel material: cities, resorts, hotels worldwide plus girls, couples and families on holiday suitable for travel brochure, magazine and newspaper use.
Markets supplied: Tour operators, airlines, design houses, advertising agencies.
Formats accepted: Digital files, 50MB.
Usual terms of business: No minimum submission but usually like the chance of placing material for minimum period of 2 years.
Commission: 50 per cent.
Additional information: World Pictures forms the central travel collection in the Photoshot group of companies.

WRITER PICTURES LTD*
90 Temple Park Crescent, Edinburgh EH11 1HZ.
Tel: 020 8224 1564. E-mail: info@writerpictures.com
Web: www. writerpictures.com
Contact: Alex Hewitt (Partner).
Specialist subjects/requirements: Photographs of authors and writers, mainly editorial-style portraiture.
Markets supplied: Publishing industry, news media.

Formats accepted: Digital preferred, minimum 30MB, but transparencies/negs always considered.
Usual terms of business: No minimum initial submission. Minimum retention period: 1 year.
Commission: 50 per cent.
Additional information: Commissions to photograph individual writers may also be available.

ZENITH IMAGE LIBRARY
Apollo 11, 18 All Saints Road, London W11 1HH.
Tel: 020 7221 1691. E-mail: info@zenithfoundation.com
Web: www.zenithimagelibrary.com
Contact: Mona Deeley (Director).
Specialist subjects/requirements: The Arab world and the Middle East – current events,
historic/recent history events, everyday lives, culture, sport, religion, and other aspects of the
unreported Middle East. Both stills and clips. Also interested in private archive collections of images
relating to the region.
Markets supplied: Newspapers, magazines, general publishing, etc.
Formats accepted: Digital.
Usual terms of business: No minimum terms stated.
Commission: 50 per cent.
Additional information: All stock is rights-managed, licensed to buyers for specified project uses
only and priced according to size.

SERVICES

This section lists companies providing products and services of use to the photographer. A number of those listed offer discounts to BFP members. To obtain the discounts indicated, members should simply produce their current membership card. In the case of mail order transactions, enclose your membership card with your order, requesting that this be returned with the completed order or as soon as membership has been verified. But in all cases, ensure that your membership card is valid: the discount will not be available to those who present an expired card.

Courses & Training

THE BFP SCHOOL OF PHOTOGRAPHY
Focus House, 497 Green Lanes, London N13 4BP.
Tel: 020 8882 3315. Fax: 020 8886 3933. E-mail: course@thebfp.com
Web: www.thebfp.com
Offers a two-year correspondence course in freelance photography and photojournalism. May be undertaken by either post or e-mail.
Discount to BFP members: On application.

NATIONAL COUNCIL FOR THE TRAINING OF JOURNALISTS (NCTJ)
The New Granary, Station Road, Newport, Saffron Walden, Essex CB11 3PL.
Tel: 01799 544014. Fax: 01799 544015. E-mail: info@nctj.com
Web: www.nctj.com
Official training body for the journalism industry. Offers basic journalism training through its accredited colleges/universities and by distance learning. Short mid-term courses are available in various disciplines for journalists wishing to progress their career.

TRAVELLERS' TALES
92 Hillfield Road, London NW6 1QA.
E-mail: info@travellerstales.org
Web: www.travellerstales.org
Training agency dedicated to travel photography and writing, offering masterclasses in London and training holidays around the world. Tutors are top travel photographers, editors and writers. Courses suitable for beginners and professionals. Hosts annual Traveller's Tales Festival featuring the world's leading travel writers and photographers. Details and booking via website.

Equipment Hire

FILM PLUS
77-81 Scrubbs Lane, London, NW10 6QW
Tel/fax: 020 8969 0234. E-mail: neil@filmplus.com
Web: www.filmplus.com
Professional rental and sales. Digital, lighting and camera equipment hire. Film and hardware sales. Also studio hire.
Discount to BFP members: 10%

HIREACAMERA
Unit 5, Wellbrook Farm, Berkeley Road, Mayfield, East Sussex TN20 6EH.
Tel: 01435 873028. E-mail: enquiries@hireacamera.com
Web: www.hireacamera.com
Hire of wide range of digital cameras and camcorders, catering for both private and corporate needs.

THE FLASH CENTRE
68 Brunswick Centre, Marchmont Street, London WC1N 1AE.
Tel: 020 7837 6163. Fax: 020 7833 4882. E-mail: hire@theflashcentre.co.uk
Branches also in Birmingham (0121 327 9220) and Leeds (0113 247 0937).
Web: www.theflashcentre.com
Hire of electronic flash and digital photographic equipment.

SFL
Unit 23 Headley Park 10, Headley Road East, Woodley, Reading RG5 4SW.
Tel: 0118 969 0900. Fax: 0118 969 1397. E-mail: info@sflgroup.co.uk
Web: www.sflgroup.co.uk
Hire and sale of AV equipment, film production and video production equipment.

Equipment Repair

BOURNEMOUTH PHOTOGRAPHIC (REPAIR) SERVICES LTD
251 Holdenhurst Road, Bournemouth, Dorset BH8 8DA.
Tel: 01202 301273. Fax: 01202 301273
Professional repairs to all makes of equipment. Full test facilities including modern electronic diagnostic test equipment.
Discount to BFP members: 5% off labour charges (cash sales).

THE CAMERA REPAIR CENTRE
47 London Road, Southborough,Tunbridge Wells, Kent TN4 0PB.
Tel: 01892 619136. Fax: 01892 540362. E-mail: info@thecameracentre.com
Web: www.camerarepaircentre.com
Repairs to all makes of photographic equipment, including camcorders and digital.

THE FLASH CENTRE
68 Brunswick Centre, Marchmont Street, London WC1N 1AE.
Tel: 020 7883 4737. Fax: 020 7833 4882. E-mail: service@theflashcentre.co.uk
Branches also in Birmingham (0121 327 9220) and Leeds (0113 247 0937).
Web: www.theflashcentre.com
Specialists in electronic flash service and repair.

A J JOHNSTONE & CO LTD
395 Central Chambers, 93 Hope Street, Glasgow G2 6LD.
Tel: 0141 221 2106. Fax: 0141 221 9166. E-mail: ajjohnstone@btconnect.com
Web: www.ajjohnstone.co.uk
All equipment repairs, including AV equipment. Authorised service centre for Canon, Olympus and Nikon. Canon and Nikon warranty repairs.
Discount to BFP members: 10%.

SENDEAN
9–12 St Anne's Court, London W1F 0BB.
22/23 St Cross Street, Clerkenwell, London EC1N 8UH.
Tel: 020 7439 8418. Fax: 0871 528 4582. E-mail: mail@sendeancameras.com
Web: www.sendeancameras.com
General repair service. Estimates free.
Discount to BFP members: 10%.

Insurance

AUA INSURANCE
De Vere House, 90 St Faiths Lane, Norwich NR1 1NL.
Tel: 01603 623227. Fax: 01603 665516. E-mail: sales@aua-insurance.com
Web: www.aua-insurance.com
Insurance for professional and semi-professional photographers. Comprehensive package policies covering equipment, liabilities, loss of income, professional negligence, etc.
Discount to BFP members: 10%.

AADUKI MULTIMEDIA INSURANCE
Bridge House, Okehampton EX20 1DL.
Tel: 0845 838 6933. Fax: 0845 838 6944. E-mail: info@aaduki.com
Web: www.aaduki.com
Specialist service to photographers for the insurance of cameras and other equipment. Range of products suitable for full-time professional, semi-pro or amateur, including liability and indemnity insurance, and high-risk travel. Bespoke policies also available.
Discount to BFP members: 15% (subject to minimum premiums).

E & L INSURANCE
Thorpe Underwood Hall, Ouseburn, York YO26 9SS.
E-mail: info@eandl.co.uk
Tel: 08449 809 520. Fax: 08449 809 410.
Web: www.eandl.co.uk/leisure-and-lifestyle/camera-insurance
Specialist photographic insurance scheme covering private, domestic or commercial photo equipment. 15% online discount.

GLOVER & HOWE LTD
12 Chapel Street North, Colchester, Essex CO2 7AT.
Tel: 01206 814500. Fax: 01206 814501. E-mail: insurance@gloverhowe.co.uk
Web: www.gloverhowe.co.uk
Insurance for photographic equipment and associated risks, for the amateur, semi-pro or professional.
Discount to BFP members: 10%.

GOLDEN VALLEY INSURANCE
The Olde Shoppe, Ewyas Harold, Herefordshire HR2 0ES.
Tel: 01981 240536. Fax: 01981 240451. E-mail: gvinsurance@aol.com
Web: www.photographicinsurance.co.uk
Comprehensive insurance cover for all photographic, video and sound recording equipment,
binoculars and telescopes, computers, home office/studio, all accessories etc.
Discount to BFP members: 10%.

INDEMNITYGUARD
Pavilion Insurance Management Ltd, Pavilion House, Mercia Business Village, Coventry CV4 8HX.
Tel: 02476 851000. Fax: 02476 851080. E-mail: sales@indemnityguard.co.uk
Web: www.indemnityguard.co.uk/bfp
Professional indemnity insurance for photographers and videographers, offering a range of cover
levels. Instant quotes, cover, renewals and changes available online.
Discount to BFP members: 10%.

MORGAN RICHARDSON LTD
Freepost CL4071, Westgate Court, Western Road, Billericay, Essex CM12 9ZZ.
Tel: Freecall 0800 731 2940. E-mail: quotes@morganrichardson.co.uk
Web: www.morganrichardson.co.uk
Specialist "Policy Portfolio" and "Photographers' Economy" insurance for photographers. Tailored
packages. Professional indemnity automatically insured up to £50,000.
Discount to BFP members: 10%

PHOTOGUARD
Pavilion Insurance Management Ltd, Pavilion House, Mercia Business Village, Coventry CV4 8HX.
Tel: 02476 851000. Fax: 02476 851080. E-mail: sales@photoguard.co.uk
Web: www.photoguard.co.uk/bfp
Specialist insurance cover for photographers and their equipment, offering a range of flexible
options. Instant quotes, cover, renewals and changes available online.
Discount to BFP members: 10%.

TOWERGATE CAMERASURE
Funtley Court, Funtley Hill, Fareham, Hampshire PO16 7UY.
Tel: 0870 4115511. Fax: 0870 4115515. E-mail: camerasure@towergate.co.uk
Web: www.towergatecamerasure.co.uk
Range of specialist insurances for amateur, semi-professional and professional photographers,
including comprehensive cover for equipment, studios, work in progress and legal liabilities (public,
products and employer's).
Discount to BFP members: Up to 40%, subject to minimum premium requirements.

WEALD INSURANCE BROKERS LTD
Falcon House, Black Eagle Square, Westerham, Kent TN16 1SE.
Tel: 01959 565678; freephone 0800 074 7016. Fax: 01959 569988.
Web: www.quoteour.co.uk
Comprehensive specialist insurance policies for professional and semi-pro photographers.
Discount to BFP members: 15% (subject to no claims).

---

*Are you working from the latest edition of The Freelance Photographer's
Market Handbook? It's published on 1 October each year. Markets are
constantly changing, so it pays to have the latest edition*

Postcard Printers

ABACUS (COLOUR PRINTERS) LTD
Lowick House, Lowick, Near Ulverston, Cumbria LA12 8DX.
Tel: 01229 885361. Fax: 01229 885348. E-mail: sales@abacusprinters.co.uk
Web: www.abacusprinters.co.uk
Quality printers specialising in colour postcards & greetings cards and promotional card catalogues.
Minimum quantity 500.
Discount for members on production of current membership details.

COLOURCARDS
Unit 2-3 Northfield Industrial Estate, Beresford Avenue, Wembley HA0 1NW.
Tel: 020 8733 9800. E-mail: sales@colourcards.co.uk
Web: www.colourcards.co.uk
7-day postcard and greetings card printing service. Any digital artwork accepted. Card design
service also available.

JUDGES POSTCARDS LTD
176 Bexhill Road, St Leonards on Sea, East Sussex TN38 8BN.
Tel: 01424 420919. Fax: 01424 438538. E-mail: sales@judges.co.uk
Web: www.judges.co.uk
Printers of postcards, greetings cards and calendars. Minimum quantity: 100.
Discount to BFP members: 10%.

THE POSTCARD COMPANY
51 Gortin Road, Omagh BT79 7HZ.
Tel: 028 8224 9222. Fax: 028 8224 9886. E-mail: sales@thepostcardcompany.com
Web: www.thepostcardcompany.com
Printers of postcards, greetings cards and product cards. No minimum quantity.

THOUGHT FACTORY
Group House, 40 Waterside Road, Hamilton Industrial Park, Leicester LE5 1TL.
Tel: 0116 276 5302. Fax: 0116 246 0506. E-mail: tara@thoughtfactory.co.uk
Web: www.thoughtfactory.co.uk
Minimum quantity: 100. Price: £50 + VAT.
Discount to BFP members: 10%.

Processing & Finishing

ACTPIX LTD
Trefechan, 2 Dolybont, St Harmon, Rhayader, Powys LD6 5LZ.
Tel: 01597 870017. E-mail: info@actpix.com
Web: www.actpix.com
Picture framing, Giclee printing, image retouching and scanning of commercial images at very high
resolution.
Discount to BFP members: 5% on orders over £150.

> *As a member of the Bureau of Freelance Photographers, you ll be
> kept up-to-date with markets through the BFP Market Newsletter,
> published monthly. For details of membership, turn to page 9*

ANDREWS IMAGING
Leacon Road, Ashford, Kent TN23 4FB.
Tel: 01233 620764. Fax: 01233 645618. E-mail: info@andrewsimaging.co.uk
Web: www.andrewsimaging.co.uk
Comprehensive range of film and digital processing, scanning and printing services.

BLUE MOON DIGITAL LTD
Davina House, 5th Floor, 137-149 Goswell Road, London EC1V 7ET.
Tel: 020 7253 9993/4. Fax: 020 7253 9995. E-mail: info@bluemoondigital.com
Web: www.bluemoondigital.com
Full film and digital imaging service including printing, processing and duplicating. Other services include mounting, CD/DVD burning and website design.

BLUESKYIMAGES LTD
2 Lakeside, South Cerney, Gloucestershire GL7 5XE.
Tel: 01285 862813. E-mail: info@blueskyimages.co.uk
Web: www.blueskyimages.co.uk
Top-quality film scanning from 35mm up to 5x4in. Also exhibition quality printing services, from film or digital.

CC IMAGING
7 Scala Court, Leathley Road, Leeds LS10 1JD.
Tel: 0113 244 8329. E-mail: ccimaging@btconnect.com
Web: www.ccimaging.co.uk
Comprehensive colour and B&W processing and printing services. E6 specialists. Specialist digital photographic print service. Full mounting and finishing services. Digital scanning, retouching and printing.
Discount to BFP members: 15%.

CPL GRAPHICS & DISPLAY
Head Office: 14 Vale Rise, Tonbridge, Kent TN9 1TB.
Tel: 01732 367222. Fax: 01732 366863. E-mail: info@cpl-graphics.com
Web: www.cpl-graphics.com
Specialist digital printing services. Professional and personal service where the photographer can talk directly to the person printing their work.
Discount to BFP members: 10% on orders over £100.

DUNNS IMAGING GROUP LTD
Chester Road, Cradley Heath, West Midlands B64 6AA.
Tel: 01384 564770. Fax: 01384 637165. E-mail: enquiries@dunns.co.uk
Web: www.dunns.co.uk
Comprehensive printing services, with online ordering. Event photography. Schools package printing and online service.

GENESIS IMAGING
Unit 1, Hurlingham Business Park, Sulivan Road, Fulham, London SW6 3DU.
Tel: 020 7384 6299. Fax: 020 7384 6277. E-mail: info@genesis-digital.net
Web: www.genesis-digital.net
Services: Large Format (Lambda) photographic prints, extra wide Giclee fine art prints, stretched canvas prints, Acrylic face mounts (perspex face mounts), aluminium mounts, Dibond mounts, Foamex mounts, foam board mounts and bespoke framing services. Drum scanning, film outputs, digital image retouching and image composition. E6 & C41 film processing, hand prints and print runs.
Discount to BFP members: 10%.

HMD GROUP PLC
Olympia House, 4 Garnett Close, Watford WD24 7JY.
Tel: 01923 237012. Fax: 01923 817421. E-mail: sales@hmdgroup.com
Web: www.hmdgroup.com
Digital printing services, mounting and finishing.
Discount to BFP members: 15%.

HOME COUNTIES COLOUR SERVICES LTD
Treelands, Oldhill Wood, Studham, Bedfordshire LU6 2NE.
Tel: 01582 873338. E-mail: sales@hccs.co.uk
Web: www.hccs.co.uk
Photographic processing services for photographers, including digital.
Discount to BFP members: On volume work only; open to negotiation.

KAY MOUNTING SERVICE
4c, Athelstane Mews, London N4 3EH.
Tel: 020 7272 7799. Fax: 020 7272 9888. E-mail: info@kaymounting.co.uk
Web: www.kaymounting.co.uk
Specialists in Diasec bonding behind perspex/aluminium with sub-frames; ready to hang frameless artwork.
Discount to BFP members: 10%

ONE VISION IMAGING LTD
Herald Way, Binley, Coventry CV3 2NY.
Tel: 0845 862 0217. Fax: 024 76 444219. E-mail: info@onevisionimaging.com
Web: www.onevisionimaging.com
Comprehensive colour processing and digital imaging services.

PEAK IMAGING
Unit 6, Flockton Park, Holbrook Avenue, Halfway, Sheffield S20 3PP.
Tel: 01142 243207. Fax: 0114 224 3205. E-mail: info@peak-imaging.com
Web: www.peak-imaging.com.
Mail order pro-am photographic and digital imaging centre.
Discount to BFP members: 10% on pro lab services.

PERFECT PICTURE COMPANY
Welbeck Way, Peterborough PE2 7WH.
Tel: 01733 393383. Fax: 01733 391825. E-mail: sales@perfectpicturecompany.com
Web: www.perfectpicturecompany.com
Specialists in stretch canvas prints. Also supply Image Bloc prints, picture frames and digital image enhancement services.
Discount to BFP members: 15% on canvas prints; other items according to size and regularity of orders.

THE PHOTOGRAPHIC CENTRE
Pinewood Studios, Pinewood Road, Iver Heath, Buckinghamshire SL0 0NH.
Tel: 01753 656229. E-mail: info@photographiccentre.com
Web: www.photographiccentre.com
Professional photo lab with full range of conventional and digital services. B&W, colour, processing and printing, scanning, framing and canvas printing.
Discount to BFP members: 15%.

211

PROFOLAB IMAGING LTD
Unit 4, Surrey Close, Granby Industrial Estate, Weymouth, Dorset DT4 9TY.
Tel: 01305 774098. Fax: 01305 778746. E-mail: info@profolab.co.uk
Web: www.profolab.co.uk
E6 processing and full digital service.

REDWOOD PRO LAB & WHOLESALER
7 Brunel Court, Severalls Park, Colchester, Essex CO4 9XW.
Tel: 01206 751241. Fax: 01206 855134. E-mail: info@redwoodphoto.com
Web: www.redwoodphoto.com
Colour and B&W processing, electronic imaging, in-house wedding album manufacture.
Discount to BFP members: 5%.

RUSSELL PHOTO IMAGING
17 Elm Grove, Wimbledon, London SE19 4HE. E-mail: info@russellsgroup.co.uk
Tel: 020 8947 6177. Fax: 020 8944 2064.
Web: www.russellsgroup.co.uk
Comprehensive colour processing services; 2-hour E6 processing, C41, machine and hand line printing, exhibition printing and mounting service. Digital services; scanning, digital printing and Giclee printing.
Discount to BFP members: 5%.

SCL
16 Bull Lane, Edmonton, London N18 1SX.
Tel: 020 8807 0725. Fax: 020 8807 2539. E-mail: davids@sclimage.net
Web: www.sclimage.net
Comprehensive colour and B&W processing plus full range of digital output services. Plus mounting and finishing, exhibition graphics, roller banners and display stands.

THE VAULT IMAGING LTD
1 Dorset Place, Brighton BN2 1ST.
Tel: 01273 688733. E-mail: info@thevaultimaging.co.uk
Web: www.thevaultimaging.co.uk
Comprehensive professional processing, scanning and printing services. Specialists in large format printing on a selection of premium papers and canvas, giclee and photo art archival prints.

Specialised Equipment & Materials

COLORAMA
Unit 18, Atlas Road, Hermitage Industrial Estate, Coalville, Leicestershire LE67 3FQ.
Tel: 01530 832570. Fax: 01530 832603. E-mail: info@colorama-photo.com
Web: www.colorama-photo.com
Suppliers of photographic background paper, background support products and light modifying solutions for professionals, including Cove-Lock infinity coving systems.

Are you working from the latest edition of The Freelance Photographer's Market Handbook? It's published on 1 October each year. Markets are constantly changing, so it pays to have the latest edition

---

THE FLASH CENTRE
68 Brunswick Centre, Marchmont Street, London WC1N 1AE.
Tel: 020 7837 5649. Fax: 020 7833 4882. E-mail: sales@theflashcentre.co.uk
Web: www.theflashcentre.com
2 Mount Street Business Centre, Birmingham B7 5RD.
Tel/fax: 0121 327 9220.
Unit 7 Scala Court, Leathley Road, Leeds LS10 1JD.
Tel: 0113 247 0937. Fax: 0113 247 0038.
Specialist suppliers of electronic flash systems, SLR and medium format digital cameras, and
associated colour management and image output services.

JESSOPS
Head Office: Jessop House, 98 Scudamore Road, Leicester LE3 1TZ.
Tel: 0116 232 6000. Fax: 0116 232 0060.
Web: www.jessops.com
Specialist suppliers of all photographic and digital imaging equipment including Portaflash portable
studio flash, a full range of darkroom equipment and accessories.

KENRO LTD
Greenbridge Road, Swindon, Wilts SN3 3LH.
Tel: 01793 615836. Fax: 01793 630108. E-mail: sales@kenro.co.uk
Web: www.kenro.co.uk
Wide variety of accessories including camera bags, batteries and chargers, Benbo tripods, Tokina
lenses, Nissin flashguns, Marumi filters, flash and lighting kit, background supports, reflector kits,
lightboxes and viewers, memory cards.

S.W. KENYON
PO Box 71, Cranbrook, Kent TN18 5ZR.
Tel: 01580 850770. Fax: 01580 850225. E-mail: swkenyon@btinternet.com
Web: www.swkenyon.com
K-Line dulling sprays for reducing glare on objects to be photographed.

OCEAN OPTICS
Archers Field, Burnt Mill Industrial Estate, Basildon, Essex SS13 1DL.
Tel: 01268 523786. Fax: 01268 523795. E-mail: optics@oceanoptics.co.uk
Web: www.oceanoptics.co.uk
Specialist suppliers of underwater photography equipment.

SILVERPRINT LTD
12 Valentine Place, London SE1 8QH.
Tel: 020 7620 0844. Fax: 020 7620 0129. E-mail: sales@silverprint.co.uk
Web: www.silverprint.co.uk
Specialist suppliers of B&W materials. Importers of Maco and Foma fibre-based and RC papers and
a wide range of other papers, toners, liquid emulsions, tinting and retouching materials. Products
for archival mounting, and archival storage boxes and folio cases. Mail order service.

---

*As a member of the Bureau of Freelance Photographers, you ll be
kept up-to-date with markets through the BFP Market Newsletter,
published monthly. For details of membership, turn to page 9*

Storage & Presentation

ABLE DIRECT CENTRE LTD
5 Mallard Close, Earls Barton, Northampton NN6 0LS.
Tel: 0844 8482733. Fax: 0844 8482766.
Web: www.able-labels.co.uk
Able-Labels – printed self-adhesive labels; rubber stamps.

ARROWFILE
PO Box 637, Wetherby Road, York YO26 0DQ.
Tel: 0844 855 1100. Fax: 0844 855 1101. E-mail: customerservices@arrowfile.com
Web: www.arrowfile.com
Archival photographic storage and presentation specialists. The Arrowfile System organises, stores and protects varying photo sizes, negs, slides, and CDs all in one single binder album.

BRAYTHORN LTD
Phillips Street, Aston, Birmingham B6 4PT.
Tel: 0121 359 8800. Fax: 0121 359 8412. E-mail: sales@braythorn.co.uk
Web: www.braythorn.co.uk
Suppliers of cardboard mailing tubes and polythene envelopes. Minimum quantities: 1000 envelopes, 100 tubes.
Discount to BFP members: 10%.

CHALLONER MARKETING LTD
Raans Road, Amersham, Buckinghamshire HP6 6LL.
Tel: 01494 721270. Fax: 01494 725732. E-mail: info@challoner-marketing.com
Web: www.challoner-marketing.com
Suppliers of Fly-Weight envelope stiffener. Minimum quantity: 100.
Discount to BFP members: 5% on orders over 5,000.

DW GROUP LTD
Unit 7, Peverel Drive, Granby, Milton Keynes MK1 1NL.
Tel: 01908 642323. Fax: 01908 640164. E-mail: sales@dw-view.com
Web: www.photopages.com
Filing and presentation systems, masks for all formats, mounts, wallets, storage cabinets, lightboxes, display boxes, viewing booths, viewtowers, ultra-slim light panels. Also CD-ROM production and replication, CD printers and replication systems, floppy disk duping, poster prints.
Discount to BFP members: 10%.

NICHOLAS HUNTER LTD
Unit 17, Chiltern Business Centre, Garsington Road, Cowley, Oxford OX4 6NG.
Tel: 01865 777365. Fax: 01865 773856. E-mail: office@nicholashunter.com
Web: www.photofiling.com
Plastic wallets for presentation of prints, slides and negatives.
Discount to BFP members: 5% on orders over £100; 10% over £500.

KENRO LTD
Greenbridge Road, Swindon, Wilts SN3 3LH.
Tel: 01793 615836. Fax: 01793 630108. E-mail: sales@kenro.co.uk
Web: www.kenro.co.uk
Professional and retail photo albums and frames, CD storage products, strut mounts and folders, lightboxes and viewers, storage and presentation accessories for digital and film.

LONDON LABELS LTD
20 Oval Road, London NW1 7DJ.
Tel: 020 7267 7105. Fax: 020 7267 1165.
Self-adhesive labels for 35mm slides, printed with name, address or logo. Also plain labels.

RICHFORDS
E M Richford Ltd, Curzon Road, Chilton Industrial Estate, Sudbury, Suffolk CO10 2XW.
Tel: 01787 375241. Fax: 01787 310179. E-mail: sales@richstamp.co.uk
Web: www.richstamp.co.uk
Rubber stamps and inks, including stamps made to order and specialist quick-drying inks.

SECOL LTD
Howlett Way, Thetford, Norfolk IP24 1HZ.
Tel: 01842 752341. Fax: 01842 762159. E-mail: sales@secol.co.uk
Web: www.secol.co.uk
Wide range of photographic storage and display products including sleeves, filing sheets, storage boxes, black card masks, mounting systems, portfolio cases and portfolio boxes.
Discount to BFP members: 10% on prepaid orders of £100 or more.

SLIDEPACKS
1 The Moorings, Aldenham Road, Bushey, Herts WD23 2NR.
Tel: 01923 254790. Fax: 01923 254790. E-mail: sales@slidepacks.com
Web: www.slidepacks.com
Binders, folders, mounts and wallets for transparency presentation, storage and filing. Custom-made service also available. Also supply labels, lightboxes, lupes and other accessories.

Studio Hire & Services

BASE MODELS
PO Box 6709, Bournemouth BH8 0BW.
Tel: 0845 2255015. Fax: 01202 524193. E-mail: info@basemodels.co.uk
Web: www.basemodels.co.uk
Commercial, fashion and glamour model agency supplying models throughout the UK and Portugal.
Discount to BFP members: 10%.

FARNHAM STUDIO
Frampton Cottage, Pankridge Street, Crondall, Near Farnham GU10 5QU.
Tel. 01252 850792. E-mail: enquiries@model-media.co.uk
Web: www.model-media.co.uk
Photographic studio based in an attractive cottage with gardens and three large studio rooms. Studio tuition and models also available.
Discount to BFP members: 20%.

HOLBORN STUDIOS
49/50 Eagle Wharf Road, London N1 7ED.
Tel: 020 7490 4099. Fax: 020 7253 8120. E-mail: studiomanager@holborn-studios.co.uk
Web: www.holborn-studios.co.uk
15 studios to hire, plus very comprehensive equipment hire.
Discount to BFP members: 10% on full week bookings.

SIMULACRA STUDIO
Railway Arch 260, Hardness Street, London SE24 0HN.
Tel: 020 7733 1979. E-mail: info@simulacrastudio.com
Web: www.simulacrastudio.com
Fully equipped studio offering characteful space under a converted railway arch. Wide range of hire equipment available.
Discount to BFP members: 25% on full-day hire

Web Services & Software

AMAZING INTERNET LTD
82 Heath Road, Twickenham, Middlesex TW1 4BW.
Tel: 020 8607 9535. E-mail: contact@amazinginternet.com
Web: www.amazinginternet.com
Website solutions for photographers. Range from fully updateable portfolio websites to large photo library systems, plus full e-commerce facilities and online sales modules for wedding and social photographers.
Discount to BFP members: 10%.

CONTACT
Surrey House, 31 Church Street, Leatherhead, Surrey KT22 8EF.
Tel: 01372 220330. Fax: 01372 220340. E-mail: mail@contact-uk.com
Web: www.contact-uk.com
Low cost web portfolio portal with international art buyer usage, plus optional annual source book.

CRUNCH
Suite 1, Dubarry House, Hove Park Villas, Hove BN3 6HP.
Tel: 0844 500 8000. E-mail: info@crunch.co.uk
Web: www.crunch.co.uk
Online accounting system and accountancy practice dedicated to freelances and other small businesses. Full end-to-end accountancy process backed by qualified Chartered Accountants.
Discount to BFP members: 10% for first two years of service.

IMENSE
William Gates Building, 15 JJ Thomson Avenue, Cambridge CB3 0FD.
3 More London Riverside, London SE1 2RE.
Tel: 020 3283 4225. E-mail: sales@imense.com
Web: www.imense.com
Imense Annotator keywording application aimed at professional and semi-professional photographers. Provides automated kyewording designed to speed up workflow and attract buyers with commercially relevant keywords.

LIGHT BLUE SOFTWARE
101 Teversham Drift, Cambridge CB1 3LL.
Tel: 07881 952510. E-mail: admin@lightbluesoftware.com
Web: www.lightbluesoftware.com
Provider of "Light Blue: Photo" business management software specifically designed for photographers. Includes contacts, shoot records, order and payment tracking, purchases and more. Free 30-day trial version available from website.

MISTERCLIPPING.COM
MisterClipping.com B.V., Hendrik Figeeweg 1M, 2031 BJ Haarlem, The Netherlands.
Tel (UK): 020 3286 9069. E-mail: info@misterclipping.com
www.misterclipping.com
Graphic processing service providing handmade clipping paths to isolate images from their backgrounds. Uploaded images can be downloaded with a path or isolated from their background within 24 hours.

SIGNUM TECHNOLOGIES LTD
Dunraven House, 5 Meadow Court, High Street, Witney, Oxfordshire, OX28 6ER.
Tel: 01933 776929. Fax: 01933 776939. E-mail: signum@signumtech.com
Web: www.signumtech.com
SureSign digital watermarking plug-ins for Photoshop, for copyright protection and notification.

SPANSOFT
8 Juniper Hill, Glenrothes, Fife KY7 5TH.
Tel/fax: 01592 743110. E-mail: support@spansoft.org
Web: www.spansoft.org
Slide Librarian shareware package for cataloguing transparency collections on PC.

THIRD LIGHT
St John's Innovation Centre, Cowley Road, Cambridge CB4 0WS.
Tel: 01223 475674. Fax: 0700 340 1284. E-mail: sales@thirdlight.com
Web: www.thirdlight.com
Provider of Image Management System (IMS), a web-based picture library and e-commerce system enabling photographers to store, display and sell images via internet galleries.

WEBBOUTIQUES LTD
1 Abbey Street, Eynsham, Oxfordshire OX29 4TB.
Tel: 01865 883852 Fax: 01865 883550. E-mail: kimberley@webboutiques.co.uk
Web: www.webboutiques.co.uk
Bespoke web design services to photographers and artists, from standard sites to complex code driven solutions. On-line ordering and printing services and a full on-line portfolio search are available.
Discount to BFP members: On application.

USEFUL ADDRESSES

ASSOCIATION OF MODEL AGENTS
11–29 Fashion Street, London E1 6PX.
Tel: 020 7422 0699. Fax: 020 7247 9230. E-mail: amainfo@btinternet.com
Web: www.associationofmodelagents.org

ASSOCIATION OF PHOTOGRAPHERS (AOP)
81 Leonard Street, London EC2A 4QS.
Tel: 020 7739 6669. Fax: 020 7739 8707. E-mail: general@aophoto.co.uk
Web: www.the-aop.org

BRITISH ASSOCIATION OF PICTURE LIBRARIES AND AGENCIES (BAPLA)
59 Tranquil Vale, Blackheath, London, SE3 0BS
Tel: 020 8852 7211. E-mail: enquiries@bapla.org.uk
Web: www.bapla.org.uk

BRITISH INSTITUTE OF PROFESSIONAL PHOTOGRAPHY (BIPP)
1 Prebendal Court, Oxford Road, Aylesbury, Buckinghamshire HP19 8EY.
Tel: 01296 718530. Fax: 01296 336367. E-mail: info@bipp.com
Web: www.bipp.com

BRITISH PRESS PHOTOGRAPHERS' ASSOCIATION (BPPA)
Suite 219, 2 Lansdowne Crescent, Bournemouth BH1 1SA.
E-mail: info@thebppa.com
Web: www.thebppa.com

BUREAU OF FREELANCE PHOTOGRAPHERS (BFP)
Focus House, 497 Green Lanes, London N13 4BP.
Tel: 020 8882 3315. Fax: 020 8886 3933. E-mail: mail@thebfp.com
Web: www.thebfp.com

CHARTERED INSTITUTE OF JOURNALISTS (CIOJ)
2, Dock Offices, Surrey Quays Road, London SE16 2XU.
Tel: 020 7252 1187. Fax: 020 7232 2302. E-mail: memberservices@cioj.co.uk
Web: www.cioj.co.uk

DESIGN & ARTISTS COPYRIGHT SOCIETY (DACS)
33 Great Sutton Street, London EC1V 0DX.
Tel: 020 7336 8811. Fax: 020 7336 8822. E-mail: info@dacs.org.uk
Web: www.dacs.org.uk

GUILD OF PHOTOGRAPHERS
30 St Edmunds Avenue, Newcastle-Under-Lyme, Staffordshire ST5 0AB.
Tel: 01782 740526. E-mail: info@photoguild.co.uk
Web: www.photoguild.co.uk

MASTER PHOTOGRAPHERS ASSOCIATION (MPA)
Jubilee House, 1 Chancery Lane, Darlington, Co Durham DL1 5QP.
Tel: 01325 356555. Fax: 01325 357813. E-mail: enq@mpauk.com
Web: www.thempa.com

NATIONAL ASSOCIATION OF PRESS AGENCIES (NAPA)
2nd Floor. Contemporary Urban Centre, 41-51, Greenland Street, Liverpool, Liverpool, L1 0BS.
Tel: 0870 609 1935. E-mail: enquiries@napa.org.uk
Web: www.napa.org.uk

NATIONAL UNION OF JOURNALISTS (NUJ)
Headland House, 308-312 Gray's Inn Road, London WC1X 8DP.
Tel: 020 7278 7916. Fax: 020 7837 8143. E-mail: info@nuj.org.uk
Web: www.nuj.org.uk

PRESS ASSOCIATION
292 Vauxhall Bridge Road, London SW1V 1AE.
Tel: 020 7963 7000. Picture Desk: 020 7963 7155.
Web: www.pressassociation.co.uk

REUTERS
Reuters Building, South Colonnade, Canary Wharf, London E14 5EP.
Tel: 020 7542 7949 (picture desk UK news); 020 7542 8088 (international). E-mail:
lon.pictures@reuters.com
Web: http://pictures.reuters.com

ROYAL PHOTOGRAPHIC SOCIETY (RPS)
Fenton House, 122 Wells Road, Bath BA2 3AH.
Tel: 01225 325733. Fax: 01225 448688. E-mail: reception@rps.org
Web: www.rps.org

SOCIETY OF WEDDING & PORTRAIT PHOTOGRAPHERS (SWPP)
6 Bath Street, Rhyl LL16 3EB.
Tel: 01745 356935. Fax: 01745 356953. E-mail: info@swpp.co.uk
Web: www.swpp.co.uk

INDEX

A

B

C

T

Join the BFP today and get next year's Handbook hot from the press!

As a member of the Bureau of Freelance Photographers, you'll be kept right up to date with market requirements. Every month, you'll receive the BFP *Market Newsletter*, a unique publication telling you what picture buyers are looking for now. It will keep you informed of new markets – including new magazines – as they appear and the type of pictures they're looking for. It also serves to keep *The Freelance Photographer's Market Handbook* up to date between editions, since it reports important changes as they occur.

And as part of membership, you receive the Handbook automatically each year as it is published. For details of some of the other services available to members please see page 9.

Membership currently costs just £54 a year. To join, complete the form below and post with your remittance to the BFP. You'll receive your first Newsletter and membership pack within about seven days.

Please enrol me as a member of the Bureau of Freelance Photographers for 12 months. I understand that if, once I receive my initial membership pack, I decide that membership is not for me, I may return it within 21 days for a full refund.

☐ I enclose cheque/po value £54 *(or £70 Overseas rate*)*

☐ Debit my MASTERCARD/VISA/SWITCH no_____Start_____

Expiry_____ Issue No (Switch only)_____ Security code_____ in the sum of £54.

NAME _____ BLOCK

ADDRESS _____ CAPS
PLEASE

_____

_____Postcode_____

Post to:
Bureau of Freelance Photographers,
Focus House, 497 Green Lanes, London N13 4BP.

*Overseas applicants must send cheque/draft drawn on a UK bank; or pay by credit card

H11

Also published by BFP Books

The *Freelance Photographer's Project Book* is a major new publication from BFP Books. It is designed to help photographers find fresh markets for their work by giving them the inside information on breaking into different sectors of the market. Each of the 20 chapters, or "projects", is written by an experienced and successful freelance who specialises in the market concerned. Each contributor provides the newcomer with the benefit of their long experience in approaching these specific markets.

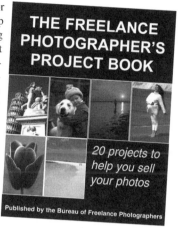

THE FREELANCE PHOTOGRAPHER'S PROJECT BOOK

20 projects to help you sell your photos

Published by the Bureau of Freelance Photographers

Subjects include Selling family photos; Selling outdoor photos; Selling wildlife photos; Selling country photos; Selling garden photos; Selling boating photos; Selling to photo magazines; Selling to local papers; Selling travel photos; Selling architectural photos; Selling generic photos; Selling transport photos; Selling to home magazines; Selling through libraries; Selling cards & calendars; and Selling stock with articles.

The final two projects cover Mounting an exhibition and Producing a book.

The contributors have been chosen not only for their expertise in their chosen subject but also their ability to impart this knowledge with clarity and precision. A short summary of the contributor's background and experience is appended to each project.

The book is fully illustrated with examples of pictures that sell, all provided by the contributors themselves.

The *Freelance Photographer's Project Book* will provide invaluable information for anyone who has ever thought of selling their pictures but does not know where to start. Whatever the subject, the *Project Book* offers a fast track to success.

144 pages Hardback £22.50

Get a special previous user's discount when you order next year's Handbook direct

Each year's *Handbook* contains hundreds of amended listings as well as new entries. To take the magazine section alone, during the course of the year, new publications launch while existing titles fold. In addition, editors change which often leads to a change in picture requirements. Similar important changes occur in every other section of the book.

the freelance photographer's market handbook

2012 edition out 1 October 2011

It's vital, therefore, to keep up-to-date by working from the latest edition. The *Handbook* is published in October each year, and you can order next year's edition from September onwards. By using this form, you'll benefit from a special previous user's discount, saving you £3 on the usual direct-from-the-publishers price. While the normal price is £16.95 (£14.95 plus £2 p&p), you pay only £13.95.

Complete the details below for your copy of next year's *Freelance Photographer's Market Handbook.*

NB. Offer closes 31 December 2010

Please send me a copy of **The Freelance Photographer's Market Handook 2011** at the special Previous User's Discount price of £11.95 plus £2.00 p&p.

☐ I enclose cheque/po value £13.95

☐ Debit my MASTERCARD/VISA/SWITCH no_____Start_____

Expiry_____ Issue No (Switch only)_____ Security code_____ in the sum £13.95.

NAME _____ BLOCK

ADDRESS _____ CAPS

_____ PLEASE

_____Postcode_____

Post to:
BFP BOOKS
Focus House, 497 Green Lanes, London N13 4BP.   H11
*Overseas readers must send cheque/draft drawn on a UK bank; or pay by credit card